The City of Lists

A novel by
BRIGID ROSE

ISBN 978094ε
Crocus

The City of Lists

The City of Lists

First published in 2009 by Crocus
Crocus books are published by Commonword, 6 Mount Street, Manchester M2 5NS

admin@commonword.org.uk
www.commonword.org.uk

Crocus books are distributed by Turnaround Publisher Services Ltd, Unit 3, Olympia Trading Estate, Coburg Rd, Wood Green, London N22 6TZ

Cover design by Tyme Design www.tymedesign.com
Printed by LPPS Limited www.lppsltd.co.uk

British Library Cataloguing-in-Publication Data: a catalogue record for this book is available from the British Library

Dedicated to John Corton and to my family, with very much love and many thanks

Thank you to Andrew May for his kind permission to use the title; to the Hebden Bridge stillness group and the non-duality north / advaita people. Finally, as many of the ideas in the book come from the teachings of Eckhart Tolle, a big thank you to him.

The City of Lists

by
Brigid Rose

Prologue

A change has taken place. He's different from how he was. His name is still the same but it's as though the person that label belongs to no longer troubles or matters. He was like a tangled knot in a piece of string, a knot that seemed so hard and tight that it could never unravel. But now the knot has undone itself and the string hangs loose and free. A memory of constriction remains but that's all.

The room is small and dim and without sunlight. But sitting on the bench, looking at the walls, he feels alive and at peace. Everything in the room looks and feels alive to him. Even the basin in the corner into which he urinates has the same bright, benign quality.

The Guarda enter from time to time. They come to apply shocks to his legs and arms but the pain isn't important. The punishments are there and then they're gone. The Guarda ask questions of him but the peace is so deep he can hardly speak.

Time goes on and it's as though the Guarda can't keep away from their prisoner. One fetches water for him to drink or brings a blanket, another even comes to empty the basin. Despite his strangeness and silence, he is alluring to them. They come just to be near it: the feeling of a knot that has finally unravelled. The proximity seems to affect them; it loosens them slightly too.

Thoughts arise as he sits there. Thoughts of his two companions. He knows that a separation has occurred but it doesn't trouble him unduly. To him there's only an apparent distance between them now. There's no end to the closeness he feels. It goes on and on and on.

'She and he and I are the same,' he thinks. 'That's what happens. That's all…'

Part One

Chapter 1

The light was starting to fade. The fairground was some distance away and Lol was in a hurry to get there. I called to him to slow down and reluctantly he slowed his steps.

I had an arm linked through Valentine's to try and move him along a little faster. His body felt frail and I could feel his ribs through his coat. All he wanted was to turn around and go home. I was trying to get myself into an upbeat mood, to gear myself up for the fair, but it wasn't working. I was too anxious.

We got nearer and I heard the churning music from the rides, the yelling and screaming. We turned a corner and there it was; a mass of lights surrounded by the growing darkness of the wasteland.

Passing under rows of lights on wires, we entered the fair. Lol whooped at the spectacle, leapt up and hit a bulb hanging overhead. He sent a chain swinging and I felt my stomach shrink. His angry excitement seemed to infuse everything he did.

The fairground smelled of the smoky fuel, and of mud where the ground had been trampled by people's feet. According to the authorities, there was nothing corrupting in the type of amusement that fairgrounds offered. Funfairs were considered acceptable entertainment. As a consequence they were all subsidised, making the rides cheap.

I glanced at Valentine. He looked overwhelmed, almost naked without his darkened glasses. Lol was casting about, hurriedly assessing the rides, feverishly jangling loose citizen tokens in his pocket as if he was in a rush to spend them. We saw a ride of carts decorated to look like chariots. They had gold wings on their sides and they sat on top of tall twisting poles. The ride looked old, paint was flaking off in patches, but Lol grabbed the sleeves of our coats and pulled us towards it.

When I was a child, my mother had refused to take me to a fairground. She'd said fairs were dangerous and instead I'd gone secretly with some other children wanting to try out the rides. That night, with Lol, I wasn't in a rush to go on anything.

Lol climbed the steep, narrow stairs up to the chariots and got

Valentine to follow him. I waited behind on a lower step, hoping Valentine wouldn't fall.

Someone was shouting.

A burly man was striding towards us roaring how only two people were allowed in the carts at a time. Lol had already made it into the chariot and he was pulling Valentine into it by his coat. The man came and stood at the foot of the steps. With his hands on the safety railings, he started to rattle them. He was trying to shake me from my place. I had to cling tightly to the rails.

Lol slammed his hand on the side of the chariot in complaint. 'Let her on!'

The man yelled back at him that maybe if I hadn't been so fat he might have let me ride.

He told me, 'Get off before I force you off.'

I waited for the stairs to stop shaking so that I could lower myself to the ground. I backed away into the crowd then, and watched as the man climbed the steps of the cart himself, collecting citizen tokens from Lol. Once he'd gone, Lol began waving and calling to me to join them.

'Come *on*, Neeve.'

I glanced in the direction the fair-worker had taken. He was busy taking payment from customers in another cart. I shook my head. 'No…'

The steps began to slide away from the carts. The carts lurched forwards and Lol and Valentine were spun away towards the rear of the ride. I stood and watched them go. By the time their chariot returned to the front, Lol's angry frown was starting to fade. At the second rotation, his mouth was wide open, catching the air.

The chariots gained speed. People on the ride started to scream. I caught flashes of Lol and Valentine strapped into their seats – Lol whooping and waving his arms, Valentine staring fixedly at a point inside the cart.

The chariots moved faster still, spinning in surprising directions, tilting at precarious angles. I saw the faces of the screaming riders and knew they weren't really scared. They were putting everything into their screams, trying to deafen themselves, getting it out while they could – safety pretending to be danger.

A door in the ride's platform opened and a large, mechanical snake emerged. The snake opened its mouth and flames of yellow cloth came out. It looked as though it meant to set the chariots on fire. The riders screamed louder still.

I'd try by turns that evening; being cheerful, talkative, quiet, in the hope it would make a difference with Lol. I thought that if Valentine and I could be more *something*, if we could be *something enough*, then things would be alright with Lol. Probably it was too late for that.

The ride slowed and stopped. Lol and Valentine climbed down and came to where I stood. Their faces were flushed from the cold air.

'How was the ride?'

Breathlessly, Lol said that it could've been faster. The grey pupils of his eyes looked like metal. He wanted to know if Valentine was enjoying himself. The way he asked, it seemed not so much a question as a threat. Valentine didn't answer.

We followed as Lol went about the fair, analysing each of the rides. He couldn't seem to find another that he liked. He kept yelling back at us how they weren't thrilling or frightening enough.

We passed a ride that was shaped like a huge black cube. The outside surfaces were so shiny they were like flat, perfect mirrors. There was no indication as to what went on inside but the ride at least looked newer than most of the others. And it was popular; a long queue was moving slowly forward. Lol had found what he wanted. He led us to the end of the line.

After scarcely a minute though, he was breathing out, irritated and impatient, complaining about the length of the wait. His hands were jittering around so much in his pockets that the front of his coat shook.

He was too restless to stay put. Without another word, he broke from the line. We watched as he pushed past people, moving away from us. We stood dumbfounded as his black head got further away.

It was as though Lol had us both on pieces of elastic that were being pulled tighter the further he went. We broke from the queue as though we hadn't any choice and went after him.

We passed several rides, the Green Wheel, the Hydra and the Monster Machine.

No sign of him.

Stretching high into the air, the next ride was the Tower.

Valentine saw him first. He pointed and I saw him too.

Lol was heading for the back of the ride. I saw him for no more than a second before he disappeared behind it.

We attempted to run after him. But by the time we'd reached the rear of the Tower, we'd lost him again. All we could see was a small patch of land lit up by the fair. Stones and litter were illuminated by the lights. Beyond that, the flat, muddy ground led away, swamped by the dark.

We stared into the darkness, trying to trace movement. Valentine called Lol's name, a weak, garbled sound that could scarcely be heard above the fair noise.

No response.

I shouted too and then waited, listening.

A noise came from behind, 'Y-yee!'

I swung back towards the ride, my eyes trying to locate the source.

'Y-eee!'

I looked up. Then further up still. Lol was at the top of the ride, clinging to the metal framework of the Tower. He was waving down at us using the whole of his arm, making his body sway unsteadily with the movement.

I yelled at him to get down but he kept waving, flapping his free arm, pretending he was about to take off. I looked about to see if people were watching us. But no-one could see us from the other side of the ride.

Afterwards, I'd have a vivid memory of Lol's face as he was high on the Tower. I'd see him in close-up; the wind frantically blowing his black hair, his mouth grinning so much you could see both rows of teeth. But that memory can't have been right because from where I'd stood, I could only just make out his face.

Something came hurtling down from the top of the Tower. Lol had thrown it. It spun through the air and hit the ground a few metres in front of us. I ran to see what it was. His wallet. Holding it in my hands, I stared up at him. Keeping his arm around the metal bar, Lol began to take off his coat. Then he threw that too. As the coat floated down the side of the Tower, the air ballooned it, making it look like a falling man.

I had the feeling he was going to jump.

Suddenly Valentine was stumbling towards the Tower. He half-ran, half-fell to get to it. He reached its framework, making a grab for one of the struts, and pulled himself on to the lowest bar. But he was too weak to climb fast.

Then I was running too. I climbed the Tower, hand over hand, foot over foot, shaking uncontrollably, the scaffolding ringing out as my shoes struck the bars.

Lol was gazing down at us. He'd stopped dancing about. Now he was just watching us trying to get to him; peering at us as though we were oddities and he was waiting to see what we'd do next. Valentine and I climbed, our faces raised, our hands gripping the freezing cold bars.

Maybe it was seeing us so provoked, seeing our desperate attempt to get to him. After a minute or so of watching us raise ourselves no more than four metres from the ground, Lol started to climb down.

His head was lowered, watching his feet as they reached for the struts. It seemed to take forever for him to get nearer. He got to a bar about five metres above us. We held on, waiting for him to get within reaching distance. But then, with no warning, he just let go.

It was a strange moment. Lol's fingers released their hold on the scaffold. His feet slipped from the bars – my eyes witnessing something that my mind couldn't process. Lol fell and my head spun away.

His body made a dull thud below us.

I waited, my face pressed against the scaffold, eyes shut. There was a noise in the bars; sound reverberating the metal. The sound was travelling through my skull, humming into my brain. I lifted my head. Valentine was climbing down. I suddenly felt too far from the ground. I clung on, unable to move.

Valentine ran to the body lying in the mud and stood staring, not wanting to touch it, maybe trying to tell whether or not it was breathing.

A shoulder moved, then the head. Lol rolled slowly over until he was on his back. His face was half-covered in mud; half a nose, a cheek, an eye, half the lips were thick with mud.

He made a noise. The sound came from his closed mouth, but loud enough for me to hear. A sort of mumbled complaint at the pain.

I thought, *Maybe he's alright...*

I had to think how to move my legs. My knees felt like they'd give way. I shut my eyes again and felt my way down.

By the time I'd reached the ground, Lol was already on his feet, swaying, trying to balance himself. He looked dazed, as though the wind had been knocked right out of him.

Then suddenly, a young man wearing fair-worker overalls came around the back of the ride and stopped short when he saw Lol staggering about, caked in mud. Lol let out an abrupt laugh at the youth's shocked expression. The force of his laugh caused him to fall to the ground again and at that, the fair-worker turned and rushed back in the direction he'd come from. It wouldn't be long before he fetched others.

We started to haul Lol up from the dirt. Somehow, between us, we found the energy to raise him. We succeeded in standing him up but he was sliding on the mud. We had to get him into the darkness of the wasteland, beyond the lights of the fair.

We only managed to take him about forty metres before we collapsed to the ground. I reached for Lol, laying a hand over his mouth, hoping to stop his groan.

Back at the Tower, a group of workmen were pacing about in the light behind it, peering into the dark. One of them had Lol's coat. We'd forgotten it when we ran. We watched as the man felt about inside the pockets. Then another of them stepped into the dark and disappeared.

Blood was banging in my ears. We held our breaths. I listened for the approach of footsteps. Each heartbeat felt like a boot on the ground.

Chapter 2

It was Valentine and me. That's how it began. I met him through work when he was moved to our sub-division, supposedly to help with the new twice-yearly Censuses. He was transferred from the Postal Department, a large building about five or so kilometres away, on the other side of Widechapper.

It wasn't common for workers to be transferred to new jobs in the way that he was. He came followed closely by a wave of rumour he wouldn't easily shake off. The rumour went that he'd been caught opening confidential letters but it was hard to believe from the look of him. Whatever he was thought to have done at the Postal Department, at our Unit he couldn't go far wrong; he'd only be mindlessly inputting numbers into a machine.

That first week he hardly spoke to anyone. He seemed like a startled animal; alert and frightened. I was struck the first time I heard his voice. A weird, whispery, unearthly voice, he had. I overheard him asking a question of the man who worked at a screen one desk away from me, and it made me look up from my file. I watched him as he spoke, his eyes consistently lowered, deferring too much. Hearing him made me want to cry. I could've let tears disappear down between the cracks in my keyboard. I could've listened and watched all day and got no work done.

From then on, I was mesmerised. In the refectory queue, I stood a little way behind, observing the way he spoke and moved. While working, I kept one eye and ear open, alert to his actions. Before he came, I used to sit at my work-station, everything around me so clean and neat. All those flat surfaces and rectilinear edges. It made me feel messy, aberrant, irregular. But then Valentine arrived and he felt like the only real, living thing to have ever entered the building.

One day I went over with some statistics to be in-putted onto his screen.

I flapped an envelope about in my hands. 'Here's some files for you.'

His blank face broke unexpectedly into a smile. He repeated my words quietly, 'Oh…some files for me, then.'

Looking right at me, his greenish-brown eyes momentarily took me in. Then, he turned back to his screen and resumed his typing. I was glad just to have seen a different expression on his face from the stunned one he normally wore.

Valentine was the sort of person you might never really fathom. He was beautiful and people would stare so fixedly at what was on the surface, they could forget there was a person underneath. His face was a vision and he used it as a shield, like a smoke-screen. I came to realise that it stopped people getting close and he liked it that way. But his appearance also drew attention that he found difficult to cope with. His beauty was the sort that looked almost unnatural and it made people suspicious. Whatever the case, Valentine had grown afraid of people's staring eyes.

Valentine's skin was a dark golden colour and his hair was a similar rich deep brown. He looked vaguely burnished, like radiant metal. His almond-shaped eyes slanted slightly upwards at the outside corners giving his face a questioning look, as though everything he witnessed perplexed him. He seemed secretive but not in a bad way – a sort of guardedness that had accumulated itself on account of his unease. And there was a rigidity to his body. His spine was very upright as he worked at his desk. But he was erect, not from a sense of pride or officiousness. His straightness was a result of tension, in the way of someone who'd kept themselves held in check too long. It looked like it must hurt him.

When I was a child my mother used to worry. She'd watch me playing, inventing things in my head and she'd stop me and say, 'Don't expect too much. Don't expect too much from this world.' She told me it over and over, until eventually I learnt not to. I was brought up not to wish for things beyond my means. Later, I realised why she'd said that, but at the time, I couldn't understand. Anyhow, when I met Valentine the part of me that had long been curbed responded too suddenly. I started going beyond the bounds of what was sensible for me and the way I'd always lived.

Slowly, Valentine came to trust me. He sensed that I was harmless perhaps, when he came over to ask me questions about replicating the data etc. At the Unit, he was circumspect and worked hard. He kept his head down. It pleased me then, when occasionally in the breaks he'd come over to talk to me. He didn't say much and it was usually work-related conversation but he didn't seem all that uncomfortable.

I found out we both lived in the Compound. I'd never seen him there. I'd have remembered him. The Compound was huge. 'Cell Stadium,' people called it because of the booths which housed the hundreds of inhabitants. Valentine lived way across in the B-wing. He kept to the buying halls and canteens over on that side.

So I knew, in that respect at least, Valentine was the same as me. He was unmarried, unattached, had no dependants. The Compounds had been set up especially to house our type – single people. Single-status people were considered unstable and in need of restraint. We were likely to come loose like so many frayed threads.

I started thinking of ways to get closer to him. I thought about asking him if he would come with me for a drink after work. He'd made no other friends at the Unit and I thought he might be glad of the gesture. I planned out my words, practising what I would say.

One noontime interval, Valentine was sitting on his own at a table in the refectory. I went over. I was efficient, almost brisk.

'Would you like to come for a drink tonight in the Compound?'

He stared at me with those odd, slanting eyes.

'This is a strictly platonic invitation I'm extending, obviously...'

My body groaned in complaint at the words.

Valentine kept staring.

'If tonight isn't suitable, then perhaps another evening?'

I hovered as he looked down into his noodle and protein pot, holding the fork very still above the food. Then he whispered, 'Yes, alright.'

That threw me.

'...Yes, alright for another evening, you mean? Or...do you mean yes, alright tonight?'

He briefly rubbed the side of his nose. A small sweep down towards his mouth, then another whispered answer, 'I meant tonight.'

That evening I made my way down to the bar in A-wing where I'd asked Valentine to meet me. It wasn't pleasant in there but there was nowhere on site that was any better. All four bars in the

Compound wings were exactly alike. Their walls were painted a pale lime colour. I'd watched them grow grimier in the years I'd lived there. The lighting was too bright, showing up the dirt. They were like run-down versions of the refectory at work. We both had to be back on our floors to be stamped in before the curfew started at a quarter past ten and I was afraid that our conversation topics would run dry before then.

When I got there, I was surprised to find Valentine already sat at a table. I saw him from the entrance. He was over on the right side of the room with his back towards the door. He was changed into his Compound uniform, like everyone else, but somehow it shocked me; I expected to see him still in his work clothes. I stood for a moment, looking at him; the taut line of his back, his shoulders hinting at their precise shape through the material. His head was slightly turned and I could see the side of his face; the shape of a cheek-bone superimposed upon the lime-green paint behind. I was struck by how removed he appeared from the people sat talking at nearby tables. He seemed outside the rhythm of the lives of even the other Compound inhabitants; much further out than anybody should be.

I made my way over to where he was sitting.

'Hello,' I said.

He looked up at me, squinting as if a harsh light was shining in his eyes.

'G'd evening.'

There was a pause. I looked around the room. He was edgy and nervous. He seemed it anyway. So did I, probably.

'I'll go and get a drink. Would you like another?'

He politely tipped his glass a little way as if to show me it was still quite full. His movements were minimal; just fractions of movements.

'No thanks. Not just yet.'

I went to the bar, all the time sensing Valentine through the back of my head. Watching him as if I had eyes there. I was willing him to stay put, scared he might make a bolt for the exit when my back was turned. I quickly bought my blackcurrant and rejoined him.

I sat down on the bench, a little distance away, letting the flatness of the tabletop lie between us. I was conscious of the way my skirt had ridden up. Under the table I could see the two big fat domes of my knees.

I began by asking him questions; easy questions with easy answers to encourage his responses.

'So, what do you think of working at the Unit?'

'It's a very good place.'

'Do you feel settled in there now?'

'Yes. People have been very kind.'

I couldn't see that they had. People were wary of him. He'd been transferred in dubious circumstances and they'd kept their distance.

'You said you lived in B-wing?'

'Yes, B-wing. Floor twenty-three.'

He omitted the booth number. I watched his fingers as he spoke. He was fidgeting with a stray end of cord that came up from a split seam in the upholstery on his bench.

'What's B-wing like? Is it alright?'

'Yes, it's okay.'

'Do the rooms have the dark brown leaf-patterned carpets? Ours do.'

'No, my carpet's plain. It's a tan colour.'

'You'll see the monument from your window over on that side, will you? I knew somebody who used to live over there. She said that she could see it from her booth and the bronze flags on the top that catch the light.'

The banality of the conversation I constructed around us seemed to ease him. He moved a little further back in the seat and looked more comfortable. He didn't clutch his glass as tight.

I continued to ask him questions in that vein and he answered them in a considered way. Touchingly thought-out answers for such easy questions. I told him about my family; insignificant details, a few of which I made up to fill in the spaces he left, but mostly to try and get him to match me in the conversation. I told him about my mother. I told him about the house where we'd lived and some other things I remembered.

'So…do you have family?'

Perhaps I shouldn't have asked such a question. Not on the first night. There was an element of risk in raising the subject with another Compound inhabitant. Mostly people steered clear.

'I've got a sister.'

'A younger sister?'

'No, older. Her name's Mauran.'

'Is she married?'

'Yes. She lives in Cliffer District.'

If I let myself, I could've have grilled him with questions. I tried to take it slowly.

'Must be nice to have a sister. I'd have liked a sister or brother. Does Mauran write to you?'

'Yes.'

I waited a few seconds. 'So you're close, then?'

His weird, hushed voice became quieter. 'Yes, I used to live with her before she married. Before that we lived with our grandfather.'

I was absorbing every word.

'He brought you up?'

'My parents weren't around after I was four.'

'No…?'

'…My sister says I take after our grandfather. She says I'm more like him than anybody…' He shuffled in his seat and seemed to leave the sentence unfinished.

I looked at the people at nearby tables. I caught two inhabitants watching us. When I met their eyes, they turned away. I wondered how Valentine and I appeared to the other people in the room; a graceful, golden-skinned man and a large, fleshy woman. I tried not to care.

'So you got on well with him, your grandfather?'

'Yes.' He paused. 'There's a lot I can't remember.' A closed look passed over his face.

I tried to make a joke. 'I wish there was a lot I couldn't remember.'

He made a short, breathy sound into his glass, and his teeth chinked against the sides. But no more information came. Valentine sat and drank his juice and didn't speak for a while. When I turned to catch a glimpse of him, his face had a faint look of surprise on it, as though he'd shocked himself by telling me the things he had. I suppose I'd surprised myself with the way I'd spoken about my own life. It was an unnerving process, getting to know a person.

I looked back across the room. Despite the Compound uniforms, you could still, with a little effort, read the people sitting around in the bar. You could pick up parts of who they were from their faces and gestures, tell if they worked more through their minds or feelings or senses. You could tell what was dominant in them, what would be dominant if there was the chance to pursue certain paths. But Valentine seemed to be unreadable according to that sort of code. He seemed removed from every aspect of it.

At a quarter to ten, the first alarm for curfew sounded through the Compound. The bar stopped serving its drinks and people began to drain their glasses and gradually move outside.

Valentine and I stood briefly in the square and wished each other goodnight. I didn't try to detain him. He had further to go than me to get to his stamping station.

I wandered back to my floor, through the dark and a light drizzle. The air was full of tiny drops of water that you could hardly feel and that you could hardly see, except when you passed the exterior wall-lights and then you could see millions. I found my way absently up the flights of steps and along the metal walkways, my head full of thoughts. By the time I reached my floor, my coat was soaked with rain.

I was in my bed, already stamped in at the porter's station, my calf still buzzing a little from the charge, when the second alarm went off. The queue at the station hadn't been long.

The lights went out. I lay in the dark going over the things Valentine had told me about himself. I cherished the information. Private things to know about a person.

I once saw someone at the Compound, a stranger, walking across the main square and knew the number of her booth. She brushed past me and the numbers flashed into my head, as clear as if they'd been written down. I followed her to her floor to see if I'd been right, and saw her going in the door that had appeared in my mind.

And I knew when there was going to be trouble for the girl in the booth next to mine. I could feel it coming towards her; it was like a stone being hurled. One night I heard banging and voices coming from next door and in the morning I woke to find the booth empty, all her things gone.

Occasionally, I knew things I had no business knowing, and for no reason. When I was a child, without meaning to, I frightened people with it and my mother tried to get me to stop. I couldn't halt it though, it kept occurring. I didn't tell anybody about it after that. What could I have said anyway? There wasn't a name for what happened in my head.

So I'd know, sometimes, when something was making a person unhappy, I just couldn't always tell what it was. The *knowing* of things would come and go but the feelings never did; even if I didn't understand what I'd sensed, the sensing wouldn't stop. It was like that with Valentine, only with him, I felt everything much more intensely.

Valentine didn't say much but his body gave off an awful lot of noise. It seemed to me that it did. His body seemed to emit a sort of restrained yelling. He was raw all the time; going to work, being at work, coming back from work. Whenever I was near him, I could hear it. It was there in the background of our conversations.

At the Unit, Valentine and I were together more often. I'd encourage him to talk. About anything. Nothing he could say would be too odd, or boring, or repellent. We'd spend the morning or afternoon intervals in each other's company. We'd walk back to the Compound together at the end of the day. I liked to imagine that Valentine was becoming more expressive in my presence. At least, he seemed to grow accustomed to me being there. Through my association with Valentine, my connections with other staff members started to drift. Without noticing, we became distanced from our colleagues. I let the couple of acquaintancesships I had at the Compound flounder as I focused on Valentine.

Already, I was becoming different because of him. My head was filling up with plans, schemes for him and me. Because of Valentine, I would stop living in the way I always had, the way I'd been taught. It meant one thing: all my poor mother's work was coming undone.

One day, I received a payment for good behaviour at the Compound. I was given three citizen tokens in exchange for some of my earnings. I'd made no transgressions in six months and so I was awarded some money to spend outside the gates. In the past, I'd broken rules, unaware they existed – regulations introduced without notification, not made explicit until they were breached. It taught people to monitor themselves more carefully and I'd got better at being cautious.

As soon as I knew I was getting the money, I started planning how to spend it. I wanted to treat Valentine, to surprise him. I wanted something different for us both. Having the tokens in place of the usual Compound tickets meant we weren't limited to the buying halls, bars and canteens inside the gates. We'd have a bit of freedom till the money ran out.

I took the tokens – dark blue metal and bronze imprinted with the symbols of the City – with me to work, carrying them around in my skirt pocket. I could hear them jangling about when I moved, hitting my leg as I walked.

I decided to take Valentine to a place on our way back from work, a venue just outside the Compound. It wasn't an adventurous choice but I didn't want to alarm Valentine by going somewhere unfamiliar. Besides, I had to keep an eye on the time. I'd been able to book us each an hour and a quarter outside the gates after work, but we had to be back at seven o'clock. We walked past this place twice every weekday, going to and from the Unit, but neither of us had even looked through the door.

It was late in the year. It was cold and a bit of snow had fallen. A fine covering lay on the streets where we walked. Soon the City would be weighed down under mounds of snow and they'd have to get the ploughers out.

I waited until the last minute to surprise Valentine with my plan. We were nearly home. The Compound was ahead of us, rearing up at the end of the street; the great mass of it with its high walls blank up to the rows and rows of tiny, dirt-blackened booth windows that ran around the building.

I stopped as we were passing the bar.

'Valentine?'

He turned to look at me.

'Should we go in here tonight?'

His expression changed, his eyes flickering and widening. How easy he was to startle. I should have given him more warning.

'I was granted these yesterday.' I held my hand open. The three coins were hot in my palm from being clutched so tight. 'I thought you might like to try a different place with me.'

He smiled, but weakly.

Above the door to the bar was a sign, 'The Trip'. It showed a picture of a figure carrying luggage, going somewhere unspecific with a vague, unprepared look on its face. I wondered if Valentine had ever been on a trip before, one where it was necessary to pack bags.

'Would you like to go in here?'

'Okay...' He sounded uncertain.

I walked up to the entrance. Valentine stayed where he was on the pavement and stared at me as I pulled open the door.

I stood, peering in, getting a sense of the place. The lighting there was much darker than in the Compound bars. It didn't have the same exposing glare. We wouldn't feel too obvious. A few of the seats and tables were occupied with customers sat talking or reading.

'It looks nice, Valentine. It's warm.'

He didn't move at first so I stepped inside, out of his sight, and then he followed me.

Inside, we made our way across the room. Nobody seemed to look at us particularly. We stood together at the bar, studying the list of available drinks. It was just as I'd hoped; there was a small percentage of alcohol in some of them, the alcoholic content shown alongside the drinks' names and prices. Alcohol wasn't banned outright any more. Initially, in an early phase of the City's Streamlining, mistakes were made and alcohol was withdrawn too fast. The feelings that it had masked, suddenly weren't subdued by anything and things became chaotic. Alcohol had to be reintroduced and removed more gradually. In the bar the drinks went up to 1.75%. Maybe we'd be able to get a little spin off them.

'Listen, Valentine...'

There was music playing. There were no words to it but it sounded good. All music and broadcastings were absent at the Compound making it hard to keep up with what had been Streamlined outside in the City. Hearing the music there in the bar, was lovely.

'What're you like when you're drunk?' I joked.

'I don't know.'

'What do you want to try? You can have anything.'

Valentine wasn't looking at the list of drinks, he was looking at a woman over at the other end of the bar who held a glass of thick silver liquid in her hand.

'I wonder what that is...?'

'I don't know.' I looked down the list. 'It must be this. It's just called 'Silver'. 1.55% alcohol.'

'May I have one of those?'

'Of course. I said you can have anything.'

Despite our discreet entrance, by now people in the bar had begun to notice Valentine and to stare at his face. I could feel his anxiousness increasing as we stood there.

'If you go and find somewhere to sit, I'll order the drinks.'

Normally I was a coward but with Valentine I could be brave. He brought a boldness out of me that I didn't know was there.

As quickly as I could, I ordered two Silvers from the bar-tender. They came in fat, wide glasses with the edges rimmed in silver to match the drink. I paid with one of my citizen tokens, calculating how many rounds the good-behaviour money would buy us.

I took the change from the bar-tender and went to find Valentine.

He was sitting at a table in a dark corner, shielded from the other drinkers by a narrow partition wall.

'This is a good place,' I said.

'Yes.'

I passed him his Silver and sat down. 'You have first taste.'

He angled his glass to his mouth and the glinting, viscous liquid inched towards his lips. I watched as he took a sip, held it in his mouth, and then swallowed.

'Mm...'

'Is it good?'

'Yes, it is.'

As he spoke, I saw inside his mouth and thought I caught a glint of silver lining his tongue.

'Valentine, open your mouth!'

He looked at me warily.

'I think the drink's coated it inside. Can I see?'

He opened up a fraction.

'Your tongue's silver!'

'Really?'

I wanted to show him the effect. 'Watch this…'

I took a sip myself and opened my mouth.

'So is yours,' he said.

The Silver didn't taste metallic at all. It had a sweet layered taste; dense and rich and vaguely flammable. As the substance entered my mouth it felt cold, but as I swallowed and it slid down my throat, it left a heat behind; a warmth that trailed after as it went to my stomach. I took another sip and swirled the liquid around my glass. I watched it clinging to the sides, leaving behind fine silver threads as it slid back down.

It wasn't long before the alcohol took effect. Within minutes I could feel the joints in my limbs loosening; my shoulders and knees particularly. I felt my thoughts beginning to ease and my breathing becoming slower. We were quiet for a while as we indulged ourselves in our drinks.

When I glanced back up at Valentine, I was struck by the grace of his profile. He looked so still, like a statue turned into a man. From his expression, it seemed he was thinking hard about something, something that I couldn't even guess at. I sat, trying to work him out with my Silver-coated brain.

What puzzled me was that he was so reticent. I thought he ought to feel as good about himself as he looked, but his appearance seemed to weigh down on him and make him awkward. He wanted to be invisible, to be forgotten. But it was a knife-edge walk. When someone tries that hard to hide, they can't help but make themselves conspicuous.

I looked down at his legs. I could see the shape of his thigh through the material of his trousers. I wanted to reach over and touch it. Instead, I slid my hands under my legs and pressed them into the seat beneath.

There was noise coming from over to the left of the bar. A group of people in work clothes had come in and were stood talking. Their neck-ties were loosened at their collars. A large man amongst them appeared to be directing the conversation. The group was listening to him talking, breaking into laughter whenever he paused.

I looked at Valentine. He was also watching the group.

'What're you thinking?'

'Look at that man, Neeve.'

'What about him?'

'Doesn't he look composed?'

'Hm?'

'…He looks confident.'

The man was undoubtedly assured. The antithesis of Valentine.

'So?'

'I wonder what it's like…' He sounded wistful.

'You're drunk already, Valentine.'

I sat redundant, as he imagined his life re-lived as the man by the bar. As he wished he was someone other than Valentine Frankland. I wanted to divert him, to steer his thoughts. I wanted to steer him away from anything unpleasant, especially on our special night. I'd only known Valentine for three and a half months, but I was about to ask him something I should have waited much longer to broach. It was a rash thing to do. It must have been an idea that had been circling around in the back of my head, waiting for a chance to break through. Otherwise, alcohol or no alcohol, I'd never have asked him.

'Valentine?'

'Yes?'

'Are you holding out for anything?'

He thought for a moment. '…Not especially.'

I waited for a little while, not speaking.

'Do you ever think of leaving the Compound?'

He looked shocked. He glanced around the bar, checking that no one had overheard me.

'Well…' His voice was markedly hushed. 'Sometimes, perhaps.' I'd grown used to the quietness of his voice, but right then I was having to strain to hear him.

'How long have you lived there? Four years isn't it?'

'Four and three quarters.'

'That's longer than I have, and I've been there too long. I can hardly remember what it's like to live anywhere else.'

'Me neither.'

'It would be good to leave, wouldn't it? To just walk away and not bother about coming back to be stamped in.'

'Yes, but don't think like that. You'll make yourself unhappy. We can't go. It would be different if we had families or spouses.'

'Did your sister never offer you a place with her and her husband?'

'They only have one spare room and they're hoping for a child. Besides, her husband doesn't think much of me.'

'Why not?'

He shrugged his shoulders. 'I don't know.'

Then he said, 'He's training for the Guarda.' He was trying to make voice sound indifferent but he was failing.

The words came out of my mouth then. I blurted them and once they'd been spoken, I couldn't take them back. 'Why don't we leave the Compound?'

'What?' He glanced around again, much quicker this time.

I must have looked like I meant it. He said, 'That's ridiculous. We're not...' He took a breath and looked away. I scarcely heard the next word, '...together.'

I felt myself blush when he said it. I looked down at my hands. I suddenly felt hot in my clothes. I sucked in a mouthful of air to try and take the colour away, but my cheeks continued to burn.

'I know that,' I mumbled.

'Only couples can leave.' He sounded agitated. He was still turned away, staring at the bar.

'I know we're not a couple.'

He didn't turn back.

'I know we aren't...I promise.'

After a few long moments, Valentine turned towards me. His eyes looked hurt and untrusting. He was scrutinising me, suddenly unsure of my motives.

'Besides they don't even consider couples until they've made a binding Engagement Contract.'

'But an Engagement Contract doesn't have to mean anything. It only lasts nine months.'

'It's binding. Don't you know what that means?'

He was right. I didn't know what to say. I was a schemer.

I pulled at my work blazer.

'I'm sorry…I just get desperate to get out sometimes. Sometimes I think I'd do anything to live in a proper home. Don't you ever think that? Don't you ever consider it? Pretending with someone, or even *to* someone so you can get out. It's been done before. It's not unheard of.'

'Forget it, Neeve.'

'Uh.'

The subject was dropped but it left behind a nasty silence. I sat quiet, feeling the effects of the Silver wearing off. I got up and headed to the bar for two more.

I'd ruined our special night. I spoilt it with my big mouth and didn't know how to remedy it. All the money I had I spent on Silvers, but even they couldn't put things right. Valentine was uncomfortable with me for the rest of the evening. We drank the drinks hurriedly and were back at the Compound before time.

At the Unit, the following day, Valentine remained distant. He concentrated hard on his statistics when I had to pass his work-station. I made a couple of attempts to talk to him but they didn't amount to anything. He wasn't rude or dismissive, just inaccessible. I let him be for fear of making things worse and bit my nails off worrying. It felt as though everything at the Unit followed Valentine into his remoteness; the halls, the corridors, the offices, the people.

But Valentine must have been lonely too. Without each other, neither of us had anyone. After three days, it seemed the idea of my harmlessness had been partially restored in his mind; he approached me at my work-station in the afternoon break. He'd brought me a cup of water from the fountain.

'I got you this.'

'Oh. Thanks.'

I thought he might say something, something conciliatory. Something about his distance over the past days, but nothing came.

I spoke instead.

'I'm sorry I offended you. I didn't mean it in that way. Not in the way you think.'

He hesitated.

'…You shocked me. That's all.'

'Sorry.'

'I understand though.'

'You do?'

His voice quietened. 'You want to get out.'

'It's stupid though. I got carried away.'

'Well…' His voice trailed off. 'I hope your water's alright.'

He went back to his screen.

I dreamt I was with a man in the A-wing bar but the man wasn't Valentine. He was just a random face that my mind had picked out from the Compound crowds. In the dream I was sitting beside him, stroking his hair. The man was reticent though. He was rejecting my advances. The only thing was, the more he resisted, the harder I tried. I was squeezing his hands, refusing to let go. I realised that I was trying to entice him into signing an Engagement Contract. But it wasn't working. The man was getting angry. He started to fight me off, wrenching himself loose. I wouldn't stop. He pushed me aside. I fell to the ground. He hurried away, shouting at me, calling me names. I ran after him, but he was too fast. I was like a deranged person then, pounding along the Compound walkways, metal hammering under my feet. I was banging on the booth doors, yelling at people to come out and sign the contract. A troop of Compound Patrollers appeared at the end of a landing. I saw them coming towards me, ready to fire. I opened my eyes.

I woke to the dark of my booth, cold and sweaty with my brain whirring. I tried to slow my breathing. The air in the room felt icy. I thought of Valentine and was ashamed. I was shocked that I could dream of trying to escape with someone else, leaving him behind.

I lay trying to block out the sound of the pipes. People said that Compound pipes cried. It wasn't the pipes though, they just carried the noise. Sometimes there was banging too; a soft, repetitive thudding. People hitting themselves against the metal. I lay there trying not to hear. It must have been between two and four o'clock because there were those usual, whispery, early-morning cries. People at the Compound said that you didn't need a clock in the night time. They said you could tell the hour from the noises in the pipes.

We purposely avoided talking to each other about it, Valentine and I. Since that morning at the Unit when Valentine brought me the water, we hadn't mentioned getting out. Valentine even made a point of telling me things he enjoyed about being at the Compound. Things you'd have to make an effort to appreciate; the leafless trees in the square, the ever-present artificial light, the secure locks on the booth doors. I made an attempt to resign myself to things as they were, to make the most of my time with him and to ignore the rest. I told myself I could spend the whole span of my life in the Compound, if necessary. Better that, than be without him, I thought.

But, that evening spent in 'The Trip' I'd astonished not just Valentine, but myself as well. I'd given voice to something and it'd set off a chain-reaction in my head. During the day I was able to control it, I could rein myself in. But at night I couldn't help myself. I started having recurring dreams. Often I was awake long before the alarms, having spent what seemed like hours caught up in frantic escape dreams that never came to anything. I'd lived all that time at the Compound without being plagued by thoughts of leaving. Getting out had always been beyond the bounds of what was possible and I didn't think about it. Not until I met Valentine. Suddenly, in comparison with him, everything seemed wrong. For the first time I saw how I'd been living and it made me desperate.

But then, out of the blue, he spoke of it again.

We'd just edged into a new year and one of the heaviest snow falls of the season had recently hit. We were at the Unit. It was the morning break and I was standing in the corridor, drinking from the water fountain. Other people from our office were in the refectory fetching drinks; cups of study-aid because a batch of Census forms had just come in.

'Neeve.' His voice was suddenly right in my ear.

I was caught off guard and I swallowed a mouthful of water the wrong way. He'd whispered it as I was bent over the spout and it set me off coughing. I tried to get my composure back while I wiped my mouth with my sleeve.

'Val-ent-ine.' I coughed out his name.

'Sorry. Are you alright?'

'–Yes.'

'I wanted to tell you something while it's quiet.' He was standing close. Even so, his voice was almost nothing. 'I think you were right about the Compound.'

'Hey?'

'I think I'd be happier.'

I looked at him, not comprehending.

He mouthed the words. I had to read his lips.

'…If I left.'

'Oh.' I was stunned.

He didn't say anything. He was waiting for me.

'…That's good.'

Still nothing.

'I'm glad.'

He nodded, then. Oddly eager. Not like Valentine.

I took another mouthful from the fountain. It was probably snowing outside but still I needed something cold.

'Neeve?'

'What?'

'What do you need to do to get an Engagement Contract?' His whispering was insistent.

'Huh? I think we need to get a form.'

'And what else?'

'Fill it in. And send it.'

'Are you sure that's it?'

'I'm not *positive*…'

People were starting to come up the corridor, back from the refectory with their cups.

'I'll find out, alright?'

'Alright.'

We went back to the office.

I discovered later, that the week before Valentine approached me with his decision, there'd been a series of reprimands in his wing, each one more severe than the last. Maybe they'd wanted to set a precedent for the new year. A woman had been caught stealing cream-filled biscuits from a shop outside the Compound. They'd stained her hands with indelible dye and were keeping her inside a containment cavity indefinitely. Some other people had come in a few minutes late for a curfew and the porters had been told to increase the power charges in their stamps. The charges had been increased so much that the offenders were lamed. And these weren't even the more severe punishments.

All the same, I found it hard to believe that Valentine could change his mind. It seemed improbable. Impossible even. Maybe it had just taken him time; time to decide that, in spite of everything, my plan wasn't stupid. It seemed he might actually have been weighing it all up during the intervening weeks. Maybe, once I'd suggested it, the idea had begun to work on him too, like it had on me. I didn't know what had been going on in Valentine's head, but one thing was clear: he was more desperate than he let on.

And significantly, he didn't say, 'we'd be happier' if we left. He said, 'I'. From the very first, he wanted to stress his singularity. He wanted to make clear his separateness, right from the start of our scheme.

I knew the leaving process wasn't an easy undertaking. A person had to be serious to attempt it. Exit applications from the Compound were only permitted once in every five years. Even then, the Compound Authorities considered some inhabitants unsuitable for Full-citizenship outside the gates. Some people would never be allowed to leave.

Firstly, we had to put in a claim for an Engagement Contract. I didn't know how to go about getting an application form. I felt awkward asking people at work. I didn't want to arouse curiosity. There was a cleaner, Cynthie, on my floor in A-wing. She lived outside the Compound and came in every day from the Winder District. She wore a ring on her finger. She only looked young, sixteen or seventeen, she couldn't have been married very long. But Cynthie was smart and knew what went on. I decided to ask her.

I heard her with her bucket one morning, working her way down the line of women's booths, knocking on the doors to be let in to clean. I went out and spoke to her before I had to leave for work.

'You have to go to one of the Commissions for Betrothals and Marriages,' she told me.

'I don't know where they are.'

'The nearest one's in TER84. You'll need to take the tunnel-trains. It's quite a way. Get off at Barrowseal and walk from there. The Commission's on Mauxhall Street.'

'Can I go on my own?'

'What d'you mean?' She stopped wiping the railings.

'To collect the form and bring it back for us to sign.'

Valentine had mentioned that he wasn't keen on the tunnel-trains. He'd used them with his sister before his arrival at the Compound. He said he'd been disturbed by the other travellers, sitting opposite him, staring.

'Don't be silly. You're a Compound inhabitant. It's only the regular citizens that just have to fill a form in. Compounders have to get interviewed. And it can't just be one of you for an Engagement Contract. Unless no-one'll have you and you're marrying yourself.' Cynthie poked me in the arm with a small, bony finger as if to bring a laugh out of me. I tried but the sound I made wasn't convincing.

'Interview? I never knew about anything like that. What sort of interview?'

'You sit down and they ask you questions.'

'But what do they ask?'

'I dunno…About your private lives.'

'How we met and things?'

'Maybe.'

'How long will it take?'

'It'll depend on the couple, I suppose.'

'Oh.'

I was imagining Valentine trying to answer their questions.

She leant in close. 'So is it not a proper alliance, then?' Her tone was conspiratorial.

'Yes! Of course it is.'

Cynthie just shrugged. 'You'll be alright. No harm in people applying, is there? They can only turn you down.' She chuckled. 'Write to the Commission. Say you want an appointment.'

'It's on Mauxhall Street?'

'That's it. TER84. Now let me get on. I've got this whole row to do.'

As I walked through the Compound building that morning I tried to detect its smell. It was an awful smell to encounter; a mix of stale food, waste-matter, cleaning fluid, damp and unhappiness. But what frightened me was the fact that I no longer noticed it. When I'd first come to the Compound after my mother died, I couldn't get the smell out of my nostrils but now I was so accustomed to it, I no longer smelled it. It panicked me that I couldn't. It made me feel as though I was so much a part of the place, I'd never get out. I walked sniffing the cold air, trying to make out its stink.

I waited until after work, until after the evening food delivery. Then I went over to B-wing, to Valentine's booth to give him the news.

Within certain hours, Compound inhabitants were permitted to call upon each other in their rooms. Every booth door had a hatch in the metal, a spy hole with a concave lens. The Patrollers could move the hatch aside and peer in. It afforded them a clear view of everything that went on. The booth doors could be locked from the inside to protect inhabitants from unwanted visits, but there was no protection from the Patrollers. All the Patrollers had keys.

When I told Valentine about the interview, his face went white.

'I thought you said it was just a form?'

'That's what I thought, Valentine. Honestly.'

'What kind of interview?'

'They'll just ask us a few questions. It'll be alright, I promise.'

'I thought we just had to send a form.'

'So did I.'

He shook his head. 'No. I can't.'

'But I'll be there too. I could even answer for you. Probably.'

'No.'

'It can't be a big a deal or else nobody'd do it. It'll be a formality.'

'No, Neeve.'

'But…'

He stopped me. 'I'm sorry. I can't.' He shook his head again, more vehemently this time, as if there was a stone inside his skull that he needed to shake loose. 'It's not that simple…For me, it isn't.'

'What d'you mean?'

That's when he told me. Sometimes I wonder how long it would have taken him to tell me if he hadn't had to. Maybe he never would have done. Even then, it took him a while to say it. He fidgeted about the room, walking back and forth, picking things up and putting them down again.

When the words came, the effort he had to summon to force them out made his voice uncharacteristically loud. For him it was the equivalent of a shout.

'*I have a Passion.*'

Silence.

'Oh…'

His whole body was trembling.

Then he whispered, 'Do you know what that is?'

'Yes.'

I'd heard of Passions but I'd never met someone who had one. At least, I wasn't aware that I had.

'You see? How're they going to take to me applying for an Engagement Contract?'

'Um…'

Then Valentine left the room. He just got up and walked out of the door.

I didn't know what to do. I sat and waited, trying to think through the implications of what he'd said.

When he came back, he seemed surprised to see me still there. He perched at the end of his bed. His body looked rigid. Every few seconds, I heard his teeth chatter.

'Where did you go?'

'To the bathroom.'

His face hadn't regained any of its colour. Maybe he'd gone to be sick. His hairline looked wet where he must have washed his face.

We sat staring into space. I tried to think of something to say to him. Everything I thought of sounded crass and tactless.

'So…do you know anyone else with…the same thing?'

No reply.

'…I wonder if they've been allowed to make Engagement Contracts?'

'I don't know of anyone else.'

'Um…'

'You're the first person I've told.'

'I *am*?'

'...Well, my family knew...but I didn't tell them. The doctors did.'

I nodded. I felt overwhelmed.

'It was diagnosed at birth. I've been taking tablets for it since I was little. It's under control.' He obviously hated having to speak about it. Even so, he seemed to want to reassure me that he wasn't dangerous.

'I felt alright about applying when I thought it was a form. I thought we'd get a refusal letter back anyway, rejecting us on the grounds of...this.'

'I see...'

'But I couldn't do an interview, Neeve. Not face to face.'

'Uh-huh.'

Valentine sunk into silence. I peered at him on the bed. His trembling had stopped. Now he just looked very still. Occasionally, his jaw persisted in its tiny judders, but the chattering sound had gone. He'd become unreachable.

I sat silently, looking at the white flecks on my fingernails.

Eventually, Valentine moved. He shifted slightly and his chest heaved.

'Valentine?'

He raised his head.

'I wondered, haven't your doctors ever told you what you're permitted? About Engagement Contracts and things?'

'No.'

'What *have* they said?'

'I just go to the clinics. They prescribe the pills and tell me it's unlawful, instigating the...problem. That's it.'

The Passions were properly referred to as Bad Passions. B.A.D. It stood for something. But Valentine didn't want to give his its full name.

'Have you asked what *is* allowed?'

'I've never needed to.'

'Never?'

'No.'

'So, you've never...?'

He was twisting his fingers into the material of his trousers. He looked like he hated himself. Poor Valentine.

I quietly breathed out and gazed about his booth: at the stark walls and the dull carpet; the window on the far side, too high up to see out of without a chair; the small photograph in a frame on the table of a girl who bore a likeness to Valentine. Attractive like him, but without his slyness. She looked happier than he did, more like a normal person.

I continued to sit. He sank further away. Ages passed.

When I finally spoke, my voice sounded booming in the quiet.

'Perhaps we should still apply?'

He looked stunned.

'Neeve, no.'

'But listen...'

He flashed me a look.

'I know you're frightened of the interview, but there might not be any need to be. For all we know, there could be thousands of people ... who ... in your situation ... and they're getting Engagement Contracts all the time. There could be though, couldn't there?'

He didn't answer me. His distrustful look didn't budge.

'As far as we know, there's no evidence to the contrary, to say that they wouldn't allow it.'

He said nothing.

'You could spend your whole life at the Compound never knowing you were always allowed to form Engagements and leave. Isn't it better to find out now, than to wait five or ten years say, before discovering you could've gone sooner? Besides, the diagnosis might be less important now. What with the tablets and everything.'

I couldn't tell whether he was listening. He was holding a section of hair, pressing it down onto his forehead with his long fingers.

'I think we should still apply. Maybe you could enquire about it at the clinic. How often do you have to go?'

He just shook his head.

'Okay. But please just let me write to the Commission to ask for an appointment?'

'Neeve…' There was a terrible resigned tone to his voice. Just that alone should have stopped me.

'If they turn down our request for an appointment, then we'll know for sure and that's it. We'll leave it alone and forget the whole thing.'

'You're pushing me,' he warned.

'I'm trying to help, that's all. I bet the interview would be fine. I bet you it would.'

He made a quiet, harassed sound in his throat. He tilted his head back, leant it against the wall of the booth and raised his eyes to the ceiling. He looked desperate, like he hoped to find the solution to his life written up there.

'Just think of what it would be like outside….compared to this.'

'*Alright*, Neeve! Make the appointment and then they can turn us down and that'll be the end of it.'

I'd beaten him down.

'D'you mean it? I can apply?'

'Whatever you want…'

'You won't regret it. I wouldn't let anything bad happen, I promise.' I realised, as the words were leaving my mouth, that I was swearing to something that I couldn't guarantee. He knew that too. I'm sure he did.

Chapter 3

Lol asked if he could move the image of the Circle from the kitchen and stick it to the wall above the bed.

'It's nice to lie down and look at it,' he said. 'It has a beneficial effect.'

'How d'you mean?'

'It makes you feel good. You should try it. Would you like to give it a go?'

'Um… Not just now,'

'No? Valentine, what about you?'

'Alright.'

I couldn't tell Valentine that they used the Circle at the Realm; that it was their special tool. I couldn't say anything. I wasn't supposed to know.

'Okay. Great. Lie on the bed. Head at this end. You don't want to, Neeve?'

'No thanks…I'll watch.'

Valentine lay down, his head at the foot-end of the bed.

Lol fetched pillows and slipped them under Valentine so that he was supported and his head was raised.

'Half-close your eyes, Val, and gaze at the Circle.'

He lay there quiet for a minute or so.

I kept remembering Willa-Rix; how excited she'd been taking the Circle from the sole of my shoe. It made me uneasy. Whatever Lol thought the Circle could do, troubled me.

Lol was laughing. 'Don't stare so hard, Valentine. Just relax. Soften your eyes a bit.'

A few more minutes and then, 'Nothing's happening.'

'Honestly, you've no patience! You've only been at it a short while.'

I watched Valentine closely as he stared at the Circle-pattern. I told myself it was only a series of shapes, that shapes couldn't be dangerous. If anything bad started, he'd just have to close his eyes.

Valentine spoke without taking his gaze away. 'It's moving…' He sounded quite relaxed now. He was breathing more deeply.

'Great.' Lol turned to me and whispered, 'It's different for each person.'

Then he gestured to me, pointing to the door, indicating that he was going out of the room.

He said, 'Just keep gazing at the shapes, Val,' as he left.

When Lol came back a minute later, he had a little metal box with him. It was small enough to be held in one hand. He went to the edge of the bed and set it on the floor. He seemed to press or switch something on its side and then a noise began to come out of it. It was a sort of gentle buzzing of a very low frequency but fairly loud.

I hurried over to whisper in his ear, 'Lol, the neighbours'll hear it!'

He turned and whispered back, 'No they won't. Even if they do they'll think it's just a noise caused by some electrical fault or something.'

Then, to Valentine he said, 'Don't just listen to the obvious sound. Relax your ears a bit. Listen to the space that carries the first sound; there should be another tone in there alongside it somewhere.'

Valentine gasped. I looked at him. There was quiet surprise on his face.

I wanted to relax my ears then, to hear the other sound too. But I couldn't do it. All I could hear was the low buzzing from the box. I wondered what was happening. Valentine looked so peaceful.

Without even meaning to, I began to pick him up. I started to feel Valentine and the peacefulness that was in him. It was like the steady peacefulness was moving gradually out, filling the area around him. I felt my guard dropping despite myself. The Circle was affecting me regardless of my concerns.

The peaceful feeling grew steadily stronger and then it wasn't just in and around Valentine; it seemed to be in the whole room. In comparison to that, the thoughts in my head began to seem small and far away. If I still had worries, I couldn't feel them any more.

I went to the bed and lay down beside Valentine. I didn't care. I wanted to participate. Lol went to fetch me a pillow and then I lay staring at the Circle through my half-closed eyes. My gaze followed the lines that ran around the design; shapes that flowed into shapes and into other shapes.

Slowly it started. It was like my eyes played tricks; the lines of the Circle-pattern were beginning to move. I blinked a couple of times but the lines still flickered. The pattern looked as though it had begun to turn, the lines leading my gaze around.

As the Circle moved I could see more shapes in it; squares, oblongs, diamonds, stars and kites jumped out. The lines oscillated and bounced off the white background.

I could hear the buzzing from the little box. I tried to relax my ears, whatever that meant, to listen in a different way. Almost as soon as I did,

I could hear another sound, a single note; it was a clear ringing of a much higher pitch than the first. Something about it was beautiful. It was like the perfect note.

Eventually, my eyes came to rest on the small circle at the centre of the design. It was just a shape but it had a sort of authority to it. It didn't move. It gave off stillness. I couldn't take my eyes away.

And then after a while, the Circle itself seemed to sink back so that all that was left was the space. There was just the space and it seemed nothing would ever be able to intrude upon it. There wasn't anything to intrude upon it because it seemed like the space was everything. And, along with all the space came a familiar feeling; a feeling that'd been there behind every thought I'd had or could remember, behind every sense or feeling, every experience, only now it had moved. It'd come right to the forefront.

Wandering round one of the Compound's second-hand buying halls I found something for Valentine; a pair of darkened glasses. There on a discount rack with some old, corrective-vision spectacles was this one pair with tinted lenses. They were made from proper glass, not plastic, and they had dark frames to match the lenses. The frames were almond-shaped just like Valentine's eyes.

I lifted the glasses for a better look, moving them about in the buying hall lights. The lenses were hardly scratched. As I held them up in front of my face everything went a little darker. I tried the glasses on, checking my reflection in the little mirror attached to the rack. I could see my eyes quite clearly, nevertheless the tint in the lenses gave a sense of protection somehow.

'They suit you,' the stall-tender said hardly looking at me.

'They're not for me,' I replied. 'They're for a friend.'

But the woman had turned away already, trying to catch the eye of another customer.

I was thinking of the potential interview. If it turned out that Valentine and I were asked to go to the Commission, the glasses might make the tunnel-trains easier to deal with. Even if the eyes of other travellers were too much for him, at least his own would be shielded a little.

I glanced about the buying hall. Everything was tinted a slight purplish-black. I watched a man at the next stall, sifting through a huge box of old Compound uniform buttons. I looked at him through the lenses and then over the top of them. Lenses. No lenses. Lenses. I kept switching, watching the man's skin and clothes changing colour and tone. The glasses seemed to give distance to things. Like the feeling you could get from the Silver: a too-keen sense getting numbed, things not mattering as much.

'Are you taking them or not?'

I turned back to the stall-tender. The broken, red blood vessels on her cheeks had turned greyish-purple. The woman had grey cheeks.

'Yes.'

'A quarter, then.'

A reply arrived from the Commission in response to our request for an appointment. They sent notification both to Valentine and to me but Valentine didn't find his letter until later. He didn't often check his mailbox. Maybe letters had bad associations for him after his dismissal from the Postal Department. In any case he didn't always open the mail he received. There was a pile of unopened envelopes on the table in his booth.

The envelope bore the insignia of the Commission so when I found it in my mailbox I knew what I was about to open. I started shaking. I tore open the paper. Inside there was a pale pink card with fringed edging.

Dear Miss N Glynnan,

Your request for an appointment at the Commission of Betrothals and Marriages has been approved. Please attend an interview with Mr V Frankland at 2pm on Friday 17th March so that your suitability for Engagement Status can be assessed.

Commissioning Officers,

Mr and Mrs J Lovejoy

I put my hand over my mouth. I wasn't sure what sound might come out. I nearly doubled over in the mail hall in front of the other inhabitants. I had to collect myself. It was only the first stage, it didn't guarantee anything. Everything was still as it was; I had to go and meet Valentine and head to work.

When Valentine saw the appointment card, he had trouble believing it.

'I told you there'd be nothing to worry about. If there was, they'd have turned us down already...'

He took the card from me and held it with both hands. He stood blinking at it, staring at it like it wasn't real. Maybe he thought I'd forged it, but why would I? He kept re-reading the appointment time, muttering to himself. Then he carefully handed the card back to me. He couldn't bring himself to speak about it. We just walked to work as usual. I didn't know if he was glad about it or he wasn't.

I could have given Valentine the glasses in his booth but there'd be nothing much to look at in there. The refectory at the Unit was on an upper floor and had large windows. Valentine would be able to put on the glasses and view the City from up there. I wanted to see the expression on his face when he did.

I managed to get us a table right by the window.

'These are for you, Valentine. For the train journey to the Commission.'

I passed him the paper bag.

'They're to say thank you too,' I lowered my voice, '...for allowing me to apply.'

He took the bag from me, unsure. He sat holding the bag on his knee.

'It's just a little present. You don't owe me for it.'

He opened it and looked inside. He seemed to be considering the contents.

'I thought they might be a good idea.'

It was hard to tell what he was thinking.

'Thanks.'

'They're darkened. Things look a little different. You feel sort of safer in them. I've checked out the rules for wearing them. They're in the bag as well.'

'Thanks, Neeve. You're kind.'

He peered into the bag for a couple more seconds, then he sealed it back up, wrapped the paper closely around the frames, and slid the package into his pocket.

For a minute or two, I felt stung. My eyes prickled. He wasn't going to try them on.

Now that our appointment at the Commission had been set, I needed to ask Mr Spinks, the department supervisor, for time off work. A person needed good grounds for not attending.

I waited for a quiet moment, a time when I wouldn't be interrupting his work.

His office door was ajar. I could see him inside. He was sat at his desk, reading a file. My knees felt weak just getting up and going over to his room.

I knocked on the door but he didn't look up. I tried again and he raised his head.

'Come.'

I went inside and stood, waiting to be addressed.

Without taking his eyes from the page, he said, 'What is it?'

'…Sir…I've a request.'

He continued reading the file.

'I need permission for…' I spoke carefully, one word at a time, studying his face for a reaction, 'an afternoon away from work.'

His expression didn't alter.

'For myself and Valentine Frankland.'

He still didn't look up. He just said, 'And your colleague can't come and ask for himself?'

'I thought that only one of us should come, Sir. So we aren't both away from our screens.'

I stared at his hands. They were large and heavy-boned. The skin was stretched tight over his knuckles.

'On what grounds?'

'Well, uh…just on the grounds that we don't waste work-time by both being… '

'*No*, Glynnan.' He let the file fall onto the desk. 'On what grounds are you requesting this absence?'

'We have an appointment…'

'Yes?'

'At a Commission.' I didn't like to say which one.

'Show me.'

He held out his hand and shook it to hurry me up. I fumbled in my pocket. He took the appointment card and I blushed at its pale pinkness and frilled edges.

Mr Spinks scanned the words and made a quiet, thinly disguised scoffing sound.

'You and that marred article, Frankland, from the department?'

'Yes, Sir.'

Under his breath, Mr Spinks said, 'What a depressing thought.'
He put the card to one side.

'It'll be passed to Attendance Authorisation. They'll verify the
appointment. Then they'll make a decision.'

'Thank you.'

'Now stop delaying your tasks. Go back to your screen.'

I blundered from the office. I left Mr Spinks sitting, shaking his
head, acting like he couldn't believe what I'd asked of him.

On the day of the appointment, we were permitted to leave the
Unit at the end of the morning session.

I'd just turned off at my work-station and was getting up from
my desk. Mrs Woan, on the screen next to mine, said, 'You'll have
to work twice as hard next week to make up the time. Not just you,
him as well. Mr Spinks'll see you do.'

I didn't say anything.

I went over to Valentine. He was still at his desk. His screen was
switched off but he was making a big deal of putting the files away,
one at a time, into a drawer.

'Valentine, it's time.'

As the morning had gone on, I'd noticed Valentine drifting
further and further into a sort of trance. It was like he'd just let
himself. Maybe he'd even done it on purpose.

We went to the property store to fetch our coats from their pegs.
It felt odd, taking our coats, leaving the others hanging there.
Suddenly we were free, but not the remaining coats, not the people
they stood for. It felt odd going down to the ground floor, walking
out the front doors. My eyes weren't quite ready for the midday
light.

We made our way to the tunnel-trains.

I badly wanted to say something to try and feel a closeness with
Valentine, but I kept quiet. It didn't seem right to pull him out of
his protective trance. We walked in silence to the trains and I kept
an eye out for him on the roads when we came to the crossings.

On the way, we passed a tree growing by the side of the road. Its
branches and twigs were rough and old-looking, empty from the
winter, but at the tips, it was starting to show new buds. *Soon the
weather will be warmer*, I thought. *Not long now*. I took the tree as a sign.
A good one for me and Valentine. The buds were the same colour as

my appointment card; pale pink. Seeing signs in things was something that I'd tried to stop doing. I thought I *had* stopped it.

We reached the tunnels and went down the great long flight of steps to the trains. When we neared the bottom, Valentine brought the darkened glasses out of his pocket. I was surprised to see them again. I didn't expect to. He slid them onto his face with both hands. He did it secretively, like he didn't want me to notice, so I pretended that I hadn't.

I read the tunnel map on the wall, tracing the tracks across the City. We had to take the Beecher-Line from Widechapper out to Dunstall Rab and then change onto the Shilleah-Line to get to Barrowseal. Tunnel-train maps were the only maps I knew. And these were localised; not linked with the tunnel-train maps in any other part of the City. There was nothing to show what particular things were where. There were only lines on the station walls showing which trains ran through certain named parts of the City. Beyond the local maps, the City stretched out endlessly, passed every horizon; an infinite expanse.

Our tickets were pre-bought for us by Compound Authorities, paid for with money deducted from our wages. We had to collect them from the ticket office. I showed our proof-papers and was handed four tickets: two *outs*, two *returns*. Widechapper to Barrowseal.

It was a good time of day to travel. The tunnels weren't so busy. Fewer eyes to stare at Valentine. It shocked me, the dryness of the air and the amount of wind blowing down there, way underground.

A train pulled in and we got on. I searched among the seats to find our numbered places. Valentine sat down immediately, leaning his head against the window. When the train started up, Valentine's skull registered every judder of the carriage, and we trundled through the tunnels, all the way to Dunstall Rab, and then again on the train to Barrowseal, with his head knocking against the glass. I kept checking his eyes behind the lenses. He seemed to keep them shut for the entire journey. He only opened them, when it was necessary; when it was time to change trains.

We arrived at Barrowseal station. I gave Valentine's coat sleeve a tug to let him know we had to get off.

Coming up from below ground, I saw that the buildings were different. They looked more ornate, not so many storeys. We stood in the breeze coming up from the tunnels and wondered where to go. I waited until I saw someone with an approachable-looking face and then I asked her.

'Go across there. Down Berdee Road. Follow it along till you get to a four-way junction. There's an old Omni-Depot on the right hand side. Take a left at the junction and Mauxhall Street's about three roads down on your right.' I had to listen carefully to the instructions because Valentine couldn't.

'Thank you.'

We went through the streets, the way we'd been told, Valentine's body moving like a contraption someone else was working. I checked my watch: 1-41.

We got near. We passed the Depot that the woman had spoken about, and turned left at the junction. Mauxhall Street was where the woman had said it would be, three turnings down.

The Commission's road was short and wide and the building was obvious as soon as we turned into it. The Commission dominated the street. It was big and ceremonial-looking, set back from the pavement. The outside wall was covered in deep red-coloured glazed tiles. Small arches dotted the building's façade, and way up, far above head height, red-brick struts protruded towards the road. At the end of each strut, sat a pair of bronze kissing doves. They looked new and strangely out of place. Like they might have been added as an afterthought, when the building took on its current use.

We went up the steps. My stomach was aching from nerves and the inside of my mouth felt dry.

I pressed the bell and waited.

A distorted female voice crackled out of the intercom.

'Give your full names, please.'

I put my face close to the device.

'Mister Valentine Duvante Deyan Kristic Frankland and...' I tried to swallow but I had no saliva, 'Miss Neeve Glynnan.'

There was a pause, then a buzzer sounded, and the door clicked. I pushed it open.

We walked into a reception area. It was small and dark, with wood panelling on the walls and tiles on the floor. There were four upright chairs pushed to the sides; two on the left of the room and two on the right. Then there was a set of inner doors. The doors had frosted windows which let in a small amount of light from inside the building. A wooden sign was attached to one of the wood panels.

Please be seated.
A Commissioner will be
with you shortly.

I whispered, 'Don't forget to take off your...' pointing to my own eyes. Valentine reluctantly removed the glasses.

We sat and waited. I was fidgety. I pressed my hand into my belly to try and ease the ache there. Valentine was beside me, staring ahead into the dimness of the little room.

A woman came through the inner doors.

She looked at us.

'Gudafternoon.' She said it quickly and the words ran together.

'Hello.'

On her lapel, there was an identity badge: 'Mrs J Lovejoy'.

'Follow me, please.'

We followed her through the doors and across a large carpeted hall. Her pace was brisk. We trailed after her, up a broad staircase. At the back of her head she wore a jewelled clasp to hold her long hair in place. Somehow my eyes got fixed on that as we followed her up.

At the top of the stairs, we were met by a man. He was tall and groomed, like the woman. He wore a similar badge. 'Mr J Lovejoy'.

'Good afternoon, Citizens. You've come to the Commission of Betrothals and Marriages for an Engagement Contract assessment?'

I nodded.

'Just so. My wife and I will be conducting the interviews. Mister Frankland, if you'd come with me and Miss Glynnan, if you'd go with my wife. We'll begin right away.'

I panicked. We were going to be interviewed separately. I hadn't imagined it that way. I couldn't believe I hadn't considered it. I thought I could feel Valentine's reaction as well as my own; two hearts pounding. I could feel Valentine looking to me, desperate. I didn't know how to respond. I just stared at the floor.

'This way, please.'

The man took Valentine away. They were headed for a room off the upper landing.

'Miss Glynnan?'

The woman meant for me to follow her.

Please be alright, Valentine. Please be alright. I was willing him to cope.

The woman led me to a door on the opposite side to where Valentine had been taken. She showed me into a small room, and followed, taking a seat behind a desk. She gestured for me to take the other chair.

I sat, distracted, thinking about Valentine. I tried to concentrate. The room was decorated like an old-fashioned study but sparse. It had traditional-looking fixtures in it; furniture made to seem like it carried the weight of time.

'Citizen, female: C.f: Neeve Glynnan.'

I looked at the woman. She had an ink pen in her hand. She'd taken off the cap, and put it to one side of a pile of papers. There were two piles lying on the desk: one pile with information about Valentine and me (I could see our names repeated down the front of the first page) and the other, a form made up of several sheets of paper, waiting to be filled in.

'Citizen, female: C.f: Neeve Glynnan,' the woman said again.

Her pen was poised ready, over the form.

I wasn't sure whether or not it was a question. I didn't want to appear impolite by not answering. 'Er…yes.'

She wrote my name in a box at the top of the first page.

'You live…' She was reading from her papers. 'in the Sixth Compound. TER57. Widechapper District.'

'Yes.' I confirmed another fact.

'Your wing is…'

'I live in A-wing. Floor 38. Room 570.' The words came out cracked and hoarse. My throat was so dry that I was losing my voice. I could see a jug of water and some glasses on a tray behind the desk but I was too afraid to ask for anything.

'You've lived at the Compound for…'

I opened my mouth to speak but all that came out was a rasping coughing sound. Without saying anything the woman turned away and poured some water from the jug.

She passed me the glass and waited while I drank.

Then she repeated the question. 'You've lived at the Compound for…?'

I knew how long I'd lived there, but right then, I couldn't trust myself to be sure. I had to add up the months on my fingers, beneath the desk. I was shaking a lot. I kept losing count.

'You've lived there for how long Miss Glynnan?'

'Three years and eleven months.'

'Your date of birth?'

'The 24th of November, 54.'

It flashed into my head that, so far, I hadn't had to lie to her. I felt a little surer. I wanted to tell her how our birthdays were exactly half a year apart; both born on the twenty-fourth of the month, Valentine being precisely a year and a half older. I couldn't tell what was significant to her and what wasn't.

'You're the daughter of Rita Adele Grommeth, now deceased, and…' Alarm shot through me. '*Flyde Janna Glynnan*.' She said his name. She said it like three dirty words. 'Convicted felon.'

'Uh. Yes.' I couldn't look at her.

'Your father was a political dissident.'

In the panic over Valentine's Bad Passion, I'd managed to ignore my own obstacles, my own unsuitability for married life. I bit hard against the inside of my cheek.

The woman was waiting for me to confirm.

'Yes.'

More writing.

'What evidence can you put forward to prove you don't carry your father's tendencies?'

'…I've been…My record at the Compound has been clean.' I said. 'It has for three years.'

The woman watched me and didn't speak.

'My father was…' It felt odd talking about him. 'He wasn't…a law-abiding person. I'm not like that.'

'You don't hold extremist beliefs?'

'No, I…believe in what's right.'

She breathed sharply out through her nose. 'And what is that in your opinion?'

'…What we have now. The laws of the City.'

'Why do you suppose, your father acted in the way that he did?'

'Because he…he was misguided. That's all I can think.'

'He was misguided.' She repeated my words, as if to stress the feebleness of my answer.

There was a pause. The woman was weighing something up in her mind. I sat quietly. I was a Glynnan. The only child of a man who had undergone Vanishment. It wasn't good.

I watched the woman's pen as she wrote something down in her tidy hand-writing. Then she shifted to another line of questioning.

'You've been acquainted with Valentine Frankland for…?'

'Seven months.'

'And you met him where?' Her eyes scanned across the page.

'I met him at work.'

'You both work in the Statistics Input Department at the Census Unit.'

'Yes.'

'On the 10th of August last year, Mr Frankland was transferred to the Census Unit.'

'Yes.'

'From the Postal Department. Is that the date from which you were first acquainted?'

'Ye-s.' Valentine's transferral, and the reason for it – what if these were also things that could count against us? I tried to explain, 'They moved him because we were busy with the extra work load. The department needed more people. A very busy time.'

She looked up at me from her page. Her eyes were very pale blue, like glass.

'Describe your feelings for Mr Frankland.'

She'd changed tack again.

It was a personal thing to be asked outright in a strange office. 'Well, I'm…' I coughed. '…in love with him.' My cheeks flushed.

The woman was unfazed. 'And what do you mean by that?'

'I mean…he's very…dear to me.'

She was waiting for more.

'And I care about him, so I want him to be alright.'

I didn't know what else to say.

'Since?'

'Since...' She was staring at me now, not writing anything down.

'Sorry, since what?'

'Since when have you felt this?' She said it like I'd been unwell.

'Since...when I met him.'

She paused, looking at me. Then she went back to filling in the boxes. I kept watching her pen as it scratched about, recording my words.

'For how long have you been courted?'

'Uh?' It was the way she phrased the questions. It took me by surprise. '...By Valentine. Er, I've been meeting him socially for six months. And...courted for five.'

So there it was; the first proper lie. I hadn't been courted by anyone.

'Didn't you just say that you'd met Mr Frankland seven months ago?'

'Ye-s, that's right. Seven.'

It was like she was accusing me of something, only I didn't understand what it was.

'But six months plus five months equals eleven.'

'Oh, no...I meant, for five of *those* months. I didn't mean five *more* months.'

'I see.'

I thought then that she might deliberately be trying to confuse me, to put me off my stride. She'd known what I meant. She must have done.

'Could you stop that please?'

'Pardon?'

I hadn't realised, but I'd been running my fingers backwards and forwards underneath the top of the desk. I was nervous, that's why I was doing it but it must have been irritating her.

I took my hand away.

She turned a page over on the form.

'Do you honour the state of marriage?'

'Yes, it's very important.'

'How so?

'Well...it's beneficial to people.'

'The state of marriage brings public responsibilities, Citizen. What does that mean to you?'

'To me…it means my duties would be to…' I looked at her hair and smart clothes, at the name on her identification badge, '…try and set an example to others…people who aren't married yet.'

She didn't respond, she just filled in another box with her pen.

'Your spouse would be your protector and guardian…'

It took a second to register. She was talking about Valentine.

'How would you view your role as his marriage partner?'

'Well, I'd try to…I'd do as much as I could. I'd be loyal and try to help him with things if he needed me to. I'd –'

She cut me off. 'Would you degrade that state to achieve inferior ends?'

'How d'you mean?'

'To be given Exit permission from your Compound, Citizen.'

'No.' I swallowed hard on nothing. 'I definitely wouldn't.'

There was a long pause. The woman didn't speak for a while, as if she was allowing me time to fully appreciate the seriousness of what was happening.

Then she spoke again, 'On a rating scale, with one being the least and ten the greatest, how committed do you consider yourself to be to this partnership? Give two examples.'

'I think maybe…an eight or a nine.'

'Which is it?'

'Er…a nine.'

The examples I gave were of buying the darkened glasses and of sharing my good-behaviour money; the first things that came into my head. I realised as I was telling her, that they weren't illustrations of commitment so much as something else. Perhaps I should've gone back and tried to think of other instances but somehow that seemed worse.

Then I was taken through a series of similar questions. I had to assess my devotedness, dutifulness, loyalty etc. But the qualities I was asked to consider were confusingly alike. I found it difficult to distinguish between them. I think I said I was a 'nine' for everything.

'What about the matter of offspring? Do you hope to fulfil this aspect of married life?'

'Yes.' I tried to smile, to look how I thought a potential mother would look.

Then, the worst part of all.

'Do you know of Mr Frankland's condition?'

'What d'you mean?'

'You're not aware of it?'

'Well, yes. I know about it.'

'Do you understand that Mr Frankland has a problem?'

'Yes.'

'What do you know about it?'

'That…he has a Bad Passion.'

'And?'

'That he's known about it from birth. He goes to clinics for pills…'

'How, do you suppose, might it affect your Engagement?'

My mind went blank. I started speaking without knowing what I would say.

'I don't know. He has the tablets. He takes them everyday without fail. We'd do our best for each other…'

She didn't look satisfied.

'And…I'd try not to draw attention to it. I'd encourage him to focus on other things. I could help him to live a good life. I wouldn't allow anything else.'

'What do you know of the *nature* of his condition?'

'Um…I don't know a *lot*.'

'No?'

I was floundering.

'Valentine's a private sort of person. He doesn't like talking about it.'

'Do you know what his Listing is?'

'His Listing?'

'Yes.'

I didn't know what she meant. I didn't know what that was – a *Listing*.

'Your answer, please.'

I was too afraid to say that I didn't understand.

'…Mr Frankland hasn't told me that yet. He says he will. When he's ready, he will.'

She wrote something on the form. I tried to lean closer to read it. *Applicant unable to answer question.* She'd written something else besides that, but the words were hidden by the pen and her fingers.

'The Engagement Contract is legally binding, Citizen.'

'Yes...'

Since Valentine's Passion had been brought into the interview, I couldn't handle it so well. Questions about my father, and then this. It was too much. I was going to pieces. I was fretting over what might be going on in the room across the landing. I couldn't concentrate so well on what the woman was saying.

'If, once it has been assessed, Engagement *is* granted, then you will be given a nine-month probationary period...' I kept drifting in and out of the words, '...end of that period you and your partner have proven yourselves suitable, then a full Marriage Contract will be drawn up...' '...deemed to have been falsifying information for the sake of obtaining Exit from your Compound...' '...resulting in prosecution for both parties for misleading an official body. You will then be ineligible for any further Engagement Contracts...Do you understand this, Miss Glynnan?'

'Yes.' I could hardly speak.

She went on to say other things too, but my brain couldn't take them in. One of her sentences seemed to end as a question.

I said, 'Yes,' but I didn't know what to.

She wrote on the form again. Longer sentences inside a large box on the last page.

'Now I will allow you some quiet time to think about the document you're about to sign.'

She picked up the papers from the desk and left the room. She pulled the door closed behind her.

I couldn't think about anything for longer than a couple of seconds. Not even Valentine. I laid my arms on the desk in front of me and rested my head. I tried to breathe but it was hard getting the air inside my lungs.

My brain slowed a little. After a while I looked up. Mrs Lovejoy hadn't come back in. I tried to listen for sounds, for signs of Valentine, for the sound of Mr Lovejoy's voice as he left his interviewing room. But the building was noiseless.

The door opened. Mrs Lovejoy came back in.

'Have you considered?'

'Yes.'

'You're prepared to sign the document?'

'Yes.'

She put her fingers into her jacket pocket and brought out a pen. I took it from her and she pushed the completed form across the desk towards me. She pointed to four places on the last page where I had to sign.

At the top of the page in bold black ink there was a printed statement. *Marriage is a public institution. It brings civic duties.* I wrote my name underneath four times, but I did it badly. My handwriting was unreadable. I felt like I'd forged my own signature. I was too nervous to make it right.

'You can go now. The interview's over. Mr Lovejoy is still conducting his interview however, so if you need to wait, you can do so in the entrance foyer.'

'Thank you.'

I followed Mrs Lovejoy out of the office and down the stairs.

As she walked she said, 'You'll receive letters informing you of the success or failure of your application.'

I spoke to her back. 'Do you know how long that'll take?'

'No.'

She took me down to the chairs in the entrance.

'Goodbye, Citizen.'

'Goodbye.'

She went away.

I sat in the dark room and waited for Valentine. I told myself it wouldn't be long before we could leave. Soon we'd be getting on the trains and going home.

It was quiet. I went over the interview in my head, trying to remember my answers. We'd practised our responses beforehand, guessing at the kinds of questions we'd be asked. I'd had to coax Valentine into doing it. It'd made him nervous to think about it. That was when I thought we'd be in the same room. But Valentine was on his own, fending for himself. I hoped he'd been able to remember.

My throat had become dry again. I badly needed some water. I wanted to go and find a bathroom, but I was afraid of wandering around unauthorised inside the building. And I was scared of not being there for Valentine when he came out.

But he didn't come. I looked at my watch, the numbers slowly moving through the minutes. Nineteen minutes had already passed. I thought somebody might come in through the doors; another couple to be interviewed. But nobody came. I wondered what Mr Lovejoy and Valentine were discussing for so long upstairs. How much could be asked about a Passion that a person had never even acted upon?

I looked at my watch again. It said I'd been waiting for twenty-eight minutes. I sat staring at it, at the seconds going by: forty-six, forty-seven, forty-eight, forty-nine.

Then I heard a voice. It was Mr Lovejoy. I could hear him approaching the inner doors on the other side. His voice was muffled. I waited for some kind of reply from Valentine, but instead I heard Mrs Lovejoy.

'He'll come to when he's outside.'

'Yes. Let the girl see to it.' He spoke brusquely.

There was a brief scuffling sound and then Valentine emerged, into the entrance. The door was shut behind him.

'Valentine…'

He looked terrible. He swayed in the place where he stood. I got up and took hold of him. His face was pale and his eyes didn't seem to be registering what they saw.

I reached into his coat pocket, pulled out his darkened glasses and put them on his face.

'Valentine?' He didn't notice or respond.

I pressed my face into his coat.

'Let's not stay here. Quick, come into the air.'

I led him through the doors, supporting his body as we went down the front steps.

'What did they do?'

No answer.

'Are you hurt?'

He didn't look hurt.

'I'm sorry. I'm so sorry.'

I staggered with him down the street, my arm around his back, trying to take his weight. I was telling him to take deep breaths but I don't think he heard.

'I'm sorry. I'm sorry…' I couldn't stop saying it.

I started to cry. I couldn't help myself. Tears went down my face as I walked. I kept my head low but I knew we were attracting glances from pedestrians. I couldn't remember the route we'd originally come and the distance to the tunnel-trains was longer than it needed to be; I took a wrong turning and had to double back.

We were stood waiting at a road-crossing point when I heard Valentine muttering. He seemed to be speaking to someone I couldn't see, or maybe just to the air. His mouth was close, just centimetres above my ear as I held on to him. In the gap of sound left by the halted traffic, I caught snatches of sentences.

'The assessment of…if it's operative…indecence.'

We crossed the road and by the time we reached the other pavement, the words had dried up. He'd stopped mumbling.

Eventually, we reached the steps down to Barrowseal station. It was as if the sudden gust of wind coming up from the tunnels did something to Valentine, because as soon as it hit us, he bent over at the entrance-railings and vomited. There was mess on the pavement. I didn't know what to do except hurry him away from it. We stumbled headlong down the steps to the tunnel-trains, Valentine still in a daze, me stifling sobs, trying to squeeze the tears back inside my eyes.

Chapter 4

Lol came back with the food. He'd managed to get mango from somewhere. It was Valentine's favourite, only this one was fresh.

'Where did you find it?' I asked.

'I got it from a friend. These come once in a blue moon. We're lucky. Smell it, it's delicious.'

Lol placed the mango-half in my hands and I smelled it. It had a wonderful, sweet aroma.

It was another black-market item.

'I got fish and potatoes to make us fish pie.' Lol was taking food items out of his bag and setting them on the table. 'The mango's for starters. Give me an hour and it'll be ready.'

Thoughts of his dream from the night before were filling my head. Strange to be troubled by something somebody has done to you only in their mind, only in their sleep. Maybe the meal was his way of saying sorry.

'Do you think Valentine will eat with us?' I asked.

'I hope so. I'm hoping the smell will make him hungry enough to lure him from his room. I'll give you a shout when dinner's ready.' He wanted to be left alone to cook.

But I couldn't let it lie. Hurriedly I said, 'Do you feel alright after last night?'

He paused, caught momentarily off-guard. It was a second or two before he replied.

'I just had a dream. I'm fine now.'

'That's good…'

Lol dropped the potatoes into the sink. They thudded against the bottom. He turned on the tap and water splashed over them.

'Do you want a hand with anything?'

'No, thanks. I can sort it.'

I went back to the big room.

Slowly the flat filled with the smell of cooking. I wondered whether Valentine would come out of his room. I couldn't imagine that he would.

'Neeve! Valentine!' Lol was calling us to eat.

I went through to the kitchen. Lol was tending to something cooking on the stove. On the table were three plates, a beautiful slice of mango on each.

'It smells good.' I said.

Lol was dipping his finger quickly into the hot pan and then tasting. 'Um. Thanks.'

No sign of Valentine.

I went to the drawer for knives and forks and got out three of each.

'Can you watch this cheese, Neeve?' Lol let go of the wooden spoon and left it resting against the side of the pan. 'Make sure it doesn't burn.'

'The cheese?' It didn't smell like cheese.

He'd picked up one of the plates from the table. 'I'll tell him he can only eat it if he comes out of his room.'

He headed out of the kitchen with the slice of mango. I heard him knock, wait and then open Valentine's door. I tried to imagine Valentine's face when he saw Lol standing there holding the plate of fresh fruit. I stared down at the two remaining slices on the table. Their colour was so bright.

Talking was coming from Valentine's room but only Lol's voice.

A few minutes later Lol returned to the kitchen with the plate.

I stopped stirring the cheese. 'What did he say?'

'Not much. I'll eat it myself if he doesn't come out.'

Lol took the melted cheese from the stove and poured it onto each plate beside the mango.

We carried the food through to the big room. As we went past Valentine's door, Lol raised his voice, 'We're eating now.'

We sat with the plates on our knees. Lol, defiant, took the first mouthful.

'Mmn. Delicious.'

I badly wanted to know how it tasted but I was stalling, waiting for Valentine. I sliced off a chunk of mango with my knife. My mouth watered. I looked at the melted cheese on my plate. Lol saw me looking, touching it with the prongs of my fork.

'It's goat's cheese,' he said. 'They get milk from goats and make it into cheese. You know, goats? Like sheep.'

'I've never had it.'

'Try it and see.'

There was a sound from the other room. Two quiet thumps. Slowly, Valentine was getting up. He appeared from his bedroom and stood in the hallway, his face looking greyer than ever.

'Attaboy,' Lol said.

Valentine came to the big room and sat on the bed.

Lol picked up Valentine's plate and passed it to him, placing it on his bent knees.

'It'll do you the world of good!'

Valentine stared down at the fruit in his lap. Then he picked up a fork and began to eat. I couldn't say whether he ate from hunger or from duty. Maybe he didn't know himself.

I ate too. I tasted the mango. It had a mixture of smoothness and roughness to it; rough where Lol's knife had cut through the fibres in the fruit, but smooth due to the sheen of the flesh. It felt odd; like another tongue in my mouth besides my own. It was strange and very sweet.

The cheese was strange too, not like ordinary cheese. It complemented the fruit; warm and slightly bitter contrasting with the mango's coolness and sweetness.

Lol said, 'What d'you think? The mango's at its peak of ripeness.'

I replied, 'It's lovely.'

Valentine managed a nod.

I looked at Valentine chewing the food painfully slowly. At least he was eating. He tried the cheese and left most of it, but ended up having the whole mango slice. When he'd finished he gazed down at the juice it'd left behind.

Lol took our plates and went back into the kitchen to get the next course. I was alone with Valentine in the big room.

I spoke, trying to reach him. '...I'm so sorry about what happened yesterday.'

He didn't look at me, he just whispered, 'They'll come for me soon...'

I knew who he meant. He meant the Guarda. He'd said it in such a flat way, as if he was resigned to the fact that it would happen.

'No, they won't, Val.'

'I need to get to the club. Neeve, ask Lol to take me to the club. I can hide there. Tell Lol to take me tonight.'

'O – okay...I'll ask him. After the meal, I'll ask him.'

Lol came back in with the food.

'There wasn't much fish to go around. I've had to pad the pie out with potatoes and white sauce.'

We ate the rest of Lol's meal, Valentine just picking at the food. The pie was good but I couldn't enjoy it. The atmosphere was too heavy. Every *time I swallowed I could feel fish bones catching in my throat, scratching me on their way down.*

After his ordeal at the Commission, Valentine didn't respond when I knocked on his booth door. For almost the entire weekend, meal-deliveries were left outside his booth and were taken by other inhabitants.

He managed to surface for work on the following Monday morning, but he wasn't himself. We walked to the Unit together, but Valentine didn't say a word. He was still wearing the darkened glasses. I wondered if he'd taken them off at all since the interview.

I wanted to know everything that had happened: what had gone on in the interview room with Mr Lovejoy; what Valentine had been asked and how he'd responded; whether our answers had matched or not; whether Valentine had even signed the contract. I kept looking for a way to ask, but Valentine remained closed-off for the whole of the journey. I tried to silence the buzzing in my head. I tried to be patient and wait. I hoped his distress hadn't been for nothing.

When he got to his work-station, Valentine sat down at his desk and set up his screen with the glasses still covering his eyes. I wanted to say something to him, quietly remind him in case he'd forgotten. But I knew that wasn't it. I sat waiting for what would happen, Mr Spinks doing his rounds.

Valentine attracted glances from the other staff, but no-one spoke. At ten-thirty, Mr Spinks emerged from his office. He crossed the room without haste, arrived at Valentine's work-station and stopped directly behind his chair.

He waited a moment. Then, to the back of Valentine's head, Mr Spinks said, 'Working well this morning, Frankland?'

It took Valentine so long to respond, I didn't think he was going to answer. He remained facing forward, gazing at his keyboard.

'Yes, Sir.' I presume that was what Valentine said. I couldn't hear him from my work-station.

Another pause. Then, in an even voice, Mr Spinks said, 'Whatever it is you're wearing on your face, remove at once.'

That was it.

He turned and went back to his office.

Everyone was quiet, watching Valentine. Watching to see that he did what he was told. Even from where I was sitting, I could see that his hands were shaking as he reached up to his face. He folded down the side-arms and laid the glasses on the desk, beside his screen. It was as if he needed to keep them near him in order to feel safe.

People went back to work. I tried to lose myself in the figures on my screen and let my worries over Valentine recede. About half an hour later though, I was brought back to the room by a sudden loud thud. I swung around in my seat, and there was Valentine, lying on the department floor. He was sprawled with one of his legs caught up with his over-turned chair.

I got up to rush over to him but somebody stopped me.

'Don't make a fuss, Glynnan.'

I watched as Valentine was made to stand. Somebody had to hold him up. Orderlies were summoned. A man and a woman arrived to take Valentine to the treatment rooms. I watched as they led him to the door and away.

Someone went over to Valentine's screen and peered at it. I heard them say, 'Doesn't look like he's done anything all morning. The slacker's just been staring at his screen.'

Mr Spinks, who'd observed the event from his office door, turned and went back to his desk.

Valentine started to wear the darkened glasses all the time. After the interview, they became part of him. I don't think he even took them off when he was alone, except maybe to sleep or wash. The only times he needed to remove them were when he was wandering around the Compound grounds, which he did less often, and also when he was at his work-station at the Unit. On his way to and from the Compound gates, going from his booth and back, he took to walking briskly with his eyes almost shut, trying to replicate the effect of the glasses. I had to adapt myself to addressing two flat, darkened lenses instead of his beautiful, slanting eyes.

A week after the trip to the Commission, on the Saturday morning, I went over to Valentine's wing to see if I could convince him to leave his booth and come for a walk with me. The sky was bright and cloudless. I thought a walk might help to bring

Valentine out of himself. I thought it might encourage him to talk, to tell me, at last, about his interview. There'd been no word from the Commission.

When I knocked on his booth door, Valentine didn't open it. That wasn't unusual. Since the interviews, he'd been reluctant to let me in. But this time, I heard another voice inside the booth. A woman's voice.

She said, 'Aren't you going to answer that?'

The hatch lay across the spy hole, covering it. I suppose I could've slid it away, seen what was happening inside, but I wasn't about to do that.

Footsteps came towards the door. It opened a small way and Valentine stood in the gap. I got a shock when I saw his face. He didn't have his glasses on and he had a look of panic about him.

'I wondered if you wanted to come for a walk?'

'I can't.' His face was pale and he was trembling.

'Well, never mind. Uh…not to worry.'

I couldn't just go. I couldn't not ask. I lowered my voice to a whisper. '…Have you somebody with you?'

He nodded. He was twitchy, looking past me. He couldn't keep his eyes still.

'A Compound Administrator?' Sometimes they did spot checks.

'No.'

'W-ell…who?'

'A follow-up.' He stated it blankly. 'From the Commission.'

I think I gasped when he said that.

Valentine was about to close the door.

I put my hand out. I silently mouthed, 'Mrs Lovejoy?'

He shook his head. One quick shake. Then he shut the door.

I walked away but only got as far as the end of the first walkway. I stood at the top of the steps, trying to think. Somebody had turned up unannounced. That couldn't be right. They were unlikely to come like that, with no warning. Then I remembered; Valentine didn't check his mailbox. Maybe he hadn't for ages. There'd be a letter that he hadn't found. I was kicking myself for not getting him to check. But why would Valentine need a follow-up?

I had a horrible feeling – as though I was wrecking his life. I didn't want to hang around inside the Compound, not that morning. I still had an hour left of my weekly quota of recreational time outside. I made my way to the Compound gates, not knowing where I would go. I said I was going for a walk and got myself signed out. The woman did a body search, but I scarcely noticed it. I was to be back within forty-five minutes, she said.

I was only partially aware of the direction I was heading. I kept seeing Valentine's frightened face in my head.

I smelled the dank odour of the water before I saw it. I'd made my way to the canal. I followed the smell down the steps to the tow-path.

I stood and looked at the canal snaking away to either side of me. The sky was reflecting on the surface and for a minute, I was blinded by the long strip of light. I leaned against the wall with my eyes closed, waiting for the spots in my vision to clear, waiting for my nerves to calm.

The canal ran down behind the Compound's D-wing. I couldn't see it from my booth window and sometimes I forgot it was there. I didn't know where the canal went; I'd always had to turn back for the Compound before I'd got very far.

I started along the path. I told myself, *just walk, Neeve.*

I looked at the weeds growing out of the wall; weeds with wiry, scarlet stems and tiny, yellow flowers. They were forcing their way between the stones, trying to get to the daylight. I wandered close to the edge of the water and stretched my arm out to see its reflection on the surface of the canal.

A man and a woman were coming towards me. They looked like they were from the Compound. They glanced at me and nodded a greeting as they passed. I nodded back. I'd noticed before how, in the sun, you could see quite clearly through people's hair, see light on their scalps beneath. That's what happened, it was said, after years of Compound food. There weren't enough nutrients and eventually poor health made your hair fall out.

I walked on for a while until a shadow fell abruptly across the path. I looked up. I'd come to one of the Waterways bridges. Its wide stone arch lay across the canal. I felt instant coldness as I stepped into the shade.

'Hey there!'

The voice startled me. It came from the back of the arch. The sound rang out and echoed against the opposite wall. I peered into the dimness to trace it and saw a face come forward. It was Willa-Rix from C-wing, Willa-Rix who I'd known since childhood. She had her paper stall set up under the bridge. There she was, earning citizen tokens without the knowledge or permission of the Compound Authorities. On top of a fold-out table, in sectioned-off compartments, she'd lain piles of different types of paper. Small stones were placed on top of the piles to keep the sheets from blowing into the canal when the wind picked up. If she'd needed to, she could have had that table folded up and away within seconds. I felt like a criminal just standing near her.

'Hello, Willa.'

'Now then, Miss, how's life?'

'Okay...'

'Looks like you've lost a bit of weight, girlie.'

'...Maybe. I'm not sure.'

Sitting with Willa-Rix, behind the table and the piles of paper, was an elderly woman. I knew her too. It was the woman from the Compound who scrubbed her skin to get the dirt off. Some days you saw her and she would be red-raw, almost to the point of bleeding.

'I hear you're on your way out. Won't see you for dust soon, eh?'

'How d'you know about that?'

'Oh, you know, word gets about.'

'Well...we'll have to wait and see. I don't know yet if we will.'

'So you've got yourself a bloke?' Willa grinned at me.

Hearing Valentine mentioned made the awful, sick-feeling worse. I shook my head and mumbled into my chest.

'What is it with him, anyway?'

'What d'you mean?'

'He's stunning, Neeve. He is. But he's an *odd* one.'

I looked at her. 'Is he?' I didn't know anything any more.

'Yeah, well, who isn't around here, eh?' Willa nodded her head sideways towards the older woman, and then let out her rowdy laugh. She always laughed like that. Like everything was just an easy game. Willa was the only person I knew who seemed impervious to life at the Compound. Normally, it was nice to hear that laugh, but that day the sound went through me. It jarred inside me with the nervous aching over Valentine.

I looked at the other woman. She was sitting, perched on her tiny stool, brushing invisible mess off her lap. A long time ago, she'd been housemaid to important City officials. Now, between the sounds of water dripping from the arch into the canal, over the rumble of traffic moving steadily along the road above our heads, I could hear her muttering, 'Filth. Everywhere's filth... Meddlesome, meddlesome.'

'Tell us about these Engagement plans you're making. I like a good love story.'

I wanted to walk away. I didn't want to talk about it, not right then.

'...Well, we might be getting an Engagement Contract.'

'Oh, yeah?' Willa was canny. I thought her voice sounded teasing, sceptical maybe.

You know we're trying to fake it to get out, Willa-Rix. You know. I bet you know.

'Be good if you did. Get out, I mean.'

Compared to Valentine and me, Willa more closely fitted the profile of the type the Compounds claimed it was necessary to contain. She'd be at the Compound for years and years. Even if she met someone to form an Engagement with, they wouldn't let her leave.

I looked beyond the shade of the bridge, back towards the sunlight. The air smelt mossy under the arch. I was trying to think up an excuse to leave.

'Can't you move your stall out there, into the sun a little?' I asked. 'It's so cold under here.'

She gestured her head upwards. 'No way. There's Guarda up there. Patrolling the top of the bridge. I don't want them looking over and spotting me.'

Certain people came specially to see Willa. She'd slip fliers in between the sheets they bought. That way bits of information got passed round. Willa often saved up her weekly quota of outside-time so she could spend two hours on a Saturday doing it. She had to keep finding places outside the Compound gates to hide her table and the papers. I couldn't believe that she'd lasted as long as she had.

'Don't the Guarda come down here, onto the path?'

'Haven't seen them in a while. It's less now the boats have gone.'

'Oh…'

Willa was moving from one foot to another, her hands in her pockets, trying to keep warm. My eyes fixed on the way her shoes took it in turns to lift off the ground but I was thinking about Valentine's interview. Wondering if it was over.

'D'you want some of this stuff then?'

'Hey?'

Willa was looking deliberately down at the piles of paper. 'Do you want some of this stuff?' She said it in a way that suggested something else.

'Er…not really. Thanks all the same.'

'Suit yourself.'

Willa-Rix had grown up in the same part of the City as me. We'd played together when we were young. She knew about my father and my aunt joining one of the Movements and the consequences of that. She knew how changed my mother had been by it all. Willa always said the City was to blame for what happened. She never found fault with my family. She said it was seeing what happened to my parents that made her decide to get involved with the Movements. She also said that it *was in my blood* and always assumed I'd want to be more involved with things than I did. Whenever I saw Willa, she tried to draw me in. I'd had to learn how to deflect her requests.

'What're you going to do when you get out?'

'*If* we get out.'

Willa had lowered her voice. 'You can achieve so much more on the outside, you know. There's places I could tell you about. You'll be starting up at the clubs again, won't you? No more stamping station and curfews for you, eh? I remember you loving the dancing.'

The dancing. She made me remember. In my head was back there; coloured beams from the club lights shining through my closed eyelids as they twirled across and over me. It was true, I used to love that.

'Mm…Maybe we'll go.'

'That reminds me. I've heard about this place. It's meant to be good.'

'Yeah?' I had a quick look at my watch to try and discourage her.

'You and whatsisname should try it.'

'Valentine. Look, Willa, I've got to make tracks.'

'Hang on a minute. Just one more thing. Listen, I thought of you when I heard about this place. You'd like it. It's out in the Wantsworth District. It's called "The Realm". I've met some people who go there.'

'But –'

'Listen, Neeve. They've organised things. They know what they're doing. Just go to the club. Go for the music. It'll be better than any of those dumb places in the Dance District that you'll end up at.'

'Willa, I don't even know if we'll be getting out of the Compound.' I whispered. 'Even if we did I wouldn't take Valentine. Not somewhere dangerous. He's nervous. It wouldn't be worth it.'

'It's not even a *tiny* bit dangerous, Neeve. The place has been running for I don't know how long. The security's never been breached. Look, I'd go myself if I could. You know I would, if it wasn't for the curfew…But *you* could go. Just go once. Report back to me on what it's like. I could get you passes. I reckon I could get you in on the strength…' Her eyes shifted to the side and her thumb flicked at the corner of a pile of paper, 'of your relatives.'

I flinched, hearing them mentioned. I stared at the scanty light from the water that was reflecting on the dark arch of the bridge, pale lines moving about behind Willa-Rix's back.

I thought about my father – that last evening. At the time I didn't know it was the last evening and that he was leaving. Nobody said anything. The only reason I remembered the evening so clearly was because I was taken, as a treat, to a public screening. The screening was about a talking mouse with big ears who wore clothes and had a dog as a pet. My father took me to see it. My mother didn't come.

When we got there, we saw my aunt outside and we asked her if she wanted to watch the feature with us. I sat between them in a long row of seats and my father held my hand through the screening. While we were watching, my aunt passed me something in the dark. It was small and hard and shaped like a thick triangle. In the dark of the screening hall I couldn't see what it was. I held on to it not knowing what I ought to do with it or if my aunt would ask for it back. I didn't understand and got anxious. Holding on to it, I forgot to watch the mouse and his pet dog. Maybe the oddness of the evening was seeping into things. Things felt unfamiliar, confusing me to the point that I didn't recognise even ordinary objects.

The edges of the triangle started to melt between my fingers. Slowly it dawned on me; *a confection*. My aunt hade given me a sweet. I was supposed to eat it. I felt stupid, so stupid that I couldn't move or lift the sweet to my mouth. I kept hold of it and the heat from my hand melted it down to a sticky mess. I hid my soiled fingers under my coat. At the end of the screening I asked to go to the washroom. I stood in a cubicle and tried to wipe traces from my fingers with a handkerchief.

That night my father put me to bed. My mother was already asleep. Before he wished me goodnight he said, 'Sometimes the best way to protect the people you care about is to go away. You understand that, Neeve?'

I nodded. I don't think I did though – not really.

In the morning my father was gone. The neighbour that I fetched to come and see to my mother said, 'She's stricken. That's what your mother is. *Stricken.*'

'…Because it's quite a big deal getting people in.' Willa had broken into my thoughts.

'Getting people in?'

'Yes, not just anyone can get a pass.' Willa-Rix was still talking about the club. 'It's quite a big deal.'

'Yes?' I didn't care if it was or it wasn't. I felt worn down.

'Yeah, but I'd do that for you. For a *special* friend.'

'Mmn.'

'Will you go then?

'…I'll think about it. *If* we get out, I'll think about it.'

'Great. Honestly, you'd have to see it. It'll be really something. And nothing would happen. I wouldn't tell you to go if I thought something would.'

'I've really got to go. I've got to get in before my time's up.' I started to back away.

The old woman was glaring in my direction. As I moved off, she yelled something at me. An insulting kind of shout. It sounded like *filth-mongerer!* The noise rang about, under the archway.

It was late afternoon before I went back to Valentine's booth. I kept putting it off. Part of me thought things would be better for Valentine if I never went near him again. But I suppose it wasn't in me to just leave things alone.

When I got to his booth, I found that his door wasn't quite closed. There was a narrow crack of light around the edge of the door jamb. I couldn't hear anything from inside. I nudged the door with my finger and it opened a little way. I could see Valentine lying on his bed facing the wall. The blanket was under him, ruffled up on the mattress. I pushed the door again and its hinges squealed as it opened. Valentine lifted his head. For a moment he stared at me; his eyes vacant. Then he lowered his head and rested back down on the bed.

I stood, wavering, trying to work out the best thing to do, dithering between going and staying. In the end, I moved, machine-like, towards Valentine. I went over to the bed and lay down on it, behind him. The mattress sunk under my weight, but Valentine made no reaction to my movements. I lay close to him, careful to keep a space between us, along the length of our bodies.

Valentine was very still. I could hear him breathing.

After a time, I lifted my arm, brought it down over his side. Every centimetre of movement was slow and measured. I rested my arm tentatively on his body. He felt strange beneath my touch, submitting to the situation the way a bird might submit to a person's hands; frightened, quiet, waiting to be released. I wanted to think that he was able to gain comfort from my holding him, that he was responding a little to the warmth, but I couldn't really say that he was.

We lay like that until the bell for evening meal deliveries sounded and the attendants came round with the trays.

After thirty-two days of waiting, a letter from the Commission finally appeared in my mailbox. I'd been waiting expectantly all that time, but now seeing it lying at the bottom of the box, I almost wished it wasn't there. It was so flat, white, precise. Four perfect corners. The Commission's insignia printed on it. I held it in my hands. I couldn't bring myself to open it, not straight away. I had to take it back to my booth.

I carried the envelope up to the thirty-eighth floor, clutching it hard like it might work itself loose from my hands. I'd been in and out of my booth door thousands of times. Even so, I had to stand in front of it, checking and re-checking the number '570' before going inside. I knew I was being absurd but I needed everything to be right.

I closed the door and stood thinking about the difference between right then and a few seconds time. What would it be like once I'd read? I thought about two opposite futures. How it might be better to just hold on to the hope I had; not to open the letter at all.

I tore it open. I closed my eyes as I pulled out the paper and unfolded it. They were closed till the last moment.

First thing I saw was that I'd ripped the letter. I could still read it though. All it said was,

The Probationary Engagement of Valentine Duvante Deyan Kristic Frankland and Neeve Glynnan has been approved by the Commission of Betrothals and Marriages, 114 Mauxhall St, Barrowseal, TER84. Probationary Engagement Status commences as of 29th March to be reviewed nine months from this date. After the probationary period, the approval or denial of marriage status will be decided.

It was signed by Mr and Mrs Lovejoy.

I thought, *there's been a mistake.* I thought, *they're going to change their minds.* It felt like a hoax. Like the letter was fake. I was too stupidly suspicious to be glad right away. But the letter bore a fancy stamp showing it was Commission paper. I stood, trying to trust the words. Each time I read, they were the same.

I held the paper together where it'd been torn. The rip ran from the top of the page, down through the first '*n*' in Valentine, tearing his name and coming to a stop a millimetre above the '*E*' in *Engagement.*

There was another page of *Additional Information.* That piece of paper had also been ripped. I read a small segment of the writing. I wasn't in a fit state to take in much more than that.

…Custody of any offspring produced during the probationary period will fall to the Infant Care Division until such a time as the marriage status of the above is granted. If marriage status is denied, the Infant and Child Care Divisions will retain custody of the aforementioned offspring until adulthood.

Valentine hadn't said anything but I knew he was waiting for me to come and tell him the news from the Commission. Waiting, trying not to wait. Trying to forget a letter was coming at all. If Valentine's sister had written to him, he wouldn't have known about it. He hadn't been near his box in weeks.

I knocked on his door.

Nothing. I waited for about ten seconds.

Then, 'Who's there?' I could hear the strain in his voice.

'It's me. It's Neeve.'

'What is it?' His voice moved nearer till he was standing on the other side of the door.

'The letters have come…from the Commission.'

There was a sudden silence from inside. I could almost feel his dread coming through the metal.

I couldn't keep him hanging on. I said, 'You did it. They approved our Engagement.'

I heard a strange noise. Something scraping slowly along the wall inside his booth. Then another silence.

When he eventually spoke, all he said was, 'I don't believe you.'

'I'm telling the truth. I wouldn't lie to you. Not about this. Open the door and I'll show you.'

I waited to be let in, but Valentine was in no hurry. A man came out of the neighbouring booth. He had the blanket from his bed, wrapped around his body. He looked like he might not have anything on underneath it. If one of the Patrollers caught him, he'd be in trouble. He leant against the door jamb.

'I heard you knocking,' he said.

'Mmm.'

'Congratulations.' But he didn't sound happy for me.

'…Thanks.'

'You're Engaged to him?' He gestured his head towards Valentine's booth.

'Yes.'

'Hmm. Shifty fucker, that one.' He said it loudly, so that Valentine could hear.

I knocked harder.

'Go for weird ones, do you? Well, he's getting weirder by the minute, looks like he'll be kooking down the walkways soon. They'll have him shunted off to the loon-rooms before you can get your Exit form stamped.'

'*Valentine...?*'

'There you are, getting Engaged, and he won't even answer the door to you. What's all that about?'

'He's just coming... *Valentine?*'

'Least I won't be having to see him around here much longer. Might get decent company next time. Gives people the creeps with those glasses he wears. Wears them while he fucks as well, does he? Well, I would too if you were what I was having to look at.' The steel railings and floor seem to reverberate with the sound of his mocking laughter.

My face was against the door. '*Valentine, please. Open up!*'

I heard the latch being undone at last. I sprang at the door as it came open and crashed into Valentine. He was knocked aside as I burst in. I fell against the end of the bed, banging my knees on the frame.

I felt shaken and my legs were hurt. I adjusted myself, relocated Valentine. He was standing in a corner, looking stunned, rubbing his shoulder. More than ever, it hit me that I was in his private space. I felt like a trespasser.

Outside, the man was still talking. 'Nah...he couldn't tell his cock-end from a flea bite, that one. Wouldn't know how to sh – ' I went to the door and shut it, re-did the latch. The adjacent booth door closed then too, cutting off the rest of the words.

Without thinking, we both backed away from the door, to the middle of the room.

'I'm sorry I bashed into you.'

'It's alright.'

'You can't leave me out there though, Valentine. Not with somebody like that.'

Then I remembered the letter in my hand.

'Look...from the Commission.' I held it towards him. 'It came today.'

He looked at the paper.

'Here.'

'It looks ripped.'

'I know. It was an accident. When I opened it, it tore.'

He took it from me and started to read.

'You'll have one exactly the same in your own box.'

He didn't look up. I waited for him to finish.

'…can't believe it.' He whispered it, more to himself than anything.

'That's how I felt. But see? They must've been impressed with your answers? You did it, Valentine.'

He nodded.

'It's good, isn't it?'

I wanted to hug him, to congratulate him, but his mood didn't warrant it.

'I've been wanting to say for a while. I wanted to say thanks for everything you did. For going through with it all.' It was the first time I'd alluded to that day at the Commission, or to his follow-up meeting.

'…S'okay.'

'I'm sorry you had to.'

'Doesn't matter.' He said that about a lot of things, things he didn't want to talk about.

I could feel my chance slipping away. My chance to know what had happened to him in the interviews. I could ask now or not at all.

'Was it horrible?'

'Mm…'

I had to push it. 'Because of the Passion?'

He turned and looked at the wall. '…Yes.'

'So did they…,' I paused. Valentine was hitting a corner of the letter against his leg. '…have to test it?'

Valentine kept looking away. 'Yes. A physical.'

'A physical what?'

'A test.'

'…Like a medical? They didn't make you undress and things, like when you enter the Compound?'

'…Bit the same. Bit different.'

I could see the trembling in his jaw, the effort it was taking to contain himself. I thought I could feel him more clearly than I could feel myself; his hurt blocking out everything else. I knew I shouldn't ask him anything more.

Over by the door was a mark scratched into the wall; the mark Valentine had made when I'd announced the Engagement. I kept gazing at that. I wondered what it would cost him when it was found, what the Compound Patrollers would do.

I queued in the Compound square to use the wires. The queue went all the way back to the laundry rooms, but I was okay just waiting. I stood amongst the wafts of hot detergent and steam, thinking how one day we'd be Mr and Mrs Frankland. For now, we were the intendeds and how dignified that sounded. I was thinking about our new home.

By the time it was my turn, I felt light-headed from not eating enough – I would have missed my midday meal tray. I stepped into the cubicle, bolted the door and pulled back my sleeve to reveal the code for the Housing Agency, written on my wrist. I spun in the numbers, along with my identification.

A woman answered and I explained to her about our Engagement.

She said, 'I'll put you through to the relevant office.'

Another woman picked up. I explained about the Engagement again. It came out in a rush.

'You need to speak more slowly. You're babbling.'

'Sorry. There's a queue.'

She took some details: our names and birth dates; our address; the date from which the Engagement commenced; the names of the endorsing Commissioners. Some other things as well.

Then, 'One moment, please,' and she went away from her voice piece. I could hear it being laid down on a desk. I could hear talking; small, far away voices from the room I was calling. I waited. It was taking a while. I watched the cost of the call increasing, the numbers flashing on the display. I felt the eyes of the people queuing behind me. They were staring through the glass. I didn't need to turn around to know that.

The woman came back to the line.

'I've the address of a property. A property selected for its proximity to the place, or places, of work. I have the name of a flat in the locality of your employer. Take this down.'

I didn't have anything to write with. I hadn't expected to be given an address so quickly. I checked my pockets but they were empty. I'd have to try and memorise it.

She was reading the address to me.

'Sorry, could you say that again?'

She sounded annoyed as she repeated the words. I listened hard, trying to mentally recall the address as she said it. I thought I knew the street where the property was located.

'The rent is forty tokens a week. Twenty each to be deducted directly from both your wages.'

Then the woman said something else but the man in the queue behind me was banging on the cubicle door. I stuck a finger in my ear to block out the sound.

'Pardon? I *am* listening. It's a bit noisy here.' I was looking through the windows to see if the Patrollers were nearby. A couple of them were over on the other side of the square, addressing a woman.

The man outside the cubicle shouted at me through the glass. 'Get a move on, dozy bitch.'

'…I said, you have three days. If you decide to take the property, call again to confirm. If you haven't confirmed by the end of the working day on Tuesday, the property goes back on the lists. And I need to make you aware that this property is your first and only option.'

'What d'you mean?'

'If you decide it isn't suitable, you remain in your present accommodation and you have to apply to the Commission again at a later date as the Engagement becomes –'

The man outside slammed on the door with the flat of his hand. I'd heard what she'd said, though. She said, *'becomes invalid.'*

I tried to think of a way to persuade Valentine to come and see the flat with me but he seemed too distressed. In the end, I decided to just show him when we were walking home from the Unit, just like that night at the Trip. I thought once he'd seen the property he'd be so impressed that he'd want to use the wires to confirm our place himself.

On the Monday evening, I hurried us out of the Unit.

'Let's walk home this way, Valentine.'

'Why?'

'Just for a change.'

'But it's longer. We'll be late in.'

'Only a tiny bit longer. We can walk quicker.'

'No, Neeve.'

I started to walk away. He could either follow me, or go back alone. I knew he disliked going through the procedure at the Compound gates without me being there.

I was a quarter of the way down the street and he still hadn't moved.

I called out, 'I've got a surprise for you. Come and see.'

More seconds of hesitating.

'Come on. It's special.'

Very reluctantly, he walked towards me.

We were going down Glory Way. I could see Canal Bank Court up ahead. On the front of it there was a large sign with its name in tall letters. The building was shaped like a shoe box lying on its side. It looked to be about ten storeys high. It had rows of uninterrupted windows, running the length of it. When we were near I saw that the windows were at least four times the size of my screen at work. Not tiny like the ones in our booths.

I whispered, 'Valentine, d'you know what?'

'What?'

'This is our new home.'

He shot me a horrified look.

'No, it's alright. Look, somewhere up there!' I pointed. 'Flat 92.'

I could feel him beside me, emitting scrambled feelings. We were back, once again – Valentine out beyond the limits of his endurance. This time, I was more obviously to blame.

'You're...You're...' He was so upset and angry, he was having trouble finding the right word, '*deplorable*.'

'I just wanted you to see the place. I'm sorry I've sprung it on you. But look. Look where we could live. I know it's a lot to think about after all that's happened but – '

He breathed out, agitated. I knew there was something else coming.

'I...I don't want to move.'

'*Hey?* What d'you mean? Look at it, it's *wonderful*.'

'I'm alright where I am.'

'Don't be ridiculous! You're not. You hate it...We've nearly...we're so close to getting out. All we have to do is apply for Exit and then we can leave.'

'No.'

'No what?'

'No. Just...' Then, more weakly, 'no.'

I tried to understand.

'Is it me? It's me, isn't it?'

He shook his head.

'It's me you can't stand. That's it. You can't live with me. You hate me for doing all this.' I wasn't angry with him. I was angry with myself.

He gave a heavy sigh, 'No...I've...appreciated what you've done...very much.' It was the fondest thing he'd ever said to me.

His head made an odd twitching movement and then he did a funny thing. He took his glasses off in that big, open street. I got a shock when I saw his face. I realised that I hadn't seen his eyes properly in weeks, that the tinted lenses hid him better than I'd thought. When I saw his eyes, I knew it wasn't because the new place was no good, or because the Compound was alright, or even because of me. He was trying to explain something without having to explain it. His eyes looked raw. Like something newly born. Like something forced out too soon. They were full of fear. The lids were rimmed with it. He couldn't take more of anything.

We just looked at each other for a bit.

I didn't mean to say it aloud. I said it as a statement of fact, confirming something to myself. 'He's too afraid...'

Valentine didn't speak.

I couldn't think of anything then. I felt exhausted. I stood quietly crumpling on the pavement, giving up, energy running out of me. I needed to lie down.

Chapter 5

The man on the stage began his speech.

'Citizens, today there is cause for celebration; celebration of our cherished municipality. And what is the cause...?'

Lol said, 'Can we stay for a few minutes? I just want to get the gist of what the rally's about. We can go to the Museum straight after.'

'Yes, but please hurry.'

Further back, across the square, away from the audience and the Guarda, there was a statue of a man in uniform carrying an old-fashioned gun. Passers-by were sitting on the wide stone steps that encircled its plinth, listening to the speaker.

'We could go and sit back there and rest our legs, Val. We'll be out of the way.' I didn't care about the rally. I just wanted Valentine to be alright.

'Are you coming, Lol?'

'I'll be right there.'

I took Valentine to the steps. But by the time we reached them, more people had gathered and there wasn't much room. Valentine sat down on the top step. He preferred to be at the back, where nobody much would see him. You could tell by the hurried way he lowered himself that he was glad of the rest. I found a space a few steps below.

'...The City has spread its dominion throughout the known world. We have conquered those who would threaten our way of life, those who so envied the way in which we lived. There are none now from without equal to our force. There are none from without. All that is, is the City! The City is supreme. The City is the known world...Citizens, this is no cause for complacency, however. We must remain vigilant of the threat that continues to come from within our midst. There are still those, as we shall see today, who would try to bite the very hand that sustains them...who would wish to destroy all that we work so hard to uphold, all that we hold dear. Those who would attempt to take our freedom from us with their hateful lies. I am asking you therefore to unite with me in this fight...These are dangerous men and women ...'

I sat and tried to think about the wall, the massive wall that Verna said she'd seen. I tried to take in the idea of a wall that big.

'The future is our salvation and we are marching boldly into it. It is full of hope and promise for all those that are faithful...'

I tried to picture the bricks and mortar of it – brick upon brick upon brick – so that in my head I could climb up. Right to the top of the wall and over...

'Reporting crimes has never been easier with the opening of the new Reporting Centres... Now let us see some of those who have tried to deceive us. Those who have tried and failed and now must pay the price of their atrocities...Let them be brought before us.'

I looked up, searching the crowd for Lol. I could see him. He was about a hundred metres away, walking towards me, away from the rally. He was staring ahead, walking fast. I waved to him and he got nearer. Then his expression changed. His face looked suddenly fierce. He broke into a run.

'Lol...'

He flew past me, up the steps.

I turned to look. Some people had gathered, standing around the memorial's plinth. I saw Lol throw himself into the clustered bodies.

He was shouting, 'Move. MOVE!' People looked aghast and got out of his way.

I couldn't see Valentine. He was obscured by the crowd. It didn't occur to me at first what was happening. Then I saw a hand rise above the heads and it held the pair of darkened glasses. The glasses were being waved, tauntingly in the air.

Somebody shouted, 'Eye Offence! Eye Offence!'

Lol had cleared a path to the centre of the gathering. I saw Valentine. He was crouched with his hands covering his head.

Lol flew at the man who was holding the darkened glasses. Lol's movements in those few seconds were strange. It was like, all of a sudden, a different type of energy fuelled his muscles. His body tremored with the exaggerated focus. It seemed to inhabit a different time frame. Everything was speeded up.

Lol had the man by the throat.

The glasses fell to the ground, landing amongst the feet of the crowd. The lenses shattered against the stone. Someone kicked the empty frames off the step and they were lost in a forest of legs.

I saw Lol. He was about to pummel the man.

I think I shouted, 'Lol!' I was too frightened to know what had come out of my mouth.

Somehow, it was as though Lol heard that it was my voice. He stopped. He seemed to click out of the other time frame, back to now.

He pushed the man away. The man staggered and fell back against the stone.

Then Lol made a grab for Valentine. Half-dragging, half-supporting him, he pulled Valentine from the crowd and down the steps. The fierce look was still in his eyes. Nobody dared stop him.

There was a roar from the front of the rally's audience. An offender had been brought onto the stage. The roar was deafening, not human-sounding. Like animals or thunder.

A voice called out again from the top step of the memorial, 'Eye Offence! Eye Offence!'

Some Guarda from the rally, seeing the skirmish at the statue, hurtled over.

I turned back to find Lol and Valentine. They weren't there. I swung my eyes in every direction. Nobody was running, nobody running from the crowd. I couldn't work out where they were.

The Guarda dashed over and members of the public gathered round them.

'Down to the tunnel-trains. They went down to the tunnels!'

Guarda ran to the other side of the memorial and disappeared in the direction that Lol and Valentine must have gone.

People began shouting accounts of the scene to the remaining Guarda, their voices raised, trying to out-do each other. I heard snatches of sentences, distorted descriptions of Valentine, a Valentine I didn't recognise. 'He was a protestor...an obvious Eye-Crimer.' 'Darkened glasses...He was Contemplating behind them.' 'Purposefully undermining the rally.'

My head swam. I thought I might black out. I backed away from the crowd, trying to lose myself in the confusion.

I reached the other side of the memorial. There were railings at the top of the steps that lead down to the tunnel-trains. I leant against them momentarily and looked down into the gaping entrance. A part of me didn't want to go. I didn't know what I'd find there. I teetered at the railings.

Another roar came from the crowd. Another offender had been brought onto the stage. A list of crimes was being read out. More booing and roaring. I turned and plunged down towards the trains.

My behaviour from then on wasn't what it should've been. Even though I knew that Valentine couldn't take much more, I still went ahead. I was doing it for him and it would all be worth it in the end, that's what I told myself. We were nearly there. I just had to haul Valentine along with me for the final effort.

For a second time I used the wires to call the Housing Agency. I called from the staff cubicle in the entrance hall at work. I spoke to a receptionist and gave her our names saying that we'd like to live at Canal Bank Court. She told me that my confirmation call had been registered and I should now instigate Exit from my Compound. I didn't tell Valentine what I'd done.

I got two Exit Consent forms from the Compound's Main Office. I filled in mine, and I filled in Valentine's. I was committing an offence, but I barely thought about it. It seemed to me that I was merely doing what was required. I didn't consider success or failure. I didn't consider penalties or consequences, the rights and wrongs of what I was doing, I just planned and acted. I moved doggedly down a fixed path, pushing myself on till the end of it.

I practised writing in Valentine's hand before I committed the words to the form. I copied the strange, concentrated scratches Valentine made with his pen, the letters slanting off at all different angles. The deliberation of his handwriting made it easier to forge. I put his signature at the end of the form; a mass of small, barely readable letters trying to make up a name.

It took the Compound Administration more than two months to come to a decision over the Exit applications. For most of that time I was on tenterhooks, fretting that there were suspicions over Valentine's forged form, expecting to be taken at any moment to a containment cavity for what I'd done. And all the while the flat at Canal Bank Court stood empty, waiting for us. In my imagination, the rooms there were loyal to us, patiently hoping that one day we'd come and occupy them.

When, in June, the letter finally came, I wasted no time in pulling it from the box. I didn't bother going back to the privacy of my booth. I opened it where I stood. I tried to read slowly so as not to jumble the words. The Compound Authority's decision was stated plainly. Valentine and I had been granted Exit.

I didn't even breathe. For a few seconds I was frozen. Everything had worked. I couldn't believe we'd done it. Both applications had gone through. I was stunned. I tried to explain it to myself; maybe there was no real reason for them not to let us go – Valentine's passion was under control, he was taking his pills, we'd behaved well at the Compound. Maybe, in their eyes, we weren't as culpable as I knew us to be.

I stood in the mail-room with the letter. I had the impulse to shout out to people but nobody there would be happy to hear I'd been granted Exit. I couldn't even tell Valentine. He would panic. I knew he was unlikely to check his own mailbox so I'd be able to keep the news to myself. I couldn't tell him, not yet. He needed more time.

I went to my booth and began to take things from the shelves. I needed to do something. The letter stated the date of our Exit: one week away, but I couldn't wait. I had to do something to make leaving more real. I moved like a mad person, dismantling my booth. I even packed away my night clothes, my soap and towel, things I'd need in only a few hours time. When everything I owned had gone from the room, I stood staring at the empty space. It was like I'd never even been there.

The foolishness of what I'd done hit me then; people granted Exit Consent had been attacked. Inhabitants had sometimes lashed out. My empty booth would arouse attention. I had to be more discreet, especially if Valentine wasn't to find out. I had to unpack, put everything back.

But as I returned my belongings to the booth they felt almost too heavy for my hands. They seemed to settle back into place with alarming permanence, like they'd never move from there again. I only had to wait one week but right then, I felt I wasn't going to survive it.

The days ticked on and still Valentine knew nothing of our Exit. The Saturday of our removal came and I'd still given him no warning.

I woke very early that final morning. As soon as I was awake, my mind began racing through the events of the day. I made myself giddy going over what was ahead. I kept thinking how that night, at the end of it all, we'd lay our heads down on beds outside the Compound walls.

I was dressed ages before the first alarm. When it sounded, I rushed to get stamped at the porter's lodge. There wasn't even the beginnings of a queue when I got there. I took the last ever charge into my leg and then headed to B-wing with my arms full of boxes; cardboard boxes I'd collected from the buying halls.

I knocked on Valentine's door. Maybe he thought I was a Patroller, banging so early, but I didn't care. I just wanted him to open the door.

He answered it slowly as usual, inching the door away from the frame and peering through the gap. When Valentine saw that it was me, his body seemed to relax. He opened the door more fully. He was still in his nightclothes. Under the rims of the darkened glasses, I could see red marks on his skin where the frames had been pressed into his face as he lay in bed.

Then Valentine noticed the boxes at my feet and his body tensed up again. Reflexively he tried to shut the door but I stopped him.

'Let me in.'

'What are they…?'

'Boxes. Let me in.'

'Why've you got them?'

'Why d'you think?' I was almost hissing. I was desperate. I didn't want him to ruin it. Not now. 'We're getting out. We're off. Just let me in.'

For a moment he couldn't speak. I pushed past him, with the boxes, into the booth.

I went straight to his shelves and started to collect up his belongings. He didn't move from the doorway.

'Better get dressed.'

He managed to find his voice again but it was thin and weak. 'What're you doing?'

'You can see what I'm doing. Please, get dressed.'

He was looking at me, incredulous. 'I'm not leaving.'

'Yes, you are.'

I knew what I was doing. I felt very clear, unaffected for once by Valentine's feelings. I was working quickly, sorting the regulation Compound items from those that were personal to Valentine.

'What've you done?'

'I couldn't let on to you. It's better like this. If I'd said, you wouldn't have agreed.'

'I told you…I told you I didn't want to go.'

'I didn't believe you.'

I took his work uniform down from the peg and folded it up in the bottom of a box. 'We were sent our Exit Consent confirmations a week ago. There'll be one for you in your mail box. The morning alarm's sounded already. You need to hurry up and get dressed and stamped, and then go and get your Consent papers. We're going to need them.'

'*I haven't applied for Ex–*' His voice was suddenly shrill and panicked.

'Shh!' I pulled a face, 'I took care of it.'

His mouth dropped open. He fumbled with a button on his nightshirt, trying to make sense of things. Or trying to summon the strength to fight me, maybe.

I turned away and started on the little cupboard under his sink. I needed to hurry. I had to maintain the urgency, to refuse to feel him or else I wouldn't be able to do it.

I emptied the cupboard of its paltry contents; things Valentine had no use for but couldn't let go of – things from years ago, from before the Compound. Trinkets from his parents' and grandfather's homes.

I could see him out of the corner of my eye as I worked. He'd moved away from the door, towards the table. I could see him picking up the framed photograph of Mauran and two other objects from the table top. He held them defensively against his body and backed off towards the wall.

I was trying to ignore him as I sifted my way through his possessions but he got to me. I stopped what I was doing and stood up. Valentine was leaning there, attempting to hide himself behind the semi-darkness of the lenses.

I went a step nearer. 'Just *try* to help me, Valentine.'

He didn't say anything.

I was getting exasperated. 'We *have* to do this. Everything's ready!'

No reply.

'What's the *matter* with you? I've done this for your sake too. All we have to do is pack and walk out of the gates!'

Again, Valentine failed to respond. Always nothing with him.

Before I could stop myself, I'd gone to him. I'd made a grab for the framed photograph he was clutching but Valentine had too tight a hold on it. I tried to wrench it from his grasp and the two other objects dropped from his arms to the floor; his wallet and a Compound library book. It was absurd. We each had hold of one side of the frame. Neither of us would let go.

'*Give* it to me, Neeve!'

He'd spoken at last.

I let go of the photograph. Valentine fell back against the wall.

I said something that I'm not even sure I meant. 'If you don't come now, if you make us stay, I won't see you any more. I don't know what'll happen to you. You'll have no help. You'll have no-one.'

It was low of me, but I didn't care. I watched the words sinking in. Maybe it was the way I said it; he seemed to believe me.

There was a moment when neither of us moved or spoke. Then suddenly Valentine moved towards the bed. He swung away from me, his movements unusually sharp. At first I didn't know what he was doing. Then I realised. He'd started to strip. He was undoing the buttons on his nightshirt. Instinctively, I shut my eyes and covered my face with my hands.

When I opened my eyes again several seconds later, I saw, through the gaps between my fingers, that Valentine had taken off his nightshirt. I could see his bare back. I stared at the spectacle through my hands. This was his way of punishing me, maybe, displaying what I couldn't have.

'Get out,' he said.

I didn't move. It didn't register that the words had come from Valentine's mouth. He was about to untie his trousers.

'Get out.' Louder this time.

I left the booth. I stood outside the door, hesitating, dumbly waiting.

Valentine appeared. He was standing there, painfully upright, in his Compound uniform.

'I'll fetch your stupid papers.' He spat out the words and then stalked to the stairwell and down.

The rest of the day was like a weird dream. Valentine and I went through the Exit procedures: Patrollers came to inspect our rooms; Valentine was fined heavily for the scratch he'd made in his booth wall; the stamps were removed from our calves in the infirmary rooms, the numbing injections leaving us dizzy and nauseous; our papers and belongings were thoroughly gone over by Compound officials; a final body-search was carried out. That's the order in which things occurred, but in my head, it was a jumble of unconnected events. We moved through each process like a crude substance through a refinery. With each command complied with, we felt ourselves more and more subdued. By the end, when they eventually marked our papers and declared us Excepted, I felt invisible, hardly there at all.

Three Patrollers escorted us out through the main gateway and onto the street. I watched as the gates were closed behind us and then we were alone on the pavement.

I remember feeling the brightness and heat of the sunlight, nothing more than that. I hardly had the presence of mind to move. I had to summon myself back from somewhere. I could scarcely take in the significance of the moment. I gazed down at our belongings.

We moved through the streets carrying our boxes of belongings. Even then none of it seemed real or lasting. It seemed that we were still inhabitants of the Compound. I kept expecting someone to call us back.

As we walked, Valentine wouldn't look at me. He hadn't all day. He was still furious. We trudged steadily side by side in the heat of the day but neither of us spoke.

Canal Bank Court smelled of fresh paint. The walls were painted white. Dried paint globules lay in the dust on the ground. Drips had dried on the walls suggesting they'd been covered in a hurry. Ahead of us stretched a corridor of flats, doors on both sides. I couldn't hear much. After the noise of the Compound the place was so quiet – no footsteps clanging on the walkways, no doors slamming, Patrollers shouting, no alarms or bells or drills.

A man in a pale blue uniform, the Caretaker, came out of his office to see who we were.

'What're your names?' he said looking at Valentine for an answer. But Valentine was staring at the floor.

I said, 'Valentine Frankland and Neeve Glynnan. We're due to move into flat 92.'

'Show me your proof-papers.'

The Caretaker took his time looking through our papers. He carefully analysed the thumb-sized photograph of Valentine on his identity slip, then told Valentine to remove his glasses. Valentine shakily took them off and I looked away as the Caretaker scrutinised his face.

'Alright.' he said eventually. Valentine put his glasses back on.

The Caretaker went back into his office then, and called out a name. A young man appeared.

'Bring up the boxes,' the Caretaker said and the younger man began piling our belongings so he could lift them. We moved to help carry them but the assistant shook his head. He put the boxes he couldn't manage inside the office.

The Caretaker gestured to us to follow him. He led us to a flight of stairs. Up we went, nine floors. At the top floor the Caretaker led us to a door numbered '92'. I stood there, out of breath from so many stairs and it struck me how the door was made of wood. Only the handle and lock were metal. There were no spy-holes like in the booths.

The Caretaker unlocked the door and we followed him inside. We stepped from the corridor into a small kitchen. There wasn't quite room enough for the three of us to stand in there, so the Caretaker backed further into the flat, watching us from the doorway.

There was a stove. There was a table that folded out from the wall. There was cupboard space and a worktop on which to prepare food. There was a sink with two taps; cold and hot. There was linoleum on the floor. The surfaces were covered with a layer of dust and I wondered how long the flat had been empty, although there was a faint smell of cooking. The sudden smell of it shot me into a memory of my old house and to living with my mother, sitting at the kitchen table, watching her peel the skins off things. She hated to eat anything with its skin on: apples; potatoes; even peas. Remembering her made me feel oddly tender and suddenly tired. I held on to the porcelain rim of the sink and stared into the basin.

'Not what you're used to, eh?' the Caretaker said. 'Rather different from where you've come from, I'd bet.'

I nodded my head and glanced at Valentine, trying to read his expression, his reaction to the room, but he was totally impassive.

'It's lovely isn't it, Valentine?'

'Lovely.' He said it like a child who copies an adult's words, not seeming to understand their meaning.

The Caretaker turned and stepped towards the next room, a shower room; a tiled cubicle with a drainage hole and a waterproofed door. Random tiles on the walls had pictures on them; bowls of fresh fruit and vegetables. Most probably kitchen decoration, but still impressive. I noticed the temperature gauge on the taps. You could adjust the heat of the water to suit yourself. And there was an extraction fan to take away the steam.

'It's very nice,' I said again because nobody else had spoken.

Next to the shower room, was the main bedroom. The Caretaker ushered us inside. It was spacious, and light because of the windows. The floorboards were bare but there were rugs scattered about. Again, the walls were freshly painted white. There was a dressing table, an armchair, a small wooden chair, a wardrobe, a set of shelves, and in the middle of it all, a big bed. A two-person bed. We stood staring at it, at the bare mattress, at the two case-less pillows that had been placed next to each other at one end, at the two little mats on the floor, one at either side of the bed so that you didn't have to get cold feet in the morning. A couple's room. I blushed just looking at it.

The Caretaker walked over to the window. With his back to us, he surveyed the City.

'Decent view of the sun coming up…for when you get tired of waking up and looking at each other.' He laughed but he sounded dull and bored. His words sent a jolt through me. *Waking Up. Seeing each other.* 'Take a look at it.'

We walked dutifully over to the window, to see the Caretaker's view. There was the City. Buildings followed by buildings followed by buildings. Streets, alleys and tower blocks. I looked down and saw the canal below, and, not far from the water, the back yards of people's homes. On someone's washing line I saw a knitted quilt made up of different coloured squares sewn together;

the brightest coloured object in view. A few houses back from that I saw a full line of white washing hanging up; a family's clothes, all different sizes. I stared at the baby's nappies drying in the day's intense heat.

Next, the Caretaker showed us the washroom. A toilet and a sink. The same fruit and vegetable tiles on the walls there too, but a different patterned linoleum. Then, the last room. The Caretaker opened the door and motioned for us to peer inside. It was the smaller bedroom. Big enough for a bed – a little bed with about thirty centimetres to spare down each side and a little more along the bottom.

'For a little one?' The Caretaker was grinning. His eyebrows were raised and his eyes were narrowed. I thought he was mocking us.

We stared blankly at him, dumbfounded.

'Y-es.'

'Well, that's it.'

We were back outside the flat, in the top floor corridor.

'The rent is forty a week as you probably know. Instructions for the use of appliances are in the drawer. Any questions?'

I had a question. Even though I was sure of the answer, I still had to ask it. 'So there isn't a curfew time? There isn't a time we have to be back in?'

He smirked. 'This isn't your Compound, is it?'

The Caretaker was looking at me now when he spoke. He'd stopped aiming his comments at Valentine.

'There *are* rules, of course. Don't think you can do whatever you please now you're in. I've seen that happen over and over with your lot. You get out of the Compounds and go wild. Don't know how to manage a place. Don't know how to even manage yourselves. No respect for the buildings. I always have to keep an eye out. Anyway, the rulings are posted inside the front door. You're to note that there's to be no gatherings of more than four people and no guest is permitted to stay longer than three days in any one season. Each guest that stays overnight must pay a charge, inform me and…'

He must have seen, looking at our washed-out faces, that we weren't taking in much of what he was saying. It'd been an exhausting day. The Caretaker handed us a set of keys each and left us to go back down to his quarters.

We were suddenly alone in the corridor and shy of each other. Valentine was staring at the keys in his hand. It was a relief to have to move, to fetch our belongings in from outside.

My body was ringing from all the Exit procedures but I was still able to register it; the feeling of shutting the door, shutting out everything that could be bad or hurtful.

Without speaking Valentine took his belongings into the smaller bedroom and quietly closed himself away. Probably right then, to him I was one of those bad and hurtful things that needed to be shut out.

I waited a few minutes and then called through his door. '...You can have the big bedroom if you want, Valentine...I don't mind which one I have.' I listened for an answer. If he responded, I didn't hear him.

I picked up my boxes and took them through to the big bedroom. I lay down on the double bed and gazed around at all the space, trying to make it sink in that we were really living there. Even if Valentine stayed shut inside his room for ages, it was still a good feeling, knowing he was with me in the flat. He was angry because of the way I'd gone about things, but the fact was we weren't in the Compound any more. It would be alright. Soon he'd be glad. Despite all his reticence, there he was, in the next room.

All that remained of our old lives were our jobs at the Unit. Every weekday morning around 8-15 we left the flat and walked to work. At the end of the working day, we left the Unit at 5-30 and came home again. We still passed some of the same buildings. They towered up from the pavement the same way as always with their endless bricks, one on top of the other. But whereas before, the sight of them might've disheartened me, now my footsteps going along those streets were not so sluggish.

In the mornings, it was the sound of the clock in the flat that roused us. We could set its alarm for any time we wanted. At night, we chose the hour to go to sleep and turned the lights out ourselves.

Our wages were paid to us in citizen tokens and so we could shop where we wanted. We bought our own food from the market stalls and prepared it ourselves. We made several ruined attempts before we'd grasped the techniques involved in cooking a proper meal. We bought things we hadn't eaten for a long time, things we could only vaguely remember eating with our families. Food was a revelation after the tasteless Compound servings.

Of course, our Compound uniforms had been taken from us the day we left our booths and now we were afforded more choice in the way we were obligated to dress. I was within the requirements as long as I wore a skirt and an un-patterned blouse. Valentine needed simply to stick to plain trousers and shirt, jumpers in autumn and winter.

But despite all these new freedoms, somehow it was still strange, getting used to the new life. Things didn't come back easily after the years in the booths. Living side by side with just one other person again was almost uncomfortable after the impersonal distance of the Compound. It was odd discovering a hundred intimate, inconsequential things about each other's daily habits.

On each floor in our block of flats there was a communal area. I was excited to discover a Set in each area so I was able to catch the broadcasts again. The Set in the communal area on the floor below us had broken down and so people came up from downstairs to watch. The room was quite full, but people weren't ill-tempered; they made space for each other on the benches.

At that time, the City was on the tenth phase of its Streamlining. It was odd coming out of the Compound, discovering what'd changed and what'd stayed the same; what publications were commended, which ones had been banned. Many of the programmes that I remembered were no longer shown. A lot of the programmes seemed to be of a certain type. They were mostly stories of villains and heroes and you soon got to know what was going to happen, who was going to win. But it was still enjoyable, going in to watch.

Valentine didn't go to the communal area. He preferred to be quiet in his room in the flat. Whenever I invited him to join me for a broadcast, he declined. I suppose he'd just be sitting, feeling tense in front of a screen and he did that all day at work.

After a while I stopped going to the communal room too. I didn't want to waste time by being without him. Valentine remained suspicious of me for several weeks after all my scheming. But, through our daily closeness and shared routines, his defensiveness slowly lessened. He spoke to me rarely, mostly only when he had to, but still, in a layer below words, it's like we had our own sort of bond.

Despite my constant nearness to him, I never grew accustomed to how amazing he was. I liked to look at him when he was busy with something, when he didn't know I was watching. As a way of coaxing him from his room in the evenings, I bought a pack of playing cards. I tried to engage him in the games I remembered playing as a child. It seemed to work. We sat together at the kitchen table and I'd stare at him over the top of my cards while he arranged his hand.

When we first moved in, Valentine wrote a letter to his sister to tell her that his address had changed. Private, unofficial mail into and out of the Compound had always been opened before it reached its recipients, but Valentine received a reply from Mauran about a month after our arrival at Canal Bank Court and the envelope remained intact.

I was in the kitchen when it came through the door. I tried not to be curious, but after he'd read, I must have kept glancing at the letter.

'Read it if you want,' he said.

I picked up the paper from the kitchen table. I was struck by the handwriting. There was something cautious and considered about the words and their arrangement on the page.

Dear Brother,

Thank you for your letter. I was very glad to receive the news that you have moved. As you have now left your rooms in the Sixth Compound, I can only assume that you have met someone to share your life with and that the City has, at least preliminarily, approved your union. This being the case, then I am very pleased for you. I have always wished to see you happy in this way. I trust that the woman in question is worthy of you, and I wish you the very best for the future.

I hope you have settled into your new home. All is well with us both here, thank you for asking. Dean sends his regards.

Best wishes,
Mauran

I folded the sheet of paper and handed it back to Valentine. 'That's a nice letter.'

He shrugged. 'She wants me to be happy…'

'What did she mean by leaving your *rooms*? Didn't she know how you lived at the Compound?'

'No. I never described it to her.'

'She didn't ever come to see you on one of the guest days?'

'No.'

I was shocked.

'Her husband didn't like her to, she said. I met up with her outside the Compound instead.'

'So, how long is it since you saw her?'

'About two years…' He was vague, trying to shrug this off too.

I kept thinking, *She only lives in Cliffer District.*

There were other things about Valentine's life that I hadn't known, that I slowly got to know as a consequence of living with him. Valentine was an insomniac. He only managed to sleep for a few hours each night. I often heard him running the tap in the kitchen in the early hours of the morning, getting himself a drink. I worried about it at first, thinking he couldn't settle in the flat, but when I asked him about it he said he'd always been like that. The pills he took for his Passion caused him to sleep very little. He just didn't feel tired enough. I wondered how he'd managed at the Compound during the curfews. Nights there must have seemed very long.

Valentine had to take his tablets three times a day. He never forgot and he always took them at precisely the same times: seven, three, eleven. I got used to hearing the rattling sound of tablets coming from the kitchen as he shook them from the bottle.

Eventually, Valentine grew restless of the card games we played. One night in the flat, he said, 'I'd like to try some Silver again.'

It was late summer and we'd had time to get used to our new lives by then. The next evening after work, we went out.

The streets were warm. The sun was big and low in the sky. It seemed to follow us as we went between the bars, turning the buildings from grey to gold. Even the presence of the Street Sweepers rolling through the zones, spot-checking pedestrians, couldn't take the edge off things.

Everywhere we went the bars sold Silver. Valentine drank it fast, even though it wasn't the type of thing you'd rush. We sat at tables on pavements, out in front of the buildings, watching people go about their business. It was fascinating just watching – people with real lives, not the worn-down characters from A-wing. The Compound felt a million miles away. Even Valentine didn't seem to mind being out, confronting the eyes of strangers. He'd make a special effort for some Silver, perhaps.

At the end of the evening, as Valentine was finishing off his last drink, he said, 'I never told you "thank you", Neeve...' His voice was low and drowsy-sounding.

'What for?'

'You know what for…Getting us out.'

He took me by surprise. He'd never wanted to discuss it.

'I'm sorry I had to push you. I was too hard on you. I never meant to be.'

'It's alright…' he said. 'I feel differently about it now.' He nodded slightly as he said it.

A tension I didn't know I'd been holding, gave way with his words.

We grew gradually bolder. By the autumn, just as Willa-Rix predicted, we decided to go on to some nightclubs after the bars had closed. The clubs stayed open after midnight and we could dance.

Valentine had never been clubbing before. He'd never even danced but it seemed to come to him well enough. It must have been the Silver loosening his limbs. I shuffled around on the dance floor knowing Valentine was there too, swaying about in the dark. I danced beside him, not touching, just accidentally banging arms.

The venues we went to were not brightly-lit places and so with the darkened glasses and the Silver, Valentine could just about manage himself. We didn't stay all that long in one place because Valentine's looks drew attention. We went from club to club. We spent an hour at Cryptor, then on to Arrabella's, then on to The Drome. These were all big clubs in the Dance District.

Dancing became a regular thing for us. It seemed to ease the monotony of Valentine's lack of sleep. A night out could numb him and he wouldn't feel so raw. Sometimes the clubs' temperature-control systems would act up and then they'd be almost too hot to move about in. Even the walls seemed to sweat in the heat. At other times, as the weather got chillier, the clubs got so cold that people had to dance in their coats and the dampness on the walls would turn to ice. But the dancers didn't bother about the heat or the cold. Sometimes I'd go up to the DJ's nest and ask them to play a song. Sometimes they'd nod nonchalantly at me and just never play it, and sometimes they'd say, 'No, that one's out,' meaning it'd been Streamlined. There was one song I used to really like. It was so long since I'd heard it that I'd forgotten its name. I had to sing it to the DJ so he knew which one I meant. The singer sang of how she was rapt by the dancing, how she'd let everything go so that she could stay lost inside the music.

> *'I leave my life behind me,*
> *Shake my way out of yesterday,*
> *Dance to the music they play…'*

It had nice words but they'd Streamlined that one too. It must have been offensive, but I couldn't see how. Occasionally though, something we'd requested *would* get played and maybe I'd remember the lyrics right through to the end. Valentine would murmur along too, trying to match his words to the song as he danced.

If I got too tired to keep awake, I'd lie with my head on the table as I sat next to Valentine. If it looked as though someone was on their way over to talk to him, Valentine would tap me on the shoulder, wake me. I'd rouse myself and we'd pretend to be talking. We'd keep on like that until the person had moved away.

But sometimes on a night out, I'd wonder how well Valentine's Bad Passion tablets actually worked. Some nights you might think he still had it. There wasn't so much alcohol in Silver but it seemed to make the Passion more noticeable. You could almost sense it coming off him. He was careful not to direct anywhere, he was cautious with it, but it was like he was letting himself touch in with it ever so slightly, trying to sense it more fully, while at the same time trying to keep control of it. It can't have been easy.

We'd stay out late, until Valentine had finally grown tired and his weariness had started to overwhelm him. Riding the tunnel-trains home after the clubs, Valentine might start to doze. As we rattled along under the City, his head would sometimes drop to my shoulder. I'd look at us reflected in the dark windows opposite and gaze at his face. I'd worry in case the way I felt, with him laying against me, would show through. I'd have to try to breathe steadily to make myself calm.

When we got back in, sometimes Valentine still wouldn't be ready to sleep. If it was a night during the weekend, I might stay up with him, into the early hours, in the hope he might tell me things – stories from his past, anything at all.

One particular night we were talking at the kitchen table. It was long after the clubs had shut. I was very weary and getting past the point of being as scrupulously careful about what I said.

'Valentine?'

'Yes…?' His elongated eyes were tired. His eyelids were heavy, beginning to close. 'Is it time for bed?'

'No, it's not that. I was just wondering what it's like…' I watched his face as I spoke. He was gazing at something on the floor. '…to look like you do?'

He answered slowly. 'How do you mean?'

'You know, what it feels like to be that…er…' I didn't want to say the word out loud. It took an extra breath for it to come, 'beautiful?'

He grew instantly more awake, like a cat suddenly pricking up its tail and swirling it. I tried to make light of what I'd said.

'What about all those people who're admiring you all the time?' I said it as jokingly as I could.

He relaxed a little.

'I know they do…' he said eventually, 'but I can't feel it.'

'Oh.'

He spoke deliberately, as if he was having to think about each word. 'No matter what, I still feel…no good. As though whatever it is about my face…' The protractedness of his speech made everything he said sound like the last words he'd utter before bed, '…isn't mine…As though it's been borrowed from somebody else and…one day they're going to ask for it back.' He shifted awkwardly in the chair. 'If a person stares…it feels as though they're looking at the man…I've borrowed my face from.'

It was obvious in the tone of his voice that it was depressing him to talk about it.

'Sorry,' I said redundantly and sat with him in a ponderous silence for a while.

Eventually, I summoned the energy to push myself up to standing.

'Are you tired enough to sleep yet?' I said.

'Not long now…'

'I better turn in. I'm really tired.'

'Okay.'

'Goodnight then. Sleep well.'

'Goodnight, Neeve.'

He couldn't contribute much, but he contributed what he could.

As a consequence of our nights out, my work at the Unit began to deteriorate. I was too tired some mornings to remember the identification number to my work-station. I would set off a buzzer because it had taken me too many attempts to key in the code. You weren't supposed to tell anybody your number. But I told mine to Valentine and he'd type it in for me. Then I'd sit at my desk, trying to be industrious, waiting for the tiredness to wear off.

Valentine was never sleepy like I was. He worked as diligently as always and took up my slack, secretly finishing tasks I failed to complete. In the noontime intervals I'd set my watch to wake myself up so that I could sleep in the toilet cubicles, even if it was just for fifteen minutes. I'd rest sitting on the toilet lid, my feet wedged up on one wall, my back against the other. I could catch up properly at weekends. Then I'd sleep for hours on end without waking.

One Saturday I awoke in the early afternoon, having slept away the whole morning. The flat was silent. Valentine had an appointment at the clinic to monitor his medicine. I imagined him sitting in the waiting room, wishing he could put his darkened glasses on, waiting to get seen.

I lay with my head sunk into the pillow, gazing at my room. I had such a pride in the flat. I wasn't a neat person, not at all, but I'd become fastidious. It meant so much to be there, I couldn't bear to see it messy. I might be tired from the clubs but I'd still tidy.

I got up from the bed and opened the curtains. It was bright outside. Clouds had been thick and low over the City for the last week, but that afternoon, any clouds there were, were thin and high. Birds sped over the City and it shocked me, the height at which they flew.

Alone in the flat for once, I felt the novelty of being there without Valentine. (Valentine rarely went out, leaving only to go to work, to the shop or to the clubs, and then I was always with him.) I thought about his bedroom, about it empty with him gone.

I didn't intend anything but I found myself going to his room. My bare feet crossed the floor, out of my bedroom and into the hall. I was standing looking at Valentine's door. I had my hand on the door-knob and I was turning it.

It was sparse inside. There were no signs that anyone regularly slept in there: a precaution in case a spot check was carried-out – an engaged couple didn't need separate beds. Most of his possessions were scattered around the rest of the flat. But the starkness, the lack of personal touches somehow made the room even more suggestive of Valentine.

The bed looked small. Too small for comfort. Its covers had been pulled taut across the mattress and tucked under; a hang-over from Compound life. I lay down on the bed and looked up at the ceiling. I considered the way the room would look to Valentine as he drifted off to sleep and when he woke up. I gazed at the high corners where the walls and ceiling met and made right angles. Then I turned over onto my front.

I felt the soft texture of the blanket on my cheeks. I thought of Valentine asleep; his face with his eyes closed. I breathed in. The smell of him had got into the material. I pressed my face deeper into the blanket and drew air into my nose. I imagined his pores giving out a honey-like sweat. And Silver; I thought I could smell that too – a powdery sort of Silver, mixed in with his quiet body-smell.

Then I heard a noise.

Somebody was outside. Valentine was back already. Coldness flooded me and I leapt from his bed. I was out of the room like a shot, my heart thumping into my throat. I pulled the door shut behind me and stood in the hall, waiting for Valentine's key in the lock.

But there was no key. Just a repeat of the shuffling from before. And then a knocking.

It isn't him.

I had a different fear then; somebody wanted to come in.

We'd never had a visitor at the flat. If the Caretaker wanted to see us he'd put a note through the door, summoning us to his office. My mind flashed through a list of possible people. The grey-faced neighbour from next door, Mr Hadden. Maybe he'd seen Valentine going out. I went to the door.

'Who's there please…?'

A voice came back, loud like the person was very close, stood with their mouth right up to the wood. 'Tis only me, girlie. Tis only me.'

It was Willa-Rix.

I unlocked the door.

'…You surprised me.' My legs felt weak. I felt stupid for being anxious. 'I didn't know who it was.'

'Relax, Chick. Are you going to let me in, then?'

Willa came into the flat and I shut the door behind her. I watched as she removed her coat. Beneath it she wore a jacket. She took that off too. She looked to be all clothing, hardly any Willa there at all. I took her coat and jacket and hung them on the back of the door.

'Have a seat.'

'Thankee kindly.' Willa took a stool from under the table. She sat glancing round the kitchen. 'A nice place you've got here, Miss Big-Shot.'

'Thank you.' I was still shocked at having someone turn up at the flat.

'Took me a while to track you down, though. You've been here a good few months already, I'll bet. I'd have come sooner if I could've. You should've left me your address. I had to ask around.'

'Sorry.'

'Not to worry. Not to worry.'

'Who did you ask?'

She tapped the side of her nose. 'It all comes down to contacts. You'll learn, you'll learn.' She laughed loudly and clapped her hands. 'Ah, not really. I ended up having to enquire at the Housing Agency. I used the wires, called from outside the Compound. It was a cinch actually. I made out that I was an old friend of your mother's. Mrs Arkle-Royd, I said I was. D'you remember her?'

'Ye-s. *Whoo, Willa*...' I couldn't believe some of the things she did. It didn't feel safe having her in the flat.

'Thing was, I couldn't remember the number when I got here. I knocked on next door's before this one. Nobody answered.' She was looking over her shoulder, into the hallway. She shook her head and whistled. 'It's alright for some isn't it, Treacle?'

'Hmn.' I felt embarrassed of the life I had suddenly.

'Are you going to offer me a cuppa?'

I lit the stove to heat the water and started rinsing out some cups for the drinks. I was wondering why she'd come. Maybe it was a genuine visit.

'Show me round in a bit?' She nodded her head towards the doorway into the hall.

'Okay...'

Water from the taps was splashing over my hands into the sink. An image of Valentine's bed popped into my head. I jolted. I'd messed up his sheets. I had to straighten them before he came back in.

Willa said, 'I've brought you something.'

I had my back to her. I carried on setting out the tea things.

'Guess what it is?'

I shook my head.

'Don't you remember, at the canal side?'

'Uh?'

'You don't remember?'

I turned around. Willa was reaching about inside her skirt pockets bringing out a handful of things: some Compound money-tickets, a crumpled piece of paper, some tatty-looking string and two odd-looking, flat, transparent, plastic, geometric discs with glittering red flecks inside. She separated the plastic discs from the other bits and moved them across the table towards me.

'Passes to the Realm,' she announced. 'Remember now?'

I nodded.

'One each. One for you, and one for whatsisname. Valdek.'

'Valentine.'

'See? I told you I could get you in.'

'Um. Thanks.'

'And that's not all…'

From another pocket, she pulled a folded piece of paper. She unravelled it.

'Directions,' she explained. 'Be careful with this. Memorise it and then tear it up really well. There's opening dates for the next few weeks written on the other side. Only three of them. It's only open certain nights. Nothing regular. Get to one of those nights, Neeve. All the words and figures are written backwards. 601 is TER106. Dilcar, that's really Raclid Road. Get to Paxmore station in the Wantsworth District. The directions will guide you from there.'

'Hang on. Valentine'd never go to something like this. He'd run a mile if he even knew you were talking about it. There's no chance.'

'Don't tell him. Just say it's for the dancing. It's much better for you if he doesn't know. Then there's no chance of him turning you in. It's not like he'll walk in the place and know what it's about. They'll keep things discreet over there, I'm sure. Or you could just go on your own.'

'On the tunnel-trains coming back late at night?'

'Find someone else to go with you, then.'

'Like who?'

'I don't know. Ask one of the fellows in the other flats. It's only your name I gave: Neeve Glynnan and fiancé.'

'Willa!'

'Look, Neeve, I'm counting on you. So are the group at the Compound. I've told them you're our *envoy*. That means *special messenger*.'

The water had started to boil. Steam was billowing into the kitchen. I took the water from the flame, poured it into the pot of sherbet decoction and put the pot down on the fold-out table.

'It's like nothing I've ever heard of, Neeve. It's not like other Movements. It's just what we've been waiting for. It could really change things. I can't explain how important it is. You'll find out if you go.'

I bit at the inside of my cheek. 'Isn't there anybody else you could ask?'

'No.' She was adamant. 'You're the only person we've got.'

'I don't know…It's the risk of it.'

Her voice was slightly raised now, 'Didn't I say already? It isn't anything *like* that.'

I'd torn my cheek. I could taste blood.

'Besides…' She was looking at me. 'You owe me, Neeve.'

I owed her from before, that's what she meant. I owed her for her help after my father left, and again when he'd undergone Vanishment. Both times, when my mother had been grieving, Willa had called round to check on us, to see how we were and bring us food. It was about a year and a half after my father had first gone away, when my mother was beginning to come back to herself a little, that we were informed of my father's arrest and Vanishment. That's when my mother's grief hit into her in a manner that she couldn't quite come back from. Maybe until then, she'd always been hoping that my father would return. When the news of the Vanishment spread, pretty much nobody would come near us, but Willa-Rix did.

'This is the most I've ever asked you to do and it's nothing, Neeve. Nothing to you, but everything to me. It means *everything.*'

I tried to breathe. My lungs seemed to have gone stiff inside me. I took a sip of hot sherbet.

'There's something I need you to do when you get to the club. Find a man and woman. The Usbornes. Gene and Girda Usborne. Tell them that Willa-Rix sent you and that Willa requests one of the *Circles*. This last bit's really important. I need you to bring it back here, Neeve. Keep it safe and hidden and I'll come and get it.'

There was the sound of a key in the door; metal grinding against metal. I turned sharply on my stool. *Valentine. His bed is still messed up.*

Valentine stepped into the kitchen and hesitated at the sight of Willa-Rix. He loomed in the cramped space, awkward above us, too visible for his own comfort.

I stood up. 'How was your appointment?' He blushed red in the face. I blushed then too. I shouldn't have mentioned his appointment in front of Willa.

'Have a seat,' I gestured to the empty stool. I thought, *I've been lying on his bed.*

'No, thanks,' he said and gestured vaguely in the direction of his bedroom.

But I was standing between him and the doorway. He couldn't get past.

'This is Willa-Rix, Valentine.'

'I met him already,' Willa said flatly. 'In a queue at the Compound gates. You introduced me, remember?'

'Oh, yes.' We'd been behind Willa in line one morning. I'd tapped her on the shoulder in greeting. Now, in the flat, as on that other occasion, Willa neglected to make eye-contact with Valentine. She addressed her comments to me, or to the general space of the room. She seemed not to know what to make of him. It wasn't a big deal; neither did a lot of people. Valentine stood silently and took it.

'I was about to show the flat to Willa...May I show her your room? We'll be quick. I hope you don't mind?'

'You've got separate rooms?' Willa's interest suddenly sparked.

Valentine looked at me, stunned.

Nobody said anything for a moment. Valentine and Willa were staring at me, waiting for me to speak. I didn't know what to say. We'd never had a visitor to the flat. I wasn't prepared. In the confusion I'd forgotten our lie.

I fumbled my way through the next sentence. '...Um, Valentine has been feeling off-colour for a few days, not sleeping well, so he offered to move into the small room till he's better...so I wasn't disturbed.'

Willa's voice was oddly soft. All she said was, 'You be careful who you show around this place, Neeve. Just watch it.'

I took Willa in to see Valentine's bedroom and closed the door. Valentine stayed in the kitchen, glad to be free of us.

Willa was gazing out of the bedroom window, out across the City, temporarily mesmerised with her face against the glass. I waited for some remark from her about our living situation but she didn't say anything. She didn't need to. She knew what was going on.

The only comment she made was about the windows, 'So much bigger than the pokey glass-holes in the booths...'

I fussed with the covers of Valentine's bed, trying to re-create the former neatness. I couldn't seem to smooth the imprint of my hands out of the sheets. I couldn't fuss for too long though. Valentine would want his room back.

We came out. I called to Valentine, 'We're done, thank you...' My voice sounded thin.

I took Willa in to see the main bedroom and heard Valentine shuffle back into his own. His door closed behind him.

Willa lay down on the big bed and stretched her arms out across the mattress.

'Someone's landed on their feet here, haven't they, Miss Swish? When you become a big-shot it's nice not to forget the people you've left behind.'

'Please, Willa, I'm not the right sort of person to -'

'That's enough now. Of course you're the right person. What sort of a game do you think you're playing here in this flat? It's hardly playing by the rules, is it?'

I opened my mouth to try and come back at her with something but there was nothing to say.

I followed her out, back into the kitchen. She put the club passes and the directions down on the table.

'What time is it now?'

I checked my watch. 'It's coming up for ten past two.'

'I better head off. I have to be back inside the gates soon.'

'Didn't you do your paper stall today?'

'No. Not today. I had more important things to do. I had to come and see you...Don't forget, Neeve – the *Usbornes* and the Circle.'

She took her jacket and coat down from the hook and opened the front door.

'See you then, Citizen.' She winked at me and disappeared into the corridor.

'Bye,' I said and closed the door.

I slumped down on a stool, resting my head on my outstretched arm as it lay across the table. I gazed sideways at the kitchen. There was silence from Valentine's room.

The Realm passes and Willa's list of directions lay near my head. I reached over and picked up one of the plastic discs, turning it over in my hand. The red glitter flecks caught the electric light on the ceiling as I turned it. Then I held the disc vertically, at right angles to the table and spun it on the flat surface. It stayed upright, gliding for a few seconds, going where it wanted. But its momentum soon slowed; unable to sustain the spin, the disc wavered and toppled over onto the table.

I rose from my stool, collecting up both passes. I wrapped them inside the directions and put them away. I chucked them in a cluttered drawer by the sink, buried under a tin of half-blunt pencils and a miniature, magnetic board game that we didn't know the rules to.

Chapter 6

In the morning, when I awoke, I didn't want to open my eyes. I was petrified. I could hear sounds of the street rising up from below. Hot sun was already flooding into the room. The night's protection had gone. I was back in the world. I wanted to shrink to the size of a speck, to be a mote of dust – inconsequential, meaningless, in random motion in the light between the thin curtains. I lay under the sheet. It was like waiting for the world to end.

Lol, however, was victorious. I could hear him singing in the kitchen; an exaggerated version of the City's anthem. I was too profoundly affected. I couldn't join him in his exuberance. I felt like a piece of cloth wrenched loose from a line, caught up in a storm with nothing to anchor it.

Valentine wasn't in the room either. He was somewhere else; a safer part of the flat. I was glad. I wouldn't have been able to look at him.

Maybe it was hard for Lol to be around us that morning – his mood so jubilant and ours so subdued. It was hard for me to be around Lol too. I found it difficult to answer him when he addressed me. I was still in bed when he came to tell me he was going to Gonetotown to see about the Fountainade.

I got up very late. It was Sunday. I didn't have to go out. I stayed indoors and tidied things, trying to convince myself I could bring order and normality back to my room. But even in the performance of ordinary tasks, I felt utterly different. I was nervous even of Valentine coming out of his room, of Lol coming back to the flat. I couldn't face them. I couldn't imagine how we would be.

The longer I put it off, the worse it'd become. I thought I should try to go out just once before I had to face returning to work the following day. By evening, I couldn't leave it any longer. I forced myself to go up the street to the late-opening grocery to buy something, it didn't matter what.

My hands trembled as I opened the Exit door of Canal Bank Court. My legs shook as I walked along the pavement. I knew it was irrational but I felt people looking at me. It was as if they knew; the pedestrians that passed me in the street, the people filling their baskets in the grocery aisles, the service-girls at the counter as I paid for my shopping. I thought everyone could read in my face what we'd done.

Valentine had been searching for some thread to mend a hole in the leg of his work uniform one evening. It was more than a month since Willa had been to see us at the flat.

Valentine came through into my room. 'I found these…' He had the directions and the two plastic discs in his hands. 'They were in the kitchen drawer. What are they?'

'They're passes.'

'What for?'

'For a club.'

'What kind of club?' There was a note of suspicion to his words.

'You know, like a nightclub. Music and the dancing.' I tried to sound breezy.

'What about this?' He held up the piece of paper.

'It shows you how to get there, probably.'

He glanced at the paper. '601…'

'That's wrong. It's TER106. All the numbers and words are the wrong way round.'

'TER106…? That's not the Dance District.'

'Well, then it's not in the Dance District.'

He stood there, considering what I'd just said.

'Why are they written backwards?'

'I don't know. Maybe they make it sort of secret so they don't get just anyone coming in. It must be a sort of filtering thing.'

'Where did you get these?'

'…From a friend.'

'Which friend?' He said it with a hint of disbelief in his voice, as though he was thinking, *Neeve doesn't have other friends.*

'The lady that came here that time. Willa-Rix.'

'Why did she give them to you?'

'She can't use them. She's from the Compound, remember?'

He stood and thought about it some more. 'Why didn't you tell me?'

'The club sounded weird, what she said about it. I didn't think you'd be interested.'

'So you're not going?'

'I don't think so.'

Valentine glanced back at the paper. For some reason he seemed intrigued.

'There's some numbers. They don't look like dates though. One, one, zero, one…then two, one, one, zero. Then…'

'One, one, zero, one.' I had to trace the numbers on my palm with my finger and work the rest out in my head, '…That's the tenth of November. The other one's…er…the first of December. Those dates have gone. The dates are written back to front as well.'

He looked over at me. His body had its familiar anxious bearing but there was something oddly expectant about him too.

'And two, one, two, one. What's that?'

'Er, that'll be…' I wrote on my palm again, 'the 12th December.' It was in a week's time. 'It'd be a long way to go just for a night out. We'd have to get to Paxmore station in the Wantsworth District.'

'Yes?' he said. But his expectancy didn't go.

'I don't think it's our kind of place. I'm not sure what type of people will be there. They might be more like Willa's sort.' I said it in the hope it'd put him off.

'I wouldn't mind.'

Now the disbelief was in *my* voice, 'D'you want to go there or something?'

He didn't reply. He hesitated, trying to think how to answer.

'Valentine, this is silly. You'd be so worried going to a new place.'

'They stare in the other clubs. All the time.'

'Who do?'

'In the Dance District.'

'But we've only been going there for a few weeks.'

'It's been nearly two months.'

'You loved it at first.'

'Well, not now. I can't keep going there. I *need* to go somewhere else.'

'Oh.' I was shocked by the vehemence in his voice. 'Well, I'm sure there must be somewhere left in the Dance District that we haven't tried yet.'

'There isn't. We've done them all. The four clubs. That's it.'

'Well, I don't suppose going to this place of Willa's is the answer.'

'How d'you know it isn't?'

'*Valentine*,' I was getting exasperated. 'I don't *know* that it isn't, I'm just *supposing* it isn't.'

He said it again, 'I don't feel safe in the Dance District.'

'No and chances are you wouldn't feel any safer at this other place either. What makes you think they'd stare any less at this place of Willa's, anyway? It could be worse.'

'I just have a feeling about it.'

'For goodness sake. You're making a big deal about some stupid club that's *kilometres* away. So they stare a bit in the Dance District but *that's it*. Nothing bad has happened.'

'You don't know what you're talking about.'

'Pardon?'

'You don't know what you're talking about when you say about the staring.' Then he did an unkind imitation of my voice, '*So they stare a bit but that's it…*'

I was shocked into silence.

Valentine seemed to be weighing something up in his head. Suddenly he blurted, 'I lost my job because of the staring.'

What he said sounded like nonsense but I didn't want to offend him again by saying so. I whispered, 'How could you lose your job?'

'They moved me to the Unit because of it.'

'I don't understand.'

'A superior at the Postal Department…' he paused, 'stared at me – all day, everyday.'

He paused again. Maybe it was easier to say the sentences if he separated them out.

'After weeks of staring, there was an indiscretion committed against my…my person…There was nobody I could go to, nobody to hear my complaint.'

'Oh.'

'Then suddenly I was dismissed. A security breach, it was claimed. I hadn't done anything…I lost my job, my reputation because of *staring*.' As the last word came out, he hit himself with both hands on his brows as though by punishing his own eyes he could wipe all staring from his past.

'I'm sorry…' I said.

He nodded and didn't look at me.

'I'm sorry I was quarrelsome.'

Valentine sniffed back his upset and acknowledged my apology with another swift nod of his head.

I thought about everything that Valentine had endured – his disgrace and transferral at work, his confinement in the Compound, the loss of his parents, the diagnosis of his Bad Passion, the rejection by his sister's husband. I felt I couldn't deny him what he was asking me for, not after all the things he'd been through. It seemed petty of me not to consider the Realm if he so badly wanted to go.

I lifted my head, addressing the room. I tried to sound keen. 'So the next club night's on the twelfth of December? Well...'

But what was going through my head was that Valentine didn't actually know anything about the club. I knew I should find the words to explain it to him but for some reason it seemed that if I told him then I'd have to explain my association with Willa and my debt to her. Those truths could lead to the unravelling of other truths. What if ended up telling him about my father's Vanishment? Shame kept me silent.

I found myself haunted by Willa's words, '*It's much better for you if he doesn't know. Then there's no chance of him turning you in...*'

We said to each other that we'd at least go and see. We agreed that we wouldn't go inside if we didn't like the look of it. It might be good just to travel to Paxmore station. It was one of the furthest stations within our region, according to the train-map on the wall at Widechapper. Neither of us had been there. We could just ride out to Paxmore and come home again if we wanted. We didn't have to go any further than that.

I memorised the directions to the Realm like Willa had told me. I invented a verse to help me remember: the first letter of each street in order became 'Every Warm August Relatives Eat Under The Cooling Fan'. It was silly but it worked. I tore the directions to shreds and I told Valentine that I'd misplaced them.

The night of the 12th December came around and, despite my fears and misgivings, we took the passes from the kitchen drawer and headed for the trains.

We walked over to Widechapper. The sky was more or less clear – the sort of night to leave a frost. We arrived at the station a little before seven o'clock.

A train trundled into the station and we got on. Every now and again, as the train passed through the tunnels, I'd see Valentine's chest heave a nervous breath. He was leant right back in his chair. I watched the lights in the tunnels flash over the surface of his glasses; alternating colours – red then blue then red again. They lit up the skin on his face, giving him rapidly switching pallors. The swaying movement of the carriages was pronounced. We were like two frightened out-sized infants being rocked by a pair of giant arms.

We stepped uneasily onto the platform at Paxmore and followed in line with the other travellers going up to street level. Paxmore station didn't seem much different from the one at Widechapper. It more or less could have *been* Widechapper station when you looked at it. We went outside into the street and stood watching people as they entered and left the station building. I wondered how long it'd take us to find the club if that's what we decided to do, if we'd even manage to find it in the dark.

'What d'you think? Shall we go home, Valentine?'

'We should try first…Find it at least.'

We didn't speak to each other as we walked. The cold was exaggerating the anxiety in our stomachs. I could hear the quiet, constant sound of Valentine's teeth chattering in his head. I hoped Willa-Rix had got the directions right.

A few scattered pedestrians were out, turned in on themselves, hunching against the cold and wind. After a while the little stores and houses petered out and we entered what looked like an old industrial sector. The pavements were empty there and only a few vehicles passed us on the road. Big, featureless buildings with black walls were set back from the grid-patterned streets, cordoned off in places by sections of buckled mesh fencing.

'What a strange place…' It was such an alien part of the City. 'It's so quiet.'

Valentine nodded.

We walked on. The street lighting became more patchy; ahead of us stretched a line of pale yellow pools of light, strung out along a straight road. The wind blew uninterrupted and I could feel the cold through a split seam in my shoe. Valentine was pulled in on himself too, only his outward watchfulness detectable on the surface. I tried to lean in to feel him but he'd pulled himself so far inside that he was impossible to reach.

Large, blank factories rose up on either side of the road, no indication on their exterior walls to show their old use. I thought I could trace a burnt, chemical smell on the wind. There were lines of small, broken windows high up near the roofs – the factories' only noticeable features that I could see. Greyish light from somewhere caught on the shards of glass that remained in place in the frames.

A sign loomed up ahead written in big luminous white figures. It displayed the factory lots: for 121–130 the sign pointed left; for 131–140, straight ahead; for 141–150, turn right. Willa's directions had indicated a factory numbered 128. We turned left off the main road and down a side street: Fielden Way, the last road on Willa's piece of paper. The road ran between the black masses of the buildings. I counted the dark hulking shapes of the buildings as we passed.

125…126…127…*128*.

128 was the same as all the others. Nothing remarkable about it. The directions said to go down an alley around the back of the building. We found the alleyway. Gravel had been laid down along it, over the top of the muddy ground, making our footsteps suddenly audible. Valentine reached for the collar of my coat. I felt the itchy wool of his gloves against the back of my neck as he walked behind me.

Ahead, there was a dim blue light set onto the wall. We got nearer and saw that it illuminated a sliding metal door. I listened for club noises but there wasn't a sound to be heard.

'This can't be right.' I was whispering.

'Is it open?'

I tried the door. It was heavy but it shifted when I tugged it. Valentine helped me to push it aside. I expected it to rumble as we slid it, but it moved quietly, opening onto a long flight of descending steps. Dim strip lights ran on the underside of hand-rails on the walls at either side, faintly lighting the stone steps and the occasional puddle. We looked down into the stairway.

'I can't hear anything.'

Valentine kept staring down into the dark. His head seemed to jerk or twitch slightly, a sharp involuntary movement. Then he inched himself forward into the building.

We pulled the metal door back in place behind us. As we descended, our shoes resounded on the ceiling, announcing our arrival. Nearing the foot of the stairs I began to hear music. It was muffled and seemingly far off but growing more distinct. Valentine sighed exaggeratedly loud. In front of us there was another door with a square of mirrored glass at head-height. We saw our own scared faces staring back at us. There was no sign anywhere to tell us that we'd come to the right place, that we'd reached the Realm.

I pushed the door and it swung open.

We were looking into a tiny reception area. The room was poorly lit and airless, like a cupboard. Inside, a woman was sitting at a small wooden table. She wore a greenish-looking dress with what seemed to be netting at the cuffs and collar. The dress fitted closely over her body, displaying her shape. At first glance, I thought there was something odd about her face. Then it dawned on me; on her eyes, lips and cheeks she wore cosmetic colours.

'Passes?' Her voice was low. She sounded ill-tempered.

'…This is the Realm?'

She nodded. 'Club passes?'

I reached for the discs in my pocket. The woman took them and put them into a slot in a small machine on the table. A high-pitched beep came back at her. All the while, she was gazing at Valentine – just what he'd been hoping to avoid.

'Names?'

'Neeve Glynnan and Valentine Frankland.'

'Have you got anything to prove who you are?'

Valentine was looking at me, wondering about the unusual entrance procedure. I got out my proof-papers. Valentine did the same and the woman copied our names down onto a sheet of paper.

'I've not seen you before.' She was still looking at Valentine. 'I'd remember if I saw you.'

'No.' I spoke for him. 'This is our first time.'

'Who told you about us?'

'Um, just a friend.' I didn't want to say her name. I didn't know if it was safe.

The woman shrugged. 'You get a free drink each with these,' she said as she handed the passes back. 'Through there.' She pointed to a door to her left.

'Thank you.'

I gave Valentine a gentle nudge towards the club. I think he may have been shaking. The woman was still staring at him as we pushed open the inner door went through.

My stomach lurched as we entered. The club was full of people.

'Neeve, what sort of place is this?'

We'd come dressed according to the club codes in the Dance District, but none of that applied here. The room was crowded with bizarre outfits.

'I don't know.'

The first thing to do was to find Valentine a quiet corner.

The club was much smaller than the ones we were used to. I scanned about for somewhere to sit. I could make out the shapes of archways and partitioned spaces in a darker area and steered Valentine towards them.

There was nowhere sit in the darker area; all the chairs had been taken. We went and stood where a side wall jutted out a short way, making a sheltered corner. We took off our winter coats and placed them at our feet. Then Valentine squeezed himself into the darkest part of the corner and leaned his head back against the wall.

I looked around at all the strangely-dressed people. *Hopefully nobody will notice Valentine at this rate*, I thought. I took hold of his hand.

'I'm alright,' he said. He meant '*Let go.*'

'I'll get us some drinks.'

I went to the bar for his Silver. I just hoped they sold it.

I made my way through the crowds of people. I'd never seen anything like it. The way the club-goers were dressed seemed improper. It was alarming to see such a variety of outfits. They wore undergarments over smart evening clothes, water-proof capes and flame-resistant trousers, hats beribboned with reflective tape taken from roadsides. There was a man wearing the jacket of a Guarda uniform with a paper flower in its lapel. He must have stolen his clothing – the thought made me shudder.

I fidgeted, waited to be served at the bar. There were murals painted on the walls; images of figures wearing strips of material – strips or maybe sashes – and what must have been slogans were written in unfamiliar words along the strips. On a large wall behind the bar, two figures were painted side by side, staring out into the room. They each had a circular symbol above their head. There were words streaming out of the figures' mouths but I hardly recognised any of them.

Someone tapped my arm. It was the bar-tender. I'd got distracted, looking around at everything.

'You're next. What d'you want?'

'Do you sell Silver?'

He nodded. He was wearing a black shirt that was covered in dots. Every dot was a different colour. Valentine and I were glaringly under-dressed in our civilian clothes.

'Anything else?'

'And a nutriented water?'

He nodded again and then went away to fetch the drinks.

I listened to the music that was playing and waited. I hoped Valentine was alright. I didn't want to leave him alone for long.

A song ended and I heard someone speaking, saying thank you into a microphone. I swung my head around, following the sound. There was a woman standing on a stage with a musician beside her. I couldn't believe it. I looked at the other people in the club. Nobody seemed worried. Nobody seemed concerned. What did they think they were doing, listening to live music? Willa had said she thought the people here would be discreet, that Valentine wouldn't be able to guess the nature of club, but she was wrong. The place wasn't safe.

The bar-tender returned with the drinks. 'Three quarters, please,' he said.

Forgetting about the passes, I paid with citizen tokens.

He smiled and took the money, then went to serve another customer.

My hands were shaking as I carried the drinks back to Valentine; I could've dropped the glasses at any moment.

The music started up again, the woman singing with a haunting, yearning voice. It sounded like the sort of music my mother had described to me – the type of song that'd been Streamlined when she was a girl. The song filled the club. Valentine would be petrified.

But Valentine wasn't on his own. I could see the back of someone wearing an animal costume, a furred body-suit with a large animal's head. I hadn't had time to prepare myself for people coming over, harassing Valentine. I hadn't even had time to think about it. I thought, *Valentine will want to leave now.* I wanted to go too.

But I got near and saw that Valentine was smiling.

I stopped in my tracks, a drink in each hand. People were milling back and forth in front of me, interrupting my vision, but I could see enough to tell.

Valentine glanced up and saw me. His gaze jolted me back into motion.

I handed him his drink.

'Thank you.'

Valentine introduced me, 'This is Neeve.'

'Hello there.'

'Hello,' I said.

'This is Lol.'

'Lol?'

Valentine nodded.

'Is that short for something?'

'It's short for Lollard but I prefer Lol.' He pushed the snout of the costume back, away from his face, making his hair stand on end. The top jaw of the creature stuck vertically up from the back of his head. The long tongue hung down his back.

Even on first glance you could tell he inhabited his body more fully than either Valentine or I knew how. He was a good ten centimetres or so shorter than Valentine, but somehow you might think he was bigger. He had black hair and brows but pale skin – too much contrast in one person's face.

'Your friend tells me you work in a Census Unit.'

'Yes.'

'What d'you do?'

'Same as Valentine. Collate statistics and input them onto a screen.' My voice was flat, defensive.

The man tilted his head a little to one side, looked at me and smiled.

'You haven't been here before?'

'No.'

'Your friend was about to tell me how you found out about us?'

'It was from a woman I know.'

'Who's that?'

'You won't know her. She's never been here. She sells paper over in Widchapper sometimes.'

'Oh, right. So, what do you think of this place?'

I was uptight. 'There's someone *singing...*'

'She's good.'

'Does she have some sort of permission to do that?'

'No.'

I glanced at Valentine to catch his reaction to the conversation. He was intently following everything that was said.

Then the man reached over and tapped the edge of Valentine's glass. At the same time, he turned back towards me and grinned.

'What's this, buying Silver for your friend?' He shook his head in mock-gravity. 'Dangerous stuff.'

'It's Valentine's favourite,' I said.

'It is? Can I try it? So long since I've gone near the stuff.'

Valentine nodded, offering his glass.

'Thanks.' I noticed the man's fingers as he held the drink. His nails were bitten right down. The skin around them was frayed and red. He took a sip and handed the glass back, coughing and slapping his chest. 'It really coats your throat on its way down. Probably given me gleaming innards!'

Valentine smiled.

I was waiting for the man to go away but he seemed to be staying where he was.

'D'you want to come for a dance, Valentine?' Once I'd got Valentine alone, we could make for the exit.

'Not yet. I have to drink this.'

'Okay.'

I gazed around the club.

'I need to go to the washroom, Valentine,' I said, even though I didn't.

'Alright.'

'I don't know where it is.'

'It's just over there.' The man pointed behind me, to a door on a far wall.

'Oh, right. Will you hold my drink for me, Valentine?'

I gave him my glass and made my way through the crowd towards the washroom.

There was a sign on the door; the silhouette of a female figure. Inside the washroom, people were milling about. Two women were waiting for the cubicles. I went and stood, leaning with my back against a full-length mirror. I pretended to wait for a toilet to become free. I could feel my pulse in the back of my head. It seemed to bang against the cold glass behind me. My throat felt tight and prickly. Tears were forming at the corners of my eyes. I wouldn't let them come. I didn't want to be there. I wanted to go and get Valentine and take him home right away.

A toilet flushed loudly and a woman came out of a cubicle. She adjusted her skirt as she walked, glancing at me on her way to the sinks, at my regulation clothing. I watched her turn on the water and put her hands under the steady stream. When she'd finished, she left the tap not quite shut and water still came from the spout. She shook her hands and drips sprayed into the air. Then she came and stood in front of me.

'I can't see myself,' she said.

For a moment I was bewildered. The girl looked amused and pointed over my head. 'In the mirror.'

I moved aside and leant against the wall instead. The girl looked at herself in the glass, arranging her hair with her fingers and looming her face in close to her reflection to check herself.

'Toilet's free,' she said.

I turned and saw an open cubicle door.

'I...changed my mind.'

The girl laughed as though I'd made a joke and then left the washroom to go back to the club. I stood watching water spill into the sink where the tap had been left running. Two sinks along, a woman was sat in the basin, swinging her legs as she spoke to her friend. I went and shut off the water.

There was something different about the people in that place. It wasn't just the way they were dressed. The woman in the sink was using her hands as she spoke, her hands accompanying the words.

I watched other people in the washroom too. Their faces were animated and alert. It made me think about the inhabitants of the Sixth Compound; the staring, blanked-out expressions, eyes that seemed to look out at the world but not really, not really wanting to see. In comparison to the people at the Realm, they'd appear so dull and slow and listless. The people at the Realm weren't like the club-goers at Dance District either. They weren't like people anywhere I knew.

I wondered what I was doing in such a dangerous place, putting myself and Valentine at risk for I didn't know what. For a Circle – I didn't even know what that was. What if Willa-Rix was right: that it was in my *Glynnan blood* to come to such places? I tried not to think about it. Valentine might still be talking with the man in the weird costume. The man could be telling him anything. I headed back out, hoping that the man had gone away.

He hadn't, though. He had his hand on Valentine's shoulder. That's how it was when I'd found my way to them. Valentine was looking down at the floor, smiling like he was trying to stop himself but couldn't.

Lol addressed me, 'I was just saying about there being no dress code here. Next time you could bring along whatever you fancy. There's a place to get changed when you arrive.'

'We just came to try the place out…I don't know if we'll be back, will we, Valentine?

Valentine twitched his head to one side, neither a 'yes' nor a 'no'.

'Well, it's not for everyone,' Lol said.

'And it's a long way back home on the trains. We'll have to head off soon.' I looked at Valentine, trying to read a willingness to leave in his face.

Valentine didn't respond. He spoke to Lol instead, 'Where did you get your costume?'

Lol looked down at himself as if he hadn't been aware of what he had on until that moment. 'Oh, this. A friend made it for me. It's bit impractical though, because it's so hot. But I like it too much to take it off.' He gestured towards the stage. 'I used to wear it when I played with the group, that's what it was made for.'

'You used to *play*?'

'Yes.'

I felt Valentine's eyes move from Lol's face to mine.

'*Playing what?*'

'I was the tenor.'

I didn't even know what a tenor was. I looked at Valentine again. 'Did your group have a name?' was all he said. I noticed that he'd finished off his glass of Silver.

'We were called "The Love-Rhumbas."' Lol gave us another sideways look, out of the corners of his eyes; 'I made that up.' He spoke unhurriedly, stretching out his words so that they joined together and came out slightly slurred. And his voice rose and lowered in pitch; he could sound amused, surprised, disheartened all in one sentence.

Lol drank his drink and looked around the room. Valentine backed off a little into the darkness of the corner as though he felt he'd overstepped himself by asking his two questions. Lol drained his glass and put his hands in the pockets of his costume, searching for citizen tokens. He held them out to Valentine. 'Would you go to the bar for me?'

Valentine went rigid.

'Get yourself another Silver and a Mild-Witch for me. What about you, Miss? Same again for you?'

I hesitated, 'I was thinking we ought to be going to get the train?'

Lol said, 'It's only about nine o'clock. There's plenty of time. Please, let me buy you a drink. What'll it be? Some more water?'

'Y-yes...'

Valentine did what he was told. He took the tokens from Lol and wandered off in the direction of the bar.

I called after him, 'A Silver, a Mild-Witch and a nutriented water...'

He nodded without looking back. My eyes followed him. He'd never gone for a round of drinks.

When Valentine was out of ear-shot, I asked Lol, 'What if there's a raid? Aren't you concerned?'

'There won't be.'

I wondered how he could be so adamant. 'How do you know? With all this music, there might.'

'There won't be.' His voice had lost some of its playful edge. For a moment, I thought about leaving without Valentine. If he didn't want to go home, then maybe I should leave on my own.

Lol said, 'So, how come you're here? Why've you come?'

'We...we came for the dancing.'

'That's not really it, is it?'

'We came here for someone...As a favour.'

'To whom? To the friend who told you about the place?'

I looked at him, trying to work out how safe it was to say.

'It's alright. You can tell me.'

'Yes. To my friend.'

'So how come you got in? People don't just get given passes for doing favours. You must have some sort of connection yourselves.'

At first I didn't understand what he meant. Then slowly, it dawned on me. Maybe I wanted to prove to him that I wasn't as stupid or as dull as I looked. I just came out with it. 'My father got Vanishment. And my aunt.' After I'd said it I felt ashamed, even in a place like the Realm.

Lol looked surprised. Everybody did when I told them.

'When?'

'About fourteen years ago.'

'What for?'

'Eye Offences.'

'*Really*? How were they caught?'

'By the Guarda, I suppose. I don't know. I don't even know what an Eye Offence is, except that you mustn't be caught in public with your eyes shut.'

'Not for longer than five minutes. The Eye Offences are laws to stop people reflecting. And not just in public places. There are laws to prevent people from doing it in private too. You know that, surely?'

'Mmm...what do you mean, *stop them reflecting*?' He made people sound like mirrors.

'To stop them discovering...resources in themselves.'

'Uh.' It felt strange hearing him tell me things. It felt like he was telling me about my own father and even then, I didn't properly understand what he'd said. I didn't want to hear about my father from somebody else; not from a stranger in a strange club.

'What were their names, your father and your aunt? We're taught some of the different Vanishment cases here,' he said. 'Vanishments are very highly regarded by the Realm. I might've learnt about them.'

'My father's name is Glynnan. Fylde Janna Glynnan. My aunt was Hester Downie.'

'Mmm.' Lol was nodding. 'I've heard of them, I think.'

'*Really*?'

'Yes, rings a bell, I'm sure.'

'What do you know about them?'

'I don't really. Their names are familiar, that's all. They must've been brave.'

I was reeling in my head. He knew of my relatives. I lost track of the conversation. I could see my father's face in my mind's eye – smiling right at me.

'What about your friend?' Lol was asking another question. 'You know? *Valentine*.'

'He's not my friend. He's my fiancé.'

'Oh, I'm sorry. So, what's your fiancé's connection? What does he know about this place?'

'Well...nothing.' I was trailing behind a bit, working hard to keep up with the conversation. 'He's just come for the dancing.'

Lol looked at me. 'Why doesn't he?'

'I didn't want to frighten him. Why, what've you said?'

'Nothing. I've told him nothing. But maybe you should have.'

'Please don't tell him. He doesn't know about my family either, about the Vanishments.'

'Okay. Don't worry, I won't say anything. What about this favour you've come for? Why your friend wanted you to come. Maybe I can help.'

'I need a Circle.'

He nodded.

'You know what one is? I need to take one back. And I need to give a message to some people. The Usba–'

'The Usbornes?

'Yes.'

'They set this group up. In the form it's in now. They're not here tonight. They're away at a meeting over in Gaslands but I could get a Circle sorted for next time you're here.'

'I don't think we'll be coming back again.'

'Yes. You said already. Well, I don't know about tonight. It's short notice.'

I'd tell Willa that I'd tried to get her a Circle but that they couldn't give me one. I'd leave it at that. If there wasn't a Circle to take, then I wouldn't have to carry anything bad back with me on the trains.

'Let me get this drink first. Then I'll go and see for you.'

I didn't really want him to. 'How big will it be?'

'How big will what be?'

'The Circle?'

He turned to me. There was something odd about the way he angled himself; his bottom-half staying still, his top-half having to make more of an effort to move.

'Not big. You enlarge it later.'

'*Enlarge it*? What *is* it?'

'A Circle? It's for illimitability.'

I must have looked completely baffled.

'Not to worry. You'll see,' he said.

I let out a breath and my lungs juddered with tension. The woman on the stage was still singing into the microphone. *Illimitabilty* – the word trailed around inside my brain, taunting all my other thoughts with its incomprehensibleness. I looked around for Valentine. It'd been a while since he'd gone. There was no sign of him.

'I'm going to see where Valentine is.'

'He's only buying drinks. He'll be fine.'

'Yes, but he –'

'He'll be fine.'

My feet stayed put but my eyes kept searching the club.

'Here, look. He's coming, Neeve.'

I looked and saw Valentine walking slowly over, concentrating hard on the drinks he was carrying. I'd have gone over to help him but I was distracted for a moment by my own name in my head. *Neeve*. Lol had said it. The way it came out of his mouth, it sounded different, nicer. A soft, cloudy-like word.

Valentine handed us the drinks.

'Thank you.' Lol took his drink and swigged, tipping the glass to his mouth. Despite his bitten down fingers and mumbled voice, he seemed confident in a way that I didn't recognise. He was comfortable with himself in a way I hadn't seen before. I'd wanted to dislike him but it was hard not to warm to him.

I took my water. 'Thanks for going to the bar.'

I was embarrassed in front of Lol; conscious of making too big a fuss over Valentine. I shouldn't make a big deal of his fetching the drinks.

I glanced at Valentine's glass of Silver. It was three-quarters full. 'Is that a double?'

Valentine nodded. 'The bar-tender poured it for me. She said I could have the extra measure for free.'

'Be careful. Drink it slowly,' I said and took a mouthful of water.

Then, 'Are you part of a Movement?' I felt my heart turn over. The liquid nearly spurted from my mouth. It was Valentine, his distinctive whisper. I turned to look at him.

Lol muttered a reply, 'You know about that?'

'At the bar. People were talking.'

I shut my eyes. I should have gone for the drinks myself.

Valentine asked again. 'Are you?'

Lol placed his hand on the side of his face and then brushed his palm over his mouth. Both of us were watching him now.

'Sort of. But I'm not the right kind of person to get properly involved. I'm not disciplined enough. They want hard-grafters and I'm lazy.'

'This club's part of a Movement, though.' Valentine said it as statement but he was looking to Lol to confirm it.

'Yes. But it's just a good place to come and socialise. I wouldn't worry.'

'What kind of Movement is it?' It was odd, Valentine asking such direct questions. He was never normally engaged enough with things to bother.

'A wing of the Innate-Politicals.'

I didn't know what Lol was talking about. I didn't want to know. It couldn't be more obvious: members of Movements were the ones who disappeared the quickest.

'You've heard of them?'

Valentine shook his head.

'Are you interested?' Lol asked.

Valentine looked shocked.

I jumped in, 'No. We're not.'

Lol repeated his question, 'Are you?'

Valentine gazed at the floor and shook his head again.

After a few minutes, Lol excused himself and Valentine and I were left alone. He avoided my eyes and moved his Silver around his glass. I didn't know what to say to him. I watched the woman on stage taking a bow. The crowd were applauding her and the musician who'd accompanied her.

Valentine said, 'Did you know what this club was before we came here?'

I lied. 'No…'

'Your friend must have told you when she gave you the passes.'

'No, she didn't. Perhaps she didn't think I'd come if I knew.'

He probably didn't believe me but he didn't accuse me of being untruthful. He just said, 'It's clear now why the dates and names were written backwards.'

We stood awkwardly as some new musicians were introduced onto the stage.

'Should we go home?' I asked.

'Alright. I'll finish this.' He drank his Silver down and I stood beside him, my stomach in a knot, desperate to leave.

We put on our coats and made our way through the crowds to the exit. We'd just about reached the door when Lol intercepted us.

'On your way out?'

'Yes.'

'Hold on a minute. I've got someone here who wants to meet you.'

The woman with him was wearing all white.

'Neeve, Valentine, this is Bonny Noach.'

One minute we were shaking the woman's hand and saying hello and the next Valentine was being whisked away towards the dance-floor by Lol.

'You want a Circle?' The woman asked.

I nodded.

'Follow me.'

She took me through a door marked STAFF into what looked like a sort of sitting room where couches and armchairs were arranged in a vague circle. On one side of the room there was a sink and a stove with a kettle. Tea things were draining beside the basin. The woman invited me to take a seat. I wasn't bothered about the Circle at all. All I cared about was Valentine, out in the club on his own.

'So how come you want a Circle?'

'It's not for me. It's for my friend. The woman who got me and Valentine the passes.'

'Why hasn't she come herself?'

'She's in a Compound. She can't come here.'

'Why does she want it?'

'I don't know why… I don't even know what one is.'

The woman looked harder at me, checking my expression.

'What's her name, this friend?'

I figured if Willa wanted the Circle so much I should tell them her name. 'It's Willa-Rix.'

'Which Compound is she in?'

'Sixth.'

I heard a door open and a man entered. Bonny smiled at him as he crossed over to the stove. He was wearing clothes that looked to be made from knitted metal; a long robe down to his feet of a wire-type material. The sound of the club music had followed in briefly behind him until the door fell shut. I fretted about Valentine.

'Do you know her booth number?'

'Booth number? No.' I did, but I didn't like to say.

'Do you know her wing?'

'C-wing.'

'And your name is Neeve Glynnan?'

I glanced over to see if the man on the other side of the room was listening. His back was to us as he stood at the stove. It seemed as though he was listening with his whole body.

'Yes.'

'How do you know Willa-Rix?'

'Um, how come you need to know all this?'

'Not much more now.'

'I need to go. Valentine wants to go home.'

'He's alright. Lol's with him. Look, we can make this quick. Tell me how you know her.'

Lol's with him. It didn't make me feel much easier.

'How do you know Willa-Rix, Neeve?'

'She was a friend when I was young. She lived near my family…And then I know her from the Compound.'

'So you've known her for a long time?'

'Er, yes. For years.'

'Okay.' She stood up. 'I need to check something. I'll be back.'

The woman left the room via another door.

The man was stirring up steaming water in some cups. I wanted to make a bolt for the door. I wanted to go and find Valentine.

I could feel the two club passes still in my pocket. They were digging into my hip as I sat. I took them out and stuffed them down the back of the couch.

The man came over with a tray of drinks. He placed the tray on the floor beside me and passed me a cup. I looked at the drink in my hand.

'It's reddened tea,' the man said.

'I didn't know you could still get that.'

'Yes.' Then he said, 'I'm Nolan Jonker.'

'I'm Neeve.'

He nodded. 'I understand your father and aunt got Vanishment?'

I spilt my tea then. It was the way he came straight out with it. My hand jolted and the tea slopped over the rim of the cup. Hot water sank into my skirt and burnt my thigh.

'Sorry…' He went back to the kitchen area to fetch a cloth.

He handed me a towel and I wiped at my skirt. My leg was stinging. I could feel my eyes prickling up for the second time that night. I could feel my throat getting tight.

'I shouldn't be here.' My voice cracked.

I didn't want to cry, it just came over me, out of nowhere. I looked away and tried to blink water from my eyes. I tilted my head back to stop tears falling on to my face.

'Drink some tea.' He spoke softly. 'It'll calm you.'

He moved nearer to the couch and knelt at my feet.

I felt him put his hands on my leg. Gently, he started to rub my shin through my sock. I looked at him through my watered-up eyes. He was trying to soothe me, rubbing my leg, stroking my calf muscle. His kindness made it worse. The prickling in my eyes grew fierce.

I swallowed some more tea.

'Is the drink helping?'

I nodded. Maybe it was.

'My parents used to make it for me as a bedtime drink when I was a child,' he said.

He kept stroking my leg. 'We'll need to take your sock and shoe off.'

'Uh?'

'For the Circle.'

I stared at him. I didn't understand.

'I'm going to undo your lace.'

I watched him undo my shoe. He did it slowly, not making any sudden movements. When my shoe was loose, he slipped it off and lightly rubbed my foot, supporting my ankle with his free hand. I looked down at myself and felt ashamed; my big size nine and a half feet.

Bonny came back into the room. She addressed the man, 'I found Willa-Rix in the index.'

I thought, *he must have made the tea quite strong*. I could feel my upset starting to subside.

Then they were both at my feet.

'Nolan's going to take your sock off now,' she said.

The man peeled the sock back from my knee, down my leg and slipped it from my toes in a roll. I saw the woman pushing up the sleeves of her costume. She was attaching a wide, cone-shaped contraption to my ankle, obscuring my view of my foot.

Unusually, it wasn't bothering me so much that I didn't know what was happening. I was watching them both without too much concern. It felt almost as though my mind was switching briefly out of alertness and then back in again. I might have started missing odd seconds of time. The tea must have been really strong.

I could feel their hands on my sole. Then suddenly there was a different sensation; a pushing-pulling feeling. I couldn't tell if something had been taken out of me or if something had been put in. It didn't hurt, but it was weird and my sole felt hot.

The next thing I knew, my sock was being put back on. My laces were being re-tied.

'There. That didn't take long. You can go and join your fiancé again now,' the woman said.

She helped me up from the couch. When I stood, it felt as though my shoe was full of water, like my foot was surrounded by hot liquid. We headed over towards the door that lead back into the club.

I turned to Bonny.

'The Circle...You've given me it?'

'Yes. Show it to Willa-Rix. She'll know what to do.'

I heard the man behind me, Nolan, saying goodbye and then the door swung shut.

I was taken back into the club. Bonny told me to wait by the bar while she went to find Valentine. I felt dozy, like I'd just woken up.

When she brought Valentine, Lol was with him. They looked odd: Lol in his animal costume, his face flushed from the dancing and Valentine in his darkened glasses. I could see Valentine's eyes staring at me through the lenses.

'Let's go home, Val,' I said.

Lol went with us to the exit. We passed through the little room where the woman in the green dress had checked the plastic discs. She wasn't there any more.

Lol stood at the bottom of the steps as we climbed up, the dark down there seeming to swallow more and more of him as we went higher. My foot felt odd. I could feel the swimming sensation inside my shoe as I stepped. I took hold of the stair-rail to help me.

A mumbled voice called from below. 'Nice to meet you...'

We went up a few more steps.

'Toodle-loo.' Lol was still down there. His words echoed around us, against the walls of the stairwell, and then were followed by another sound; a door banging shut, Lol returning to the club.

Valentine waited for me at the top. I caught up with him and we went out into the freezing cold air. Outside, the night and everything around us was glittering with frost. Sparkles covered the gravel in the alley. I walked slowly, catching my breath, watching the long trails of air escaping our mouths. Away from the busy club, I began to feel clearer.

'Where did you go?'

'That lady took me somewhere. I'm sorry. I asked her to be quick.'

'Where did she take you?'

'To a staff area. They gave me a cup of tea and asked me about Willa-Rix.'

'Why?'

'I don't know. Maybe Willa's wants to be part of the Movement …' I felt my sole throb in my shoe.

The industrial district we walked through seemed wider going back. It felt somehow cleaner in the night frost, and emptier still.

'Were you alright while I was gone? I didn't feel good about leaving you, what with the place being so unsafe.'

'I was alright. Lol was there.'

The ground was icy where we trod and my feet were slipping a little on the road. My shoes had no grip. I reached out and grasped Valentine's jacket sleeve to steady myself. I walked along for a little way, holding on to his arm, feeling unbalanced, and not only from the ice.

Chapter 7

I didn't sleep deeply. I had fitful dreams in which everything was jumbled and nothing made sense. At some point during the night, I sensed Lol awake beside me and that woke me up too.

Lol was lying still, on his back, with his eyes open. He seemed alert, maybe even wide awake. I watched him through half-open eyes as he lay there. His eyelids flickered and I wondered what he was thinking. His breathing seemed quicker, shallower than normal. I wanted to whisper to him but something stopped me. This was a different Lol, a Lol without an audience of Neeve and Valentine, a Lol I didn't really know.

Eventually, he got out of bed. He moved carefully so as not to waken me. A light left on in the hallway fed under the door. It highlighted objects and furniture on one side of the room, giving a faint shape to things. Lol went to the foot of the bed and stood with his hands hanging loosely by his sides. He stared down at the mattress, half seeming to look at me and half not. I kept still but my brain was ticking so fast in the dark that I imagined the noise of my thoughts would give me away.

Lol turned away from the bed. He reached down to the floor to pick up the jumper he'd worn in the daytime. He tugged it roughly over his head, as though impatient with himself. I watched him wander over to the shelves in a dark corner of the room. He was looking for something, running his hands along the wooden slats. His back was bent as he peered at the shelves. He picked something up. It was the pack of cigarettes, liquid-lighter and stub-pot that he kept hidden behind a book.

As Lol crossed the room, the floorboards creaked under his feet. For some reason the sound seemed to bother him. For a few seconds he seemed distracted. He started swaying back and forth over a particular spot, listening to the quiet creaking in the boards. I couldn't work out what he was doing. When he seemed to have satisfied himself, he continued across the room.

He picked up the wooden chair and carried it to the window. The curtains were still pushed back, un-drawn; we'd been so tired when we'd gone to bed we hadn't bothered to close them.

Lol reached over, slowly undid the latch and nudged the window slightly open. He sat down. In the dark, his brows cast shadows over his eyes. His face was unreadable. He lit a cigarette; a prohibited, high-tar cigarette and leaned the chair back on its rear legs so that his head was resting on the windowsill. He took a drag, his eyes gazing upwards. A vague light from down below in the street, came up into the room. He raised his arm and laid it along the sill so that the smoke got drawn out of the gap in the window. I watched the little orange glow at the tip of the cigarette as it dodged back and forth from the window to Lol's mouth. His face was turned towards the room but each time he exhaled, he turned his head to angle the smoke away, out of the gap.

Lol took another long drag on the cigarette and the tip burned brighter. I saw then, that his face was wet. I saw the shine on his cheeks caught by the tiny light. I waited for the next drag. When it came I saw more clearly still.

I watched as he put out what remained of the cigarette and then reached inside the little box for another. The liquid-lighter made a sharp, quick crack as he flicked at it to get the flame up. I took it as a cue and pretended to wake up.

I opened my eyes wide in the dark and lifted my head from the pillow.
'Lol?'
'Huh?' His voice grated against his throat.
I heard him sniff.
I raised myself up on one arm. 'What's the matter?'
'Nothing. Go back to sleep.' His voice when he whispered sounded like a hiss.
'Why are you up?'
'I had a dream. It woke me, that's all. It's alright. Go back to sleep.'
I didn't say anything for a few seconds.
Then I said, 'Are you crying?'
'No.'
'You look like you've been crying.'
'I haven't.'
He wiped his face with his sleeve; a reflex to remove the evidence. I stared at the bed covers, too embarrassed to look at him.
'I had a bad dream, alright? But I'm okay. I'm coming back to bed now. I'm just going to finish this cigarette.'
'Alright.'
I laid back down, shut my eyes and waited for Lol to return to bed. But he didn't come back. A short while later I heard the window being

closed and then the floor creaking under Lol's weight again as he crossed the room. My eyes felt the room briefly brighten as he opened the bedroom door to go out into the hall. I lay for a few more moments then I pushed the covers away and got out of bed.

Lol was in the kitchen. He was leaning with his back against the sink. It took me a while to adjust to the stark light of the room but I could see his face was red and his eyes were sore. The kitchen felt very small. It seemed I'd either have to stand too close to him, or stay out in the hall. I stepped from the hallway carpet and stood with my feet just inside the kitchen. The linoleum felt cold against my soles.

Seeing me set Lol off. He started to breathe in hard snatches of air, breathing so fast that his body jolted. I went towards him, smelled his cigarette smoke. I reached my hand out and laid it on his chest as if I could slow his breaths that way. Lol put his hand over mine and pressed it hard against himself.

I didn't know what to say. I made a sound, a sound I hoped might be comforting, 'Shhhmmmhh.'

Lol was trying to breathe more calmly. I watched as he attempted to hold the air inside his lungs and then gradually let it out.

'Shhuhmmh,' I said again. Then, as a desperate measure I pulled a face. I crossed my eyes and curled out my tongue to try and make him laugh. Lol looked at me and sniggered. Some mucus bubbled out of his nose. I gave him the handkerchief from the pocket of my night dress.

'No wonder you're distressed.' I said. 'It's because of yesterday and the rally.'

'No. I had…' He had to breathe in to be able to finish his sentence, 'a bad dream.'

'Yes. Because of yesterday. That's why you had it.'

He didn't answer. He blew his nose and looked done-in.

'Come back into the bedroom. It's warmer there.'

He let himself be led out of the cold kitchen, back to the bedroom. Then we sat under the covers, waiting for his breathing to fully settle.

'What was your dream? It must've been horrible to upset you as much as this.'

'It was. I don't want to tell you.'

'No, not if talking about it'll make you upset again.'

'It's not that. It's because it was so bad it'd upset you as well.'

'I'll be alright. It's just a dream. You can tell me if you want.'

'You'd hate me if I told you.'

'Don't be silly. I couldn't hate you. Maybe you'll feel better for getting the dream off your chest.'

He didn't say anything. He just looked down at his hands lying in his lap.

As soon as we got in that night, after the trip to the Realm, I went straight to the washroom. I locked myself in and leaned against the wall to remove my shoe. Not long after we'd caught the train home, the throbbing in my foot had eased, it felt normal again, but I still had to see what they'd done. I twisted my foot so that I could look at my sole. There was nothing there. No mark, no redness, nothing. I ran my fingers over the skin. Nothing at all. Whatever they'd tried to do hadn't worked.

I became obsessed with my foot. In the following days I kept taking my shoe off to look at my sole but I never saw anything different. When I wasn't checking my foot, I was wriggling it inside its shoe, trying to make sure that I still had control of it. Even though there was nothing to see and nothing to feel, it seemed as though my foot belonged to someone else; the people at the Realm had taken it over.

Late in December, when the dates we'd been given for the Realm had passed, Willa-Rix paid us another visit. I'd have preferred to have gone and found her myself, tracking down her paper stall somewhere so that Valentine didn't have to be privy to the visit. But there was no telling where I'd find her. And it'd be ages until a guest day at the Compound came round.

It was a Saturday afternoon when Willa came. Valentine was in his room when she knocked on the door. Her face was strange. It looked almost childlike with excitement. Her eyes were so wide. We stood in the kitchen whispering to each other.

'That was a very weird place you had us go to, Willa...We were scared out of our wits...I think they even *drugged* me. I'm not going again, I'm really not.'

She nodded absently and stared at my feet. 'You've got it, haven't you?'

I glanced down. 'There's *nothing* there. It was horrible, Willa. I was taken into this room and they...' I could feel myself getting upset all over again. 'I'm not even sure what they did. Whatever they tried to do, it hasn't worked.'

'Leave it to me, Neeve. Let's go to your room.'

I took Willa through and she sat on the bed, opening the bag she'd brought.

'Take off your shoe and sock.'

I peeled off my sock and held my foot up to show her. 'See? There's nothing.'

'Um…' Willa-Rix ran her finger across the flat of my heel. Then she pulled some antiseptic cream from her bag – at least it said it was antiseptic cream on the tube.

'I'm going to rub some of this in.'

'It's not sore. There's not even a mark.'

'It's not that kind of cream.' Her voice was low and she sounded distracted.

She squeezed a little of the ointment on to her finger and applied it to the ball of my foot.

'Here it comes.'

'What?'

'Just wait.'

I could feel something on my skin. The sole of my foot was getting hot again, like it had at the club. This time though, without the tea, it hurt more.

'Ow!'

'Keep your voice down!'

'It stings.'

'Not long now. I can see it.'

Willa turned and pulled a small square of white card from her bag. But the surface of it wasn't like an ordinary sheet. It was shiny and lacquered-looking. She laid it on the floor beside the bed.

'Stand on this.'

The heat seemed to have risen up my calf and was gathering under my kneecap, making it ache.

'Stand on the paper, Neeve.'

I got up and placed my foot on the white sheet.

'Okay, now take it off.'

I had to use my hands to help me move my leg. It wouldn't move by itself.

'Beautiful.' Willa almost gasped.

I looked down. The card had a distinct image on it; a little circular pattern surrounded by the smudge of my heel.

'It worked, Neeve!'

I sat heavily back down on the bed and massaged my leg.

Willa picked the card from the floor and studied the image. 'Amazing!'

I lifted my foot in my hands. I didn't want to, but I had to see. This time there was a pattern on my sole, the skin raised up; a small relief about five centimetres across.

'How...?'

Willa-Rix shook her head. 'No idea. The paper responds to the heat, maybe.'

She passed me the card. I held it close to my face and stared.

It was a perfect circle. Within its circumference were four equal-sized triangles that over-laid one another. Their points touched the inside edges of the circle at regular intervals. At the centre of the four triangles, was a smaller triangle which contained another circle. That last circle made up the smallest shape in the pattern. It was very simple, just some interlocking lines, but Willa was right, there was something beautiful about it.

'That should go from your foot again. You won't be able to see it soon.' She took the paper from me. 'Have you got scissors?'

'They're in the kitchen drawer probably.' I wasn't fit for walking.

Willa went and fetched the scissors. She cut very closely around the edges of the Circle, making the paper as small as possible.

'What's the Circle for? I was told it was...' I tried to remember the word. It was hard enough to say, let alone understand what it meant, 'for il...limita...bility.'

She looked at me. It seemed Willa had never heard of the word either. I don't think she wanted to admit it though. 'The Circle's for relinquishing thoughts.'

'What d'you mean?'

'It's a type of reflection. It's linked to what your father got up to with the Eye Crimes but not quite. It's called relinquishing except there's nothing *relinquishing* about it; the thoughts go by themselves.'

'Uh?'

'You think less.'

'Why would you want to think less? Everyone knows it sends you mad.'

'According to *them*, girlie. They claim it's dangerous and causes mental troubles so they can ban it. Truth is that it helps you. After a while, you're not so afraid any more. One way to do it is to use the Circle, another way is by closing the eyes and reflecting. There's several different ways apparently. But that's why the authorities drew up the Eye Offence laws. They wanted to ban that type of activity – if you can call it an activity.'

'Not afraid any more?...How come?'

'That's what I'm going to find out. I'll take the Circle back and try it with my group at the Compound.'

I was thinking about my father, hoping he hadn't felt afraid when they gave him Vanishment.

'Willa?'

'Hmn?'

'When did it all start, the Eye Offences and everything?'

'I was told that about two hundred or so years ago teachings were brought from the Eased.'

'The Eased?'

'It could be a place, a distant part of the City maybe. Or it could be a group of people; people eased by the practices. Anyway, these teachings, what became the Eye Offences etcetera, had a radical effect. People began to change. They got less...caught up. They were leaving their jobs, they didn't care so much what the City demanded of them. They didn't put so much store in their old lives, not in the same way. It's said they went "beyond themselves" and that's when the institutions began to lose their hold. The old structures began to crumble, collapsing from within. So then the authorities stepped in to eradicate it. They purged the City of the teachings, told everyone they drove you mad and banned the practices. That's when they confiscated the maps; to stop people finding each other and meeting up...You use a screen at work, don't you?'

'Yes.'

'Well, at one time, people had those in their homes.'

'That's daft. Why would anyone want a screen in their home?'

'They helped people link up. They'd share what they knew. There used to be special kinds of centres where people could go to reflect too – the authorities closed all of those. They must've panicked and gone overboard, clamping down. They built the Compounds. They believed that the prescribed roles involved in married and family life would hold things in place, so they needed everyone to fit into that or else be holed up in a Compound. They brought in the Streamlining and the Adjusted Press. They got rid of certain sorts of music; anything *affecting*. But they didn't manage to purge it all. Things got hidden, kept secret. And now people are trying all over again.'

'How do you know all this?'

'I've learned more since I came across the people at the Realm.'

I'd never allowed Willa to explain things to me before. That kind of talk petrified me because of what had happened. Now I couldn't properly take it in.

'You thinking about joining us then?' Willa asked.

I shook my head. 'I can't. I've not got it in me.'

She blew her cheeks out. 'Well, I appreciate you going to the club. Thanks to you we might actually get somewhere. See, you're involved even if you don't like to think you are.'

I tried to ignore her but she was on a roll.

'I can tell who you are just by looking at you, you know? I can see it in your eyes. It's all over your face, Neeve. You're a *Glynnan*. It's just a shame you daren't look at yourself and see what's really there.'

I changed the subject. 'Anyway, I didn't manage to pass your message on to those people like you wanted. Those Usbornes. They weren't at the club.'

'It doesn't matter. They got word somehow. After you went there, someone found me on my stall. They brought me the cream and the paper. I came here as soon as I could.'

'So why didn't they just bring you the Circle? Why did we have to go to all that effort?'

'They don't like to travel with it across the City, in case they get spot-searched. I should have got you to bring your big foot to the Compound to do all this in my booth but I couldn't wait for ages for you to be allowed in. Besides you never know when a Patroller's going to look in. I thought it was better to come here. Anyway I don't have to travel far – just a walk back to the Compound from here. I'll be okay.'

'How did you get in and out of the Compound gates with the cream and stuff?'

'It didn't come with me through the gates. I hid it outside with my paper-selling things. It's only this little beauty that I need to smuggle in.' She held up the print of the Circle, 'and it's so small, hopefully it won't cause me much of a problem. I need to head off, Neeve. Things to do.'

She started packing things back into her bag. Her eyes were still flared with enthusiasm.

'Willa...'

'Mm?'

'I can't do anything like that again. Going to the club and everything. I was...I didn't like it.'

'Alright then.'

I showed her to the door.

'Promise you'll be careful.' I wasn't just thinking about her. I was panicking that if she was caught with the Circle, somehow they'd be able to trace it back to me.

'Don't worry yourself, silly-britches.'

I closed the door behind her. I hobbled back to my room with one shoe and sock still on, the other foot bare. I went and lay down on the bed to wait for the heat and pain in my leg to ease off, to wait for the little image to disappear. I lay back but I couldn't relax. I was waiting for the Patrollers from the Compound to come banging on our door, waving the print of the Circle in my face.

Later, in the evening, Valentine came from his room to get some food from the cupboard. I hung around the kitchen wanting to talk to Valentine, waiting for him to ask me about the visitor I'd received, but he didn't mention it.

In the end I said, 'Willa-Rix called today.'

'Yes. I heard.'

'She wanted to know how we liked the Realm.'

'She came for that?'

'Yes. She wanted me to tell her what it was like.'

He was spreading some paste over cracker biscuits as he sat at the table.

'I told her we wouldn't be going back. I told her what a bad time we'd had.'

I watched a cracker break under his knife.

'I didn't mind it,' he said.

Sometimes I didn't understand him at all.

He finished his snack and went back to his room. I sat in the kitchen nervously prodding my foot. I knew my foot looked normal again – unproblematic – but somehow I felt as though it had betrayed me.

A few days into the start of the new year, I got called into Mr Spinks's office at the Unit. He said it had been noted how the standard of my work had been deteriorating, that I wasn't operating at anything like the adequate speed, that I was failing in my tasks. It was a shock to me because since the trip to the Realm, Valentine and I hadn't been back to the Dance District, only to the bars for Silver. I'd tried to catch up on my sleep. I thought I'd been working better.

Mr Spinks said, 'You look half-dead, Glynnan.' He said that the Unit Managers were aware that I'd been assisted in my tasks by other colleagues and that was not acceptable. He said that a financial penalty, it hadn't yet been decided how much, would be docked from my wages. Already an amount was debited each week from staff wages to pay for Unit refurbishments. Mr. Spinks said he was taking the precaution of moving me to a work-station at the other end of the office and that while I was at work I was no longer permitted to fraternise with Valentine Frankland. If my output didn't improve he said he'd be demoting me to Influx, emptying Census sacks for a pittance.

I went back to my work-station. I had to empty my desk in front of everyone. I didn't look at anybody, not even Valentine. I switched off my screen, took my files to the desk I'd been allocated and sat and stared into the glare of the new work-station.

After work, I waited for Valentine outside the Unit.

'Where have you been all day?'

We'd walked a couple of streets before I felt safe enough, far away enough from work, to answer him.

'I've been at the other end of the office. I have to work there now. I have to work harder. Mr. Spinks has forbidden me to speak to you at the Unit. It doesn't seem right. We're engaged after all.'

'A warning was sent to my screen about helping you with your work. It said I was in danger of losing my job.'

'I'm sorry...' I couldn't talk for a little while. Discussing it was making me upset.

We got nearer the flat. '...I don't think I can go out with you in the evenings any more, Valentine. I get too tired for work.'

'But we haven't been to the Dance District for ages.'

'I know, but I mean the bars. Maybe I should give the bars a break if going out is getting me into trouble.'

We walked for a couple more streets and I began to sense his distress. He was worrying how he was going to get by without Silver if we didn't go out.

'You could still go. You could go on your own,' I said.

He shook his head.

'We've been enough times now for you to be okay.'

He shook his head again.

He wouldn't go. It was pointless to suggest it. I just said it for something to say. But I knew Valentine would get agitated in the flat in the evenings without Silver. Somewhere in the City there must have been people who'd sell you whole bottles-full if you paid them enough – criminal-type people. Although things would have to get properly bad before you thought of risking that.

A letter came from the Commission.

Dear Mr Frankland and Miss Glynnan,

It is nine months since Engagement Status was granted by the Commission of Betrothals and Marriages and therefore your probationary period is nearing its completion. It is your legal requirement to inform the Commission as to whether you will be requesting a conversion of your current status to that of married couple or whether you will return to your former single states as residents at the Sixth Compound. Should you choose to decline this opportunity for marriage, you will forfeit the right to apply for another Engagement Contract for the succeeding five years.

In the event of your choosing to apply for marriage status, a review of your situation will be carried out. Appraisal forms will be sent to your neighbours, to your property manager and other associates, assessing the success or failure of your provisional ties. It is an offence to attempt to influence the assessments of any of the aforementioned parties in any way. In addition, a Betrothal Commissioner will visit your flat at an unspecified time to review your living quarters.

Should you be successful at the reviewing stage, a marriage ceremony time will be allocated to you. The ceremony will be conducted at the Commission.

Please find relevant forms enclosed which must be filled and returned within seven days. Failure to return the completed paperwork may result in proceedings being brought against you.

Commissioning Officers,
Mr and Mrs J Lovejoy.

I read the letter in my room and then put it away. I wasn't ready to show it to Valentine. We'd scarcely discussed the matter of marriage since moving to the flat. We'd turned our minds from thoughts of our long-term future. I figured that he'd want to stay – he seemed different, more relaxed with himself since leaving the Compound – but still, with Valentine you could never be completely sure. No doubt more dealings with the Commission would alarm him. That alone might be enough to make him call an end to everything. If anything could sway his decision in favour of our staying together, it was the freedom he had. Also, he wouldn't easily give up access to Silver.

I was a coward. I couldn't bring myself to talk to Valentine about the letter. I tried to think of ways in which I could broach the subject but always in my mind I ended up with a picture of his appalled face that told me he couldn't bear the thought of our being together indefinitely. I didn't want to be witness to his reaction. So instead, I posted the Commission's letter under his bedroom door in the evening just before going to my bed. I put my own note inside the papers.

Dear Valentine,
Please read this letter. If you could let me know what action you want to take regarding the future that would be good. Unfortunately we don't have much time. They want the forms back next week so could you please let me know as soon as you've decided? Thank you.
With warmest wishes,
Neeve.

In the morning there was no sign of the forms or the letter. I was waiting for Valentine to mention them as we went to the Unit but he said nothing. Late the following night, however, I woke up to the sound of something scraping along the floor of my room. I opened my eyes and saw that a letter had been pushed under my door. I waited until I was certain that Valentine had returned to his room and then I got out of bed.

I opened up the folded papers. Inside was a return-note written in that concise way he had.

> I'd prefer to remain in the flat if possible.
> With thanks,
> Valentine.

So that's how it was decided. I returned the forms having filled in the parts relating to Marriage Status application, having ticked the relevant spaces, having filled in the empty boxes. Valentine had made his mind up: he wanted to be my husband. *My husband.* I thought how for the first time in my whole life I might actually achieve something. I might be a wife, Valentine's wife. And I wouldn't be a Glynnan any more, I'd be a Frankland. All the hurtful things from the past would drop away if I could just take my new name.

Valentine wanted to be ready for the Commissioner's call. He spent the evenings in the kitchen instead of in his room; the small bedroom should appear to be unused. He sat for hours at the kitchen table, fidgety and prickly without Silver to drink, shuffling the playing cards, pulling them randomly from the deck and laying them out in patterns. When I asked him if he wanted to play a proper game, he said no thanks. The first couple of nights like that, he fell asleep with his head on the table; afraid that the Commissioner would call on us in the middle of the night. I found him in the morning, sleeping with the cards still in his hands.

None of the neighbours mentioned whether they'd received appraisal forms. They must have dutifully filled in the papers and sent them back. I imagined the questions that would have been asked of them. Had there been raised voices? Sounds of fighting coming through the walls? Did we come and go together? Did we receive any regular visitors? But the neighbours hardly knew us, so what would there be to say?

Still, whenever I saw the elderly couple, or Mrs Broxter, from across the corridor, or when I saw the Caretaker, or Mr Hadden and his wife from next door, I'd smile at them and let them know how happy I was. When they saw me with Valentine I made an effort. I'd laugh a little maybe, touch his arm, try to look how a proper couple might look.

We re-arranged the flat, placing Valentine's things here and there around my room to make the space look shared. In the kitchen, we combined our separate food items. I imagined them finding noodles in my cupboard and noodles in Valentine's; a small, telling sign that we ate apart. We prepared ourselves, as we had for the interview at the Commission. I quizzed Valentine to make sure our responses to questions would tally.

In the end, though, that's not how it was. We came home from work one evening and as soon as we'd opened the door, even before I'd seen the card on the kitchen table, I knew the inspection had been done. There was something quick and meticulous in the air of the flat as we walked in.

> A Betrothal Commissioner called
> today to assess your living quarters.
> You will receive a decision regarding your
> suitability for marriage status shortly.

That's all it said on the visiting card. The Commissioner had been and gone. It seemed they'd come purposefully while we were out. The Caretaker must have let them in with his key. They didn't need to speak to Valentine or me. They'd gathered all the information they needed from the neighbours and from the state of the flat.

We wandered around the rooms of our home, finding signs of the Commissioner having been there: blankets moved aside; cupboard doors not quite shut; items not where we'd left them; traces of powder on certain surfaces where the Commissioner had dusted for prints, seeing who had touched what, how many times. I panicked; a print of my foot had been dusted on the floor by my bed. I had to remind myself – *there's nothing there, Neeve. The Circle's gone. The pattern's disappeared.*

If the Commission decided that we were unfit, it wouldn't take them long to move us back to the Compound. To return to the booths after our months of freedom would be particularly harsh – we knew now exactly what to expect. That's what was facing us: a married life together in the flat, or the Compound. There couldn't be two more starkly differing futures.

I didn't know what would become of us if we had to go back there, how we would cope. What if we slowly drifted apart? It might be like being right back at the beginning, before I'd met Valentine – only much worse. It would make all this, all that had happened, a nothingness. I felt sick every time I thought of the Compound.

Then the final letter came.

Dear Applicants,

The Commission of Betrothals and Marriages has evaluated the evidence collated from your associates' appraisal forms and from the inspection of your living quarters. It is the Commission's pleasure to inform you that, in this instance, it has been deemed appropriate to grant Marriage Status. The Commissioners extend their congratulations to you on your success.

Your Marriage Ceremony has been arranged for the morning of Saturday 24th February at 10.30 am. Enclosed are a set of wedding invitation cards with which to invite your family members and friends.

Wedding outfits for bride and groom only, will be provided by the Commission's storerooms to be returned after the ceremony. Bride and groom must arrive at the Commission forty-five minutes before the marriage commences to enable dress fittings. The Commission will be glad to offer refreshments to all celebrants. Please note the ceremony will be open for public viewing.

Commissioning Officers,
Mr and Mrs J Lovejoy.

I went to my room and fell on the bed. Even before I hit the mattress, the tears had started. I buried my face in the blanket. With each sob and shudder, my body forced out more tension. I couldn't have stopped if I'd wanted to.

'Neeve…?'

I raised my face from the blanket. Valentine had come to find out what the noise was.

Seeing the letter in my hand, I think he must have assumed the worst. He must have thought we were going back to the Compound.

I shook my head. 'No.' That's all I could say. I held the letter out to him.

He sat down beside me. I watched the words sinking in as he read. His shoulders fell. His body slumped slightly forwards and a sad smile flicked across his face. When he'd finished, he closed his eyes and allowed himself to lie back on the bed. We remained there together, waiting for the news to grow real in our heads. It was over; the Compound would never get us again.

Part Two

Chapter 8

Valentine sent two wedding invites to Mauran; one for herself and one for her husband. I couldn't think who to ask. In the end I gave one to the Caretaker, even though he frightened me, and some to our immediate neighbours. The invites were a 'thank you' for filling in the appraisal forms. Also I wanted them to see us doing something respectable.

I thought about inviting Willa-Rix but decided it wasn't safe. Besides she would probably think the ceremony was ridiculous and not come. Maybe the Compound Authorities wouldn't let her attend.

We arrived at the Commission – a bright, cold February morning. A woman and a man, the storeroom attendants, greeted us and we were separated, taken to the male and female dressing rooms. I followed the woman down a long corridor, towards the rear of the Commission building into one of the prettiest rooms I ever saw; gowns hung on racks, everything white – like being inside a cloud.

'I need to measure you,' the attendant said, taking out her tape. 'Don't breathe in. We've had brides pass out in the ceremonies because their dresses were too tight.'

The tape went round my body; around my waist, hips and bust. 'You're a big girl.'

The attendant went to sift through the racks. She brought down two dresses.

'These are all we have in your size. Try them on and see which is best.'

I carried the dresses to the changing cubicle.

The first one wasn't right. My hips were higher than they were on the dress making the waist too tight. I tried the second. It was a better fit. I stared at myself in the mirror. I'd never seen myself like that, wearing such a dress. I ran my hands over the material.

'Hurry up in there, please.'

I opened the curtain and stepped out of the cubicle.

'Turn around. Let's do it up at the back.' The attendant started to do the fastener but it got stuck.

'This one doesn't fit. You'll have to wear the other one.'

'But that's too tight. I really like this one.'

'You'll have to leave it undone then. It won't fasten. You're too big. I'll have to put a pin in to stop the fastener coming down. The veil will hide your back. Don't move much or the fabric will rip. What size feet are you?'

'Nine and a half.'

The attendant pulled a face.

I sat on a chair outside the Chapel of Marriage with the attendant who'd dressed me, waiting to be called through. I could hear music being played. I fiddled with the material of my dress.

A woman came out. It was Mrs Lovejoy. She smiled at me. 'This way, Citizen.'

Someone must have turned up the volume as I entered because the music in the room suddenly lurched louder. Valentine was stood with Mr Lovejoy at the end of the aisle, on a small raised stage. I couldn't see Valentine's face. He was looking towards the front. He had on a dark suit. I thought how he'd probably rather not have had to see Mr Lovejoy ever again.

I walked down between the rows of chairs. Mrs Lovejoy walked beside me. I was surprised by how many people had turned out to see us; members of the public, come watch us wed. They were angled around in their chairs to see me. A man looked at me as I passed, puffing out his cheeks, mocking my size.

I walked to the front. I tried to be dignified and not think about my dress gaping at the back. I went and stood beside Valentine. He hadn't got his darkened glasses on and he looked frightened. Frightened but beautiful – so beautiful it seemed absurd that I was about to marry him. I wanted him to turn and acknowledge me but I didn't want him to see a large girl in an ill-fitting dress; I wanted him to see Neeve.

Mr Lovejoy made a gesture with his hand and the music was switched off. He began reciting the words.

'Today we gather to witness the marriage of Miss Neeve Glynnan and Mister Valentine Frankland, brought together by their love for one another...'

Valentine stared straight ahead. I was feeling strange in front of all the people. I tried to listen to what Mr Lovejoy was saying but I was waiting for Valentine to look at me.

'...The institution of marriage, that glorious harmonising element which in time brings forth the future in the form of offspring...'

I'd woken up that morning from a bad dream. In the dream, Valentine had changed his mind; he didn't want to get married. He'd hidden in one of the many rooms of the Commission. Eventually he'd been found and had to be dragged to the ceremony.

'...Each person: man, woman, child, knows their role within that structure, each fulfilling their duties within it...'

I don't know why it had never properly occurred to me before. Maybe it was the formality of it all; the ceremony and Mr Lovejoy presiding over us, Valentine staring ahead at the wall – but it hit me then that our marriage was fake. I suddenly realised that it was and a nervous giggle started up in me. I swallowed air to try and stop myself but I was already sniggering at the state of myself. My eyes were getting wet and my nose was starting to run. I put my hand to my mouth to try and quieten the noise.

I felt something nudge my arm. Mrs Lovejoy was offering me a handkerchief. I took it and held it to my face.

Mr Lovejoy continued with his words.

'Do you Valentine Duvante Deyan Kristic Frankland take Neeve Glynnan to be your lawful wedded wife?'

Valentine's mouth had moved to form the word but no sound had come out.

'Pardon?'

'...Yes.' Valentine ran his hand across his forehead, wiping away the sweat.

'And do you Neeve Glynnan take Valentine Duvante Deyan Kristic Frankland to be your lawful wedded husband?'

I unclenched my jaw. 'Yes.'

The absurd feeling was beginning to die down.

'Now please sign here, on the marriage contract to commit to this partnership in law.' Mr Lovejoy passed Valentine a pen and gestured to the form lying on a table to one side of us.

Valentine went and wrote his name. Then Mr Lovejoy took the pen from him and handed it to me. I wrote Neeve Glynnan under the inky mess that Valentine had made and gulped down the last throes of my fit.

'I pronounce you husband and wife.'

The music came on again.

'You may kiss the bride, Mr Frankland.'

I felt the waiting eyes of the audience.

I stared at a button on Valentine's shirt and waited too. If he didn't kiss me it'd look odd.

Then Valentine did a clever thing. He angled himself so that the audience couldn't see his face, so they were seeing just the back of his head. He pressed his lips to my cheek, just a fraction to the side of my mouth. To them it must have looked something like a real kiss.

The ceremony was ending. Mr and Mrs Lovejoy stepped from the stage and led the way, back down the aisle between the chairs. Valentine and I followed, the audience watching as we were paraded before them.

I didn't want to look but somehow I found my eyes glancing across the rows of faces. I caught sight of someone familiar in the gathering of people. I knew the person but, what with everything, it took me a moment to register, to recognise who the person was.

It was Lol. The man from the Realm.

Outside the ceremony room, a photographer was waiting for us. We had our picture taken with Mr and Mrs Lovejoy at the door to the Chapel of Marriage. Mr and Mrs Lovejoy arranged themselves, one on either side of us, and held our hands as though they were shaking them in congratulation. The photographer told us to smile and the flash went off.

We were taken into the reception room and Mr Lovejoy asked us to be seated. We were to be given a forty-five minute slot to drink tea and talk to guests.

'Please excuse us,' Mrs Lovejoy said. 'We have another ceremony to oversee. Your wedding photograph will be sent to you in due course. Enjoy your reception.'

When they'd gone, Valentine got the darkened glasses out of his pocket. He wasn't allowed to put them on, but just holding them made him feel better.

I sat and looked at him beside me. I was wondering what the first thing I said to my husband should be. But Valentine spoke first.

'What happened in there?'

He meant the fit I'd had.

'I don't know. I'm sorry. I was nervous…'

We sat quiet then, stunned by all that had happened. I thought of how far we'd come to get to that point – all the way from the Sixth Compound to there. Meanwhile, outside the door, the sound of voices was growing. People had started to assemble.

Guests filtered into the room; members of the public come for refreshments. They nodded greetings to us as they made their way over to a hatch in the wall from where the tea was about to be served. I could hear the clinking of crockery. A queue formed and the hatch opened. Somebody on the other side of the wall began passing out hot drinks. I watched as people took biscuits, two or three at a time, from the plates on the tables and put them into the pockets of their coats.

I remembered Lol. 'The man from the Realm is here.'

'Which man? *Lol*?'

'Yes. We didn't invite him, did we?'

'No.'

Valentine was looking around the room.

A woman came though into the reception area and I recognised her as Mauran, Valentine's sister, the girl in the photograph. In the picture she'd looked less troubled than Valentine. In the flesh she had a similar haunted look.

She came over.

'Many congratulations to you both,' she said.

Valentine embraced her. I'd never seen him react that way to anyone; he held his sister with such fondness. Mauran allowed Valentine to hold her for a moment, then she fidgeted a little in his arms and he let her go.

Valentine introduced us. Mauran shook my hand. 'Nice to meet you.'

I felt huge beside her. She was very slight, like a bird. 'You too,' I said.

'I'm sorry that Dean isn't here. He wanted to come but he's been called unexpectedly into work. Some disturbance…' She spoke hurriedly. She explained to me, 'He's training to be a member of the Guarda.'

'Yes, Valentine told me.'

'There's a wedding gift from us both. I've put it where they showed me, in the other room.'

'Thank you.'

'I'll go and fetch us some tea and biscuits,' I said. I thought it was best to leave Mauran and Valentine alone to talk for a while. I wandered over to join the guests who were jostling each other to get to the refreshments. The biscuits seemed to be disappearing fast so I headed for the tables first.

'Please, let me help you.'

I turned. Mauran had followed me.

'Oh...I can manage, really. I'll use a tray. Stay with Valentine. You haven't seen each other for age-'

'No, please,' she was insistent.

I looked at her. Her cheeks were quite red. I thought she was about to cry. She wanted to talk to me. It was as though she couldn't keep the words in.

'Maybe we should fetch some tea things...before there's nothing left,' I said.

The plates on the reception tables had been emptied. All that remained of the biscuits were a few crumbs. We made our way to the drinks queue, my head reeling from my conversation with Mauran.

People waiting in line made way for us, deferring, it seemed, to my big white dress. The serving-woman at the hatch smiled and said *'Congratulations'* to me as I took three cups from her.

We headed back to Valentine and stood with our drinks.

'How have you been?'

'I've been well, Valentine. How about you? So much has happened since I last saw you.' Mauran was gulping her hot tea, seeming in a hurry to finish.

'It's going well.'

'It's good to see you in such favourable circumstances.'

'You should come and visit the flat.'

'Thank you, I'd like that.'

'There's no visitor restrictions any more. You don't have to wait for guest days like at the Compound. You can come when you like.'

'That's kind.' She seemed almost embarrassed of him, embarrassed of her own brother. 'We're in the middle of decorating at the moment though...decorating the spare room. Things are busy but I'll look in my diary and see if there's a good time.'

There was a short silence and then Mauran said, 'I can't stay long, I'm afraid. It's two trains back to Cliffer.' She looked around at the other guests. 'Besides, you've all these people to greet. You don't want your old sister getting in the way.'

'You're not in the way.'

'Still, I'd better go.'

Valentine's voice changed, 'Did Dean say he didn't want you here?'

'Don't be like that.'

There was another silence.

'Well, congratulations once again.' Mauran said as cheerfully as she could. 'It was a lovely ceremony. And what a lovely couple you make. I know you'll look after each other.'

Poor Mauran. She was trying so hard.

'We'll do our best,' I said.

'Please stay...'

'I can't, Val. Really, I can't.'

They looked sad. Both of them did.

Mauran stood on her toes to kiss Valentine's cheek. He put his arms around her once again but she laughed nervously as he held her and he reluctantly let her go. She stepped back and tried to smile.

'Goodbye.' Mauran said.

'Bye...'

She left the room and Valentine stood dejected in his wedding suit. I hated that he was unhappy, especially on that particular day.

He said, 'What did you talk about?'

'When?'

'With my sister. When you were getting the tea.'

'She...was telling me how much she cared about you. And she asked me some questions about myself. I think she wanted to get to know me a little, to see if I'd make a good enough wife for her brother.'

He seemed to have shut himself unreachably away so I went to the hatch for more tea.

The room was full of people I didn't know. I looked about for somebody from Canal Bank Court. It was probably a good thing if they hadn't come; I'd behaved badly in the Chapel of Marriage.

I heard a voice behind me.

'What a lovely bride.'

I turned. It was Lol.

'Here, I'll help you with those.'

He took the freshly filled cups from my unsteady hands. I felt overwhelmed; all the people, the attention, Mauran, and now Lol. It wasn't what I was used to.

'Can't have you spilling tea down your dress.'

'What're you doing here?'

'It's a public ceremony. I read about it in the paper. You look lovely.'

I rubbed my hands on my skirt; a nervous habit I have, but I shouldn't have done it on that dress.

I looked at him and wondered what was different. He didn't have an animal's jaw sticking from the back of his head. He looked relatively normal.

He followed me back to Valentine, carrying the cups.

'Congratulations!'

Lol passed us our drinks, then, for himself, picked up a half-empty teacup left on a nearby table. 'They know how to put on a good do, these people.'

He raised his drink and chinked it against mine and Valentine's. He downed the dregs inside and then peered into the cup. 'Ugh. Too much sugar,' he mumbled.

'Lol saw the ceremony advertised in the paper.' I explained.

'Oh. Thank you for coming.'

'I couldn't miss it. And I've brought you some things.'

Lol went briefly over to the other side of the room. From beneath his jacket, lying under a table, he pulled a large paper bag.

'Gifts,' he said when he came back. He handed me the bag. It felt heavy. Then he whispered in my ear, 'Make sure you're home before you open them.'

I looked about to see if anyone was watching. 'Thank you.'

I felt mistrustful of him having made so much effort for us. I couldn't work out why he would.

'How's your foot, Neeve?' Lol nodded his head towards the floor.

'It's okay.' This was the Commission. It was my wedding day. I didn't want to talk about it right then.

Valentine looked at me enquiringly.

'I hurt it at the Realm,' I said and changed the subject. 'Do you live nearby, Lol?'

'Not far. In Gonetotown.'

I knew of Gonetotown. It wasn't any nearer to the Commission than Cliffer District, where Mauran lived.

'Are you a family member?'

'No.'

'So you're married then?' I didn't mean to grill him but we knew hardly anything about him.

'No. Haven't met the right person yet.'

'So you're in a Compound…?' My voice trailed off. Even as I asked the question, I realised that he couldn't be; he went out at night.

Lol didn't answer. He couldn't, not there. I thought, *How come?* How could he be neither Compound resident, nor spouse, nor family member?

A voice came out of speakers in the ceiling. *'The reception is now over. Wedding guests have five minutes to finish their refreshments and make their way to the exit…'*

There was a rush to get the last cups of tea from the hatch and drink them down.

Lol said, 'Maybe we'll chat some more another time.'

The voice from the ceiling repeated its announcement. *'The reception is now over…'*

'I'm sure you'll make each other very happy,' Lol said over the noise.

I looked at him. He seemed sincere. That's what I couldn't understand.

'Well, thank you for coming today,' I said.

'Yes. Thank you.'

'A pleasure. It was a pleasure to see you both. Anyway, I hope you like the gifts. Careful with them when you go back through the tunnels. They might break.'

A new announcement came from the ceiling, '*Attendants are waiting to escort the bride and groom to the storerooms for the return of their wedding garments…*'

'We'd better go, Valentine,' I said.

He turned to Lol. 'Goodbye.'

'Good-bye, Newly-weds.'

Lol collected his jacket from under the table and wandered out.

I stood in the dressing room cubicle gazing at myself in the mirror.

'Have you finished in there?' the attendant called through the curtain.

'Nearly.'

I was trying hard to fix an image of myself in my memory. I didn't think I'd wear anything so beautiful again. I couldn't bring myself to take off the gown.

'You haven't even undone the fastener yet, have you?' The attendant wandered away from the cubicle, muttering to herself. 'They *never* want to get undressed…and you can always tell which ones'll be worst.'

That evening, we sat on the floor in my room and opened our wedding gifts. Mauran had bought us *Essential Guidance for the Modern Marriage: Advice for Husband and Wife.* It was a big, thick book. Mauran had entered a few words inside, on the flyleaf.

To the happy couple,
May the years be kind, keeping you faithful to the calling of married life.
Best Wishes,
Dean and Mauran.

Then there were Lol's presents; a present for Valentine, a present for me and one for us both.

I watched as Valentine opened his gift. It seemed that Lol had gone to some effort to disguise the contents. Whatever it was, was inside a cardboard box and crumpled bits of paper had been stuffed around to protect it.

It was a bottle of Silver, half full. I couldn't believe my eyes. The bottle fell from Valentine's hands as he pulled it from the box. It rolled off his lap and across the floor. For a moment or two, we were too afraid to go near it. It briefly crossed my mind to hand the bottle in at a Guarda station but I didn't know how I'd explain where it'd come from. And besides, even though Valentine was frightened, I knew he wouldn't forgive me if I took the Silver away. After that, I was anxious about opening my own gift. The package was smaller but potentially no less dangerous. I shook it first but heard nothing. I pulled back the paper wrapping. There was a small box inside and inside the box was a bottle. Not alcohol – it was a perfume bottle made from deep blue glass. On the side, some words had been engraved, *Rare Beauty*. When I held it up, the light shone blue through the bottle. At the top was a little stopper and when I opened it, I could smell the scent that had once been in there.

'If I put water in, it'd scent the water...'

Valentine looked worried. 'You couldn't wear it though. You couldn't go to work with it on.'

'No. But maybe in the flat.'

Lol had chosen well; even though our gifts troubled us, we were both secretly pleased. I re-read the engraved writing – *Rare Beauty*.

Valentine had picked up the last present. The final gift was the smallest. Valentine was feeling it all over very carefully. I thought he was never going to open it.

'See what it is.'

He slowly unwrapped it, tearing the paper aside with the tips of his fingers. Inside the little package were two glittering discs. Two more passes to the Realm. A piece of paper fell from the wrapping. It had a list of numbers on it – 3040, 3051, 3013. The dates of future club nights

A surprised noise erupted from Valentine's throat. He whispered, disbelieving, 'He's inviting us back.'

I was amazed: even though Valentine knew about the Realm's links to the Movement; even though he knew they broke music laws there; even though he knew Lol was involved with the black market, he said wouldn't mind going back to the club.

Valentine was changing. We both were. Valentine's time at the Compound had stifled him and he'd lived outside it long enough by then, to at least know that it had. He was realising there might be more to life than he'd come to expect – just as I'd realised when I first met him. It's funny what a little freedom can do.

The man who'd wanted to hide forever in his B-wing booth and never come out, the man I'd had to drag from the Compound kicking and screaming, was fading. Valentine was getting a taste for something else. He was changing and maybe I hadn't been paying attention. I wondered, *are parents too busy caring for their children to notice the gradual, daily ways in which they change? Does something have to alert them to it?* Maybe it was like that with Valentine; I'd been too busy loving him.

It was my turn to dig in my heels.

'I can't start going out dancing again. I can't get into even more trouble at the Unit.'

'We only have passes for one night...We wouldn't be going out all the time like we were at the Dance District.'

'We can't go. Just think how dangerous it is.'

'It didn't feel all that dangerous.'

'The place is full of weird folk. Those sorts of people, they don't *care* about their own safety.'

'Nobody stared. *Nobody.* It didn't feel unsafe.'

'What about the woman on the door, the one who took our passes? *She* stared at you.'

He paused for a moment, floundering slightly. '...Not much, she didn't...Only at first. Anyway, I meant inside. Inside I was safe. Nobody stared once I was in the club.'

The thing was, he was right. The people in the club hadn't really paid him all that much attention, not compared to what we were used to.

'The reason they didn't stare was because they were all too busy showing themselves off in their illegal costumes. What if there was a raid? Wouldn't you be petrified?'

'Yes, but –'

'I wouldn't be able to do anything to help you. You think I can get you out of anything.'

'No, I don't.'

'It's too dangerous. Anyway, Lol's not the sort of person we ought to be associating with. He's got no home by the sounds of it, *and* he's a black market criminal...Is this about the Silver? Would you like him to get you more?'

'No!'

I'd offended him. 'I'm sorry. I don't really think that.'

Neither of us spoke for a minute or so and I thought Valentine was angry with me. But then he said, 'I felt at home at the Realm, Neeve, that's why. I *never* felt that in a place before.'

'But you seemed so nervous.'

'At first I was. Later on I was better.'

'You felt at home amongst law-breaking dissenters? I'm sorry but I can't see it. You've never come *close* to breaking the law.'

'Until I met you.'

I always forgot, even though it was obvious. He meant leaving the Compound, he meant being in the flat – our whole life. Somehow in my head, for some reason what we'd done didn't count. I had to shut up.

'I want to go there again, Neeve.' He was beginning to sound desperate.

That's when I realised we'd have to go back. I didn't understand why, but it was too important to him. He was looking for something. There was something that he wanted to find out about the world or himself. I couldn't bear the thought that, if he had to, he'd try to find it without me.

We went back to the Realm. Only this time, we were better prepared; we thought about what to wear at least.

I had a large rust-coloured shawl of my mother's that I'd never worn because it wasn't regulation. Mostly I used it as an extra blanket on cold nights. It was old and the tasselled fringing was matted but I thought I could wear it at the Realm, over my civilian clothes. It was covered in little embroidered flowers that had once been white and now were grey. I liked to imagine the hands that had stitched them. Someone from a former time taking slow pleasure in affixing the petals and leaves. I put on the shawl and looked in the mirror. I knew it would be nothing in comparison to the other outfits at the club, still, I felt odd and attention-seeking.

From a buying hall Valentine bought a civilian shirt and two coloured pens; green and blue. He brought them back to the flat and tentatively, because it seemed wrong to mess with regulation clothes, drew on the shirt. Slowly the material was covered with blue and green swirls. When he'd finished, the shirt looked reckless but there was something artful about his design.

'It's very bold, Valentine. Are you sure you'll wear it?'

He looked uncertain.

'Why don't you try it on? See what it's like.'

He went to the privacy of his room.

'How is it?' I called. 'Will you show me?'

But he politely declined. He said it wouldn't feel right until we were at the Realm. He came back out in his civvies.

Before we left for the trains to the Realm, Valentine took a few glasses of Silver. He'd drunk most of the contents of the wedding present bottle but he'd purposefully saved some knowing that he'd need courage for the Realm. He sat at the kitchen table quietly drinking it down.

Once we were on the train, down in the tunnels, I sat in the carriage with my eyes fixed on my bag. I had Valentine's shirt and my shawl folded inside it. I stayed that way, stiff and vigilant, for the whole journey.

It was early when we got to the Realm. The place wasn't busy and there was no sign of Lol. I wondered how long Valentine would want to stay.

We stood gazing at the mosaic on the floor and at the muralled walls but the words and pictures were too cryptic despite our efforts to make sense of them. We bought drinks and sat on a couch pushed against a far wall. From there we could see people filtering in, dressed in their regulation clothes, then going to the changing-rooms and coming out altogether altered. Once again, I was struck by the variety of people and their costumes. It was as though I'd never noticed the unrelenting sameness of the City until the Realm. The Realm made the regular world seem unexpectedly narrow and uniform. And even though I was better prepared for it, the vividness of the people frightened me. It made me worry about the lives they led beyond the club.

I tried to feel Valentine before I lost him in the buzz from the growing crowd. His usual anxiety was there, heightened because of where we were, but there was something else too; a sort of quiet craving. Valentine was like a ripened person. He was ready for something, I didn't know what. All I could do was accompany him.

I was beginning to feel conspicuous in my ordinary clothes.

I reached for my bag.

'Are you going to put it on?'

'Yes.'

With movements as discreet as possible, I slipped the shawl around my shoulders and over my body. Then I leaned back on the couch and tried to relax. I wasn't sure if I felt more conspicuous or less, now that I was wearing it. I could feel Valentine beside me, trying to summon the nerve to go and use the changing-rooms.

'I could come with you? I don't mind.'

He even thought about it for a moment. 'I'll be alright.'

He got up and navigated his way to the changing-area.

Over on the stage a man was setting up equipment for live music to be played. I felt my nervousness increase as I watched him. He wore a top with something written on it in fluorescent letters – some of the same incomprehensible words as those on the walls. I felt the strain in his arms as he lifted the large speakers. It came to me like my own effort and I realised, that for some reason, I was feeling things more strongly that night. I turned away to look at something else, trying to feel my own body, no more than that.

There was a flourish; a fizzing over by the entrance. But I could see nothing. No-one was there.

Then, Lol appeared, alone.

I watched him as he crossed the club on his way to the bar. He waved to some people and they waved back at him. He was dressed in an understated way, as he had at our wedding, and compared with the elaborate outfits of the other club-goers, it made him all the more noticeable. Watching him from a distance, the way he walked, he looked more dangerous than I'd remembered, as though his body carried some sort of vague risk. He looked like someone I wouldn't dare speak to.

He stood at the bar and the bar-tender came to serve him. He ordered a drink, a type of clear drink with a mixer, and then paid his money.

He moved through the club like a ripple. People turned from their conversations to greet him as he passed. I saw their eyes and faces as they spoke to him, reflecting back what he gave. He had a magnetic quality that it seemed I ought to try and resist. I didn't want him to notice me. Maybe I was scared I'd detect indifference on his face when he did.

He spotted me on the couch. He was coming over.

'You're back!' His smile was genuine and it stunned me.

I nodded. 'And Valentine.'

Lol swung his head round, to look amongst the crowd.

'He's getting changed.'

'Oh.' Then, 'Mind if I sit down?'

'No.'

He settled beside me.

'Thank you very much for our wedding gifts. We really like them...' I was about to speak about the Silver, to ask where it'd come from but he interrupted.

'Good! I enjoyed your wedding.'

Anyway, I already knew where the Silver had come from. I was just hoping for a more innocent explanation.

'I'm glad you came back. I wasn't sure if you would.' His eyes settled on my clothes, on the rust-coloured shawl. 'I like your dress-thing.'

'It's just a shawl.' I tugged at the tasselled hem, trying to pull it further over me.

'Won't you be hot? It looks even hotter than my animal costume.'

'I didn't know what else to wear. Once the club fills up, I'll probably roast.'

He reached out to feel the material. It was the first time he'd come close to touching me and as his hand neared me, the surrounding space seemed to lurch to attention. It was as though the air suddenly stratified itself; his hand passing through different layers as it came towards me. And somehow I felt each one; some layers popped and simmered, others seemed smooth or warm or full. His hand came to rest on my arm. As he laid it down, there was a sort of rightness to it being there; separate parts of a thing put back together. I sat stunned as he lightly stroked the shawl.

'How's work been?'

'Alright. But there's been a rumour going round that they might be stepping up the amount of Censuses again, but only in certain areas. Three, or even four, per year maybe. Our work load will probably increase.'

It was boring but Lol appeared interested. 'Which areas?'

'I'm not sure.'

'The Geddohs?'

'The where?'

Lol turned away briefly and mumbled something into the air.

'Pardon?'

He turned back to me. 'I'm glad you've come, Neeve,' he said again.

'Well, we wanted to.' I didn't like to say that it'd been on Valentine's wishes alone.

Over on the other side of the club, I could see Valentine emerging from the ante-room. He moved sheepishly in the bold shirt. He seemed all shirt and no Valentine.

I said, 'Here's Valentine now.'

Lol stood to greet him. He came close and Lol shook his hand.

'You both got so dressed up! I'm letting the side down,' Lol said, tugging at the front of his shirt.

We shook our heads in unison.

Lol sat down on one side of me, Valentine on the other. I felt as though I took up more space on the couch than either of them.

Valentine was embarrassed at first. He couldn't seem to lift his head far from his chest. I thought how good the blue and green looked against his skin. I'd never seen him wear colours.

Lol tried to counteract Valentine's discomfort. 'I could do a magic trick.'

'Okay,' I said.

He took a citizen token from his pocket.

'See this?' He addressed the question to Valentine.

Valentine nodded that he did.

'Well...' He held the token in one hand and brandished the fingers of his other hand over it. He made it disappear out of sight and held up his palms to show empty hands. Then he swerved his arm to bring a closed fist close to Valentine's head and Valentine jolted at the suddenness of the movement. Lol quickly retracted his arm.

'Sorry. I didn't mean to make you jump. It's just that the money went behind your ear. Look.' Slowly, Lol reached up and slid the coin from behind Valentine's ear. He held it up for us to see, giving us another of his sideways looks.

'Here, you have it.' He passed the token to Valentine. 'It keeps wanting to gravitate your way.'

But Valentine couldn't bring himself to take it. He declined with a shake of his head. Lol didn't insist. He just did another trick, making it go wrong on purpose. He took off his wrist chain and it vanished the same way as the citizen token. Then Lol clowned that he was unable to make it reappear.

Valentine and I began to feel more comfortable, our unease lessening with each of Lol's daft jokes. I sat smiling at his tricks, wondering why he was going to such efforts to keep us entertained when the club was full of so many people he could talk to.

Lol said, 'Look at them, over there.'

We turned in the direction he was pointing. A group of men and women with their hair long down their backs were stood talking. They had all dyed their hair the same reddish colour and around their eyes they'd put circles of red paint. The most striking thing about them, though, was their pointed ears. When the lights on the ceiling swung low across the club highlighting the edges of everything, you could see the join where the points were stuck on top of their regular ears.

'Do you recognise them?' Lol asked.

'No.' It seemed a funny question. Why would we recognise people who were in disguise? I tried to study their faces to see if I did.

'Is one of them Bonny Noach?'

'No. I mean do you recognise the characters they're acting out? Remember *The Whards Chronicles*? Did you read those books before they were Streamlined?'

Valentine and I shook our heads.

'Well, that's who they're meant to be, the Whards.'

'What's a Whard?'

'I don't know. I never read the books either. But that's what they're acting out.'

'What happens in the daytime, when they go out? They've got long red hair.'

'They're wearing wigs. The paint and ears come off and then they're plain old citizens again.'

'Oh.'

'Quite a few of the people here come dressed as their favourite characters from Streamlined stories or broadcasts. They do it so the stories aren't forgotten.'

While Lol was with us in the club, people – his friends – came over to chat to him as we sat. They would pat his arms or hug him around the shoulders and then nod in greeting at us. Lol made a point of introducing each person so that we got to know them by name. Someone said Valentine had a lovely voice. Complimentary comments were made about our outfits. Each time, before they left us, Lol would say something to make them laugh and they would go away grinning.

If Lol had to leave us for something himself, he always found his way back again. He didn't leave us alone for long that night.

I plucked up the courage to ask about his life.

'Where do you live?'

'In a flat.'

'But not as a family member?'

'No, with friends. I have two or three flats I can go to. It's handy because they're all fairly near each other.'

'But how? Oughtn't you be in a Compound like other singles?'

'There're ways around that life, you know.' He took a swig from his drink. 'A few of us here have *never* been housed like that.'

'I didn't realise.' Stupidly, I thought I ought to remind him, 'It is against the law though.'

'Not if you're not registered in the first place. My mother chose not to register my birth. *She's* the law-breaker, not me.' He chuckled. 'Look there, that's Magda Thomas.' He pointed to an elderly woman, carrying a glass with a dark drink in it. 'She's one of the club's oldest members.' I think he wanted to change the subject. 'She's been coming here since it opened.'

Lol was an unregistered person. There we were, sitting beside him. But Lol didn't seem remotely afraid.

'It's a load of lost words, you know?' he said.

'What is?'

'On the walls.'

I turned to look at the words and images behind my head.

Lol was squinting up at the pictures, his forehead folded into lines. He was tracing letters with his finger, following the path the paintbrush had taken.

'They teach the lost words here. They teach what they mean and how to speak them. It's to retrieve as much as they can from before the Streamlining. Words got banned. Labels for things got taken away, things they didn't want to exist. Take the word *Contemplative*.' He looked at us as he spoke, interested in our reactions. 'Have you heard of it?'

'No.'

'Being a Contemplative meant you were more inclined to become involved with the Eye Offences, so they banned the word. And to be contemplative made you peaceful, only dangerously so. Anyway, I'm still learning.'

'Dangerous? How?'

'Because eventually Contemplatives stop feeling the need to defend themselves against anything. They become free of all restriction. Free of the City... History is taught here too. True history. The real reasons for things that went on.'

I was staring at the words painted on the wall, trying to keep track of what Lol was saying. I couldn't believe how free he was being with what he was telling us.

He was looking at the murals again. 'They're myths mainly. Myths they don't want told.'

I turned back to sit properly on the couch, facing away from the walls. The club was covered with illegal stories; smiling depictions of humans and animals, breaking laws with their painted faces. I wondered what Valentine was making of it all. I turned to look at him and got a shock. He wasn't wearing his darkened glasses.

Valentine was sitting in the busy club with his eyes on show. Anybody – everybody – could stare if they wanted. I couldn't believe he felt safe enough to take them off. What's more, Lol, without needing to be warned, had made nothing of it. Although Valentine's eyes were openly on display and Lol had never seen them that way before, he hadn't passed comment.

It got late and we had to go for our train. We prepared ourselves for the journey back. I removed my shawl and Valentine went back to the changing-rooms to take off his shirt. It was odd; over the course of just a single evening, we'd grown accustomed to our showy costumes.

As we were leaving, Lol said, 'I might come over to see you. I could come and see where you live. This Saturday maybe, when you're off work. Or Sunday – give you more chance to tidy your place.'

I was taken aback. He was inviting himself to our home. 'It…it is tidy.'

He grinned. 'Well, I'll come on Saturday then.'

'You mean in the day or…or the evening?'

'Whenever you like.'

He walked with us out of the club and up to the top of the steps. At the sliding metal door, Lol said casually, as if he were the first person in the world to notice, 'Neeve, don't you think Valentine's got nice eyes?'

I floundered for a second, not knowing how to respond. 'Er, yes…He has.'

Valentine instantly shut his eyes and lowered his chin into his chest, closing himself away. I could see from the edges of his mouth though, that he wasn't entirely unhappy. It wasn't even a half-smile, more like a quarter.

On our own again in the night air and away from the club's crowds and noise, I could sense Valentine more fully. He was weirdly serene and because of that, almost unrecognisable.

He put on his darkened glasses and we headed home.

Chapter 9

'You can stop now if you like.' I heard Lol's low, mumbled voice coming from somewhere.

I remembered the room, the bed I was lying on. I even had to remember the body I was lying in. I didn't know how long I'd been gone. I couldn't tell. It seemed like ages.

I could still hear the sound whirring out of the little box on the floor. I knew it carried another hidden note inside it, but now I heard only one.

I opened my eyes. Valentine looked as though he was still away, his sleepy eyes gazing at nothing. A ray of light fell between the curtains and across him as he lay there. The room felt warm. It was as though the Circle and the evening sun were working together to make everything slower and easier.

There was movement; Lol turning off the sound-box. Then he came around the side of the bed and touched Valentine on the shoulder.

'Val…?'

His eyes didn't register.

'Valentine?' Lol said it louder. There seemed to be a hint of concern in his voice.

Valentine's eyelids fluttered and closed and Lol relaxed.

When Valentine opened his eyes again I was shocked by the look on his face. The fear around his eyes wasn't there any more. His jaw hung loosely, relaxed. He looked so different – his expression was one of such extreme openness that it scared me to look at him. He seemed too exposed to live. I was relieved when he started to remember who he was and traces of the old anxiousness returned to his face.

'How do you feel?' Lol asked us.

'Good,' I said.

'Anything happen?'

'It sounds odd but I felt a sort of big space that couldn't be… er…overrun by anything.'

'Really?'

'And I felt something really familiar only it was…more obvious than usual, like it…' I realised how daft I was sounding and stopped myself. 'Mostly I felt peaceful.'

Lol wasn't fazed. 'That's great. Great for a first attempt. You see, Neeve? Illimitabilty, that's what you just described. Your first taste of it.'

'Really?'

'Without a doubt.'

Lol looked back to Valentine but Valentine didn't say anything. He couldn't. For once it wasn't reticence that was keeping his mouth shut. 'I knew it about you.' Lol said and I didn't understand. 'Even when I met you both, I knew. You're naturals with the Circle.' He was beaming at us. 'We should try this again.'

Maybe the Circle had done something peculiar to my brain because, that night, right on the edge of sleep, when my mind was too tired to correct itself, it seemed for a moment, as though the whole City spread out from the places where we lay. Our flat was right at the heart of everything. We were the central pivot – the City spinning around us. All the buildings, bridges, roads and vehicles; we were what made them go. If we wanted, we could say 'stop' and the City would. The City didn't matter. Right then, none of it had any significance.

'Did you notice that mark on Lol's face? There's a little gap in his eyebrow where the skin shows though?'

Valentine was washing the dishes from supper. I was taking the crockery from the rack and drying it with a cloth. It was the evening before Lol's visit.

'Yes, here.' Valentine ran a wet finger over his brow where Lol had the scar. A shiny path of water was left behind on his skin.

We'd been trying to talk to each other about that night at the Realm but we hadn't got very far. It was too big to be put into words.

I'd kept telling myself that Lol, an unregistered person, had probably never filled in a Census form in his life. He was a criminal – much worse than Willa-Rix who was limited in her actions by the Compound. It troubled me that the harder I tried to keep away from law-breaking citizens, the closer people like Lol and Willa seemed to come into my life.

The thing was, Lol didn't fit my idea of a law-breaker. He didn't fit the picture in my head of how a corrupt person should be.

It had been difficult explaining the directions to our flat and so we'd arranged to meet Lol from the trains at Widechapper at six o'clock. It was odd, but as he came up the steps from the tunnels, he looked smaller, less dangerous than at the Realm. He greeted us warmly and seemed pleased to see us, but he was quiet as he walked along. He was subdued slightly by the unfamiliarity of the surroundings in a way I wouldn't have expected. He looked up at the buildings and into the windows of the shops, weighing them up with his grey eyes, adjusting himself to our region.

We walked past the store that sold muscle supports, the one with the neon running man in the window that Valentine and I passed every day on the way to the Unit. Lol was intrigued. He stopped to look at the lights as they switched on and off; four legs that flashed two at a time, giving the illusion that the man was running.

'Look at that,' he said.

We nodded and grinned. Strange how a small sense of pride can come up from nowhere. I'd never thought of myself as particularly belonging to a place, but showing Lol around the streets near our flat made me appreciate that it was my home.

Approaching Canal Bank Court, we pointed out the corner stone in the wall that showed the building was 140 years old. Lol stopped to look at that too.

'Well I never.'

Then we took him inside and up the stairs to number 92. We opened the front door for him and there he was, with us in the flat.

We showed him around. I thought he'd just want to glance about the place but he was interested in everything. His hands felt the walls as we moved between the rooms. He studied random objects: teaspoons, batteries, pen tops, treating them as though they were significant somehow.

'Very nice. Very nice,' he said.

He studied the framed photograph of Mauran and the pictures I'd cut from newspapers and stuck to the dressing table mirror. I showed him the photograph of our wedding that had only recently arrived; us both shaking hands with Mr and Mrs Lovejoy, everybody doing their best to smile, Valentine with his eyes shut because he didn't have his darkened glasses on. It was like Lol was drinking in the flat and laying a sort of claim to us at the same time.

Valentine's room was the last room to be seen. We had to tell Lol that it was a spare. What could we say? *We're not a proper couple.*

We've never shared a bed and this is where Valentine sleeps. Maybe he'd already guessed as much, I didn't know.

When it was time for dinner, we decided to eat in the big bedroom because the kitchen was too small for any more than two. We arranged the plates and bowls on a cloth on the bedroom floor. We'd prepared a meal of meatballs and bread with two kinds of cooked vegetable and there'd be warm creamed-wheat for dessert.

'I brought you something.' Lol said as he pulled a green bottle from his holdall. There was no label on the side of it. 'Have you got glasses?'

'Is is Silver?' But it didn't look like Silver. It wasn't as thick, it was much more liquid.

'No. Wait till you taste it.'

Valentine went to fetch three glasses and Lol poured us each a drink. It was clear and colourless and had a fizz to it. When I sipped it I noticed the same cold-then-hot alcoholic taste that Silver had, only more so. It must have been well beyond Silver's 1.55%. I hesitated with the glass in my hand, wondering where Lol had found such a drink.

'It's called Fountainade,' he said. 'D'you like it?'

'It's quite strong.' I was too shocked to tell if I really liked how it tasted.

'The alcoholic content's a lot greater than say something like Mild-Witch or Silver.'

'Where did you get it?'

'I've a friend who makes it. I bring him the ingredients and then I help him to sell it. That's how I get money.'

'He *makes* it?'

'Yes…Steady, Valentine. Remember it's stronger than you're used to.'

I didn't want to drink mine but it seemed ungrateful to refuse. I sipped at it.

We brought in the dinner and Lol ate his meal heartily; so different to Valentine who chewed his food carefully as always, as if it didn't quite belong in his mouth. When he'd finished his plateful, Lol lifted his shirt and slapped his bare stomach.

'Delicious!' he said. 'My favourite!'

Valentine and I cleared away the remains of the first course. As I collected the dishes, I noticed that my thoughts and movements were less connected to one another. I tried to look closely at what I was doing but things kept flicking away from my eyes.

'My head's spinning.'

'Don't worry, Neeve. It's just Fountainade. It won't do you any harm. Drink some water for a while instead.'

I was too far gone by then to feel properly worried by what I'd been drinking. I knew I should be more anxious than I was. 'I feel weird.'

'Here, let me help you.' Lol took the plates from me and we went into the kitchen. We came back in with the dessert.

When we sat down to eat the creamed-wheat, without seeming to think about it, Valentine took off his darkened glasses. His movements also seemed less controlled and his voice had grown slightly louder, emboldened by the Fountainade. Once again, Lol knew not to make a big deal of Valentine's face.

Then, out of nowhere, Valentine laughed. It was an ordinary enough laugh but it was odd in that it came from Valentine.

'Why are you laughing?'

'Because I'm still hungry.'

'You can't be. We've had loads.'

Valentine hardly ever laughed and now he was laughing because he was still hungry. He had an odd sense of humour.

I watched as he helped himself to another serving of creamed-wheat; I'd never seen Valentine take a second helping. Then Lol was laughing too.

After the meal, Lol had questions. He wanted descriptions of our time in the Compound, of our duties at the Unit, of the people who lived around us in Canal Bank Court. The combination of Fountainade and Lol's promptings helped to loosen our tongues. He questioned us on things that to him must have seemed small and inconsequential, but still, he made us feel important by asking. We couldn't help but feel flattered.

Prior to that night, we'd spoken to Lol surrounded always by the noise of public places; at the Commission or at the Realm. But as we talked in the quietness of the flat, our conversations took on a different quality. They had a closeness they hadn't had before.

Lol listened carefully to everything we had to say and didn't seem interested in speaking about himself that night. If we asked him questions about his own life, he'd say he was bored of himself and then he'd change the subject by asking us something else.

It grew late. I tried to stave off my weariness, but in the end I couldn't. One thing that wasn't affected by Fountainade was Valentine's insomnia; he was still wide awake.

'I need to go to bed,' I said. 'I might go and sleep in the spare room, then you can talk for longer.' I looked at Valentine to catch his reaction. It took him a few seconds to register what I'd said. He seemed quite drunk now.

Lol checked his watch. 'I better get my train soon too,' he said. 'Thanks for coming to visit us.'

Lol stood to say goodnight to me. 'Thanks very much.'

'Goodbye then.'

I went and laid down in Valentine's carefully made bed. My head was still spinning. I let myself relax into the mattress. I could hear talking coming through the wall; Lol chatting in his slurred way, his speech more considered now, as though he was adjusting himself to being with Valentine alone.

I lay and thought how different our lives were, how altered they were from our time in the Compound; we'd had a guest visit us for the evening, we'd eaten a meal and now it was late. I remembered the Compound's early curfews, the lights going out every night at a quarter past ten. I remembered the long summer evenings and how they'd bring the shutters down – complete blackness in the booths, no evening light. Sometimes, so that I could sleep, I'd had to train my brain to think better thoughts. I'd tried to think like I was someone in better circumstances. That way my body would be less tense and I'd cheat myself into sleep. But now in the bed in the flat, with the mumbled conversation going on in the next room, I didn't have to think like I was anything. I was already being it.

I drifted off to the sound of Lol's muffled questions and the empty spaces that followed them; Valentine's replies, inaudible through the wall.

I awoke to find a foot lying across the threshold of the room. I lay on my side in bed staring at it as it stuck through the doorway. It wasn't Valentine's foot. I'd have known Valentine's foot if I'd have seen it and this wasn't his.

I got out of bed and went to the door. Lol was lying on his back, fully clothed, with a towel over him for warmth. One foot was pushed through into the bedroom and the other through the doorway of the washroom. He'd spent the night in the hallway. It was the place with the thickest patch of carpet.

I was thirsty and my head felt heavy. I needed to go to the kitchen for some water. I stepped carefully around Lol, watching where I put my feet. I tried to be quiet as I turned the tap and filled a cup. Lol didn't stir. I sat at the kitchen table drinking, transfixed, watching his chest rise and fall. I followed his breaths going in and out, so definite and regular that they reminded me of *tide mode* on the alarm clock in the flat. I often pressed that button in the mornings when I woke up, lying and listening to the tinny-sounding tide.

Valentine came, disorientated, out of my bedroom. The darkened glasses were back on his face.

He looked down at Lol and then back up at me.

He whispered apologetically over the sleeping body. 'He missed the last train. I offered him the big bed but he wouldn't take it.'

'Doesn't look like he's had trouble sleeping on the floor.'

'Could you get me some water, Neeve? I don't feel good.'

'Me neither. I don't think we should have drunk that stuff last night.'

I fetched the water and passed it to him.

Lol began to stir and open his eyes. He blinked and twisted his head around to look up at us through narrowed lids.

'Good morning,' I said.

He smiled and mumbled, 'Where am I?'

He knew well where he was, but from the moment he woke up, he wanted to play.

'You're in the flat, remember? In Canal Bank Court.'

'Oh, yes…' He closed his eyes again for a few moments and it almost seemed as though he'd fallen back to sleep. But then he said, 'It must be Sunday.'

'Yes.'

He made no effort to get up from the floor.

'Did you sleep alright there?'

'Snug as a bug.'

We showered and dressed, my head and Valentine's thick and aching. Then Lol asked us what our plans were for the day. On Sundays we sometimes went to the café around the corner for breakfast. Then we'd come back to the flat and maybe read library books in our rooms or I'd cut pictures from the newspaper.

'We don't have any plans...'

'Well, I'd be interested to see what your average Sunday's like if you don't mind showing me.'

We took Lol to the café, *The MT Feeling*. We ordered three breakfasts of Rashes & Mashes with cups of tea because that's what Valentine and I always had. Lol paid for everything. He didn't seem short of citizen tokens. Then, rather than going back to the flat, to make the day more interesting, we took Lol around the TER58 and TER59 areas. We went past the buying hall where Valentine had brought his shirt for the Realm and down to the canal and then along to the municipal park where sometimes, when it got warmer, you'd see squirrels in the trees.

While we were out, we walked through a Sunday market and Lol insisted on buying vegetables, yellow beans, marrowfat peas and some green onion powder from one of the stalls. He wanted to bring the food back to the flat and cook it for us. He said it was to say thank you for letting him stay.

As we stood buying the items, some women who'd been browsing at an adjacent stall stopped and turned their attention to Valentine. Sometimes it didn't even matter that he had his darkened glasses on; it's as though he had an aura of beauty around him so that people might stare even though they couldn't fully see his face. When Lol saw what was happening, he laughed and shrugged it off. He acted like he didn't understand what the fuss was about. I think Lol's indifference helped Valentine. It made him feel freer of something.

Right then, I couldn't find it in me to care all that much what Lol did; whether he was a criminal or whether he wasn't. I was enjoying the day too much. Fears around his visit had sunk into the background. Maybe I even put them there on purpose to stop them from spoiling things. Anyway, it seemed that anxiousness couldn't easily survive in his presence. He was too playful, too ridiculous.

Later, back at the flat, Lol banished Valentine and me from the kitchen and began to prepare the food. He told us to go and relax.

We went and sat in the big bedroom but it wasn't easy for me to rest. I'd remembered the Caretaker – we hadn't been down to tell him about Lol's overnight visit. We should have gone down to pay the charge for Lol having stayed but I'd completely forgotten. What with the Fountainade last night and the day we'd spent, the rules of Canal Bank Court had slipped from my head. I told myself I'd go down to see him as soon as we'd eaten dinner.

Warm food smells were coming from the kitchen.

'Nearly there,' Lol shouted.

Maybe he's intending to stay another night, I thought.

When the food was ready, Lol brought it through to us acting as though he was a table-tender in a café. He carried the dishes high over his shoulders and then brought them down in front of us.

'Ta-dah!'

At the centre of each dish were little sprigs and leaves from the vegetables.

'That's the garnish,' he explained.

It turned out that Lol was a good cook. The meal was delicious. Lol said he was only good at it because he'd had so much practice.

'The Compounds don't breed such marvellous cooks. Not when people just wait for their food to be brought to them and it arrives cold on a tray,' he said.

I watched Valentine as he put the food in his mouth. His eyes were closed, trying to savour it. He was struggling between eating slowly to make it last and gulping it down because it was so tasty.

We ate until our bellies were stuffed, until there was nothing left in the dishes. I sat on the bedroom floor then, too full to move, trying to summon the will to go and see the Caretaker.

Lol took our plates from us and carried them away to the kitchen. I was about to ask Valentine if he'd go downstairs with me but I heard something above the clatter of pots that stopped me.

Valentine was humming. He was leaning back against the bed, quietly humming to himself. I followed the tune for a moment. It was *The Hands That Hold You* – a song everyone learns as children. I'd never heard him hum a tune before.

As soon as I'd recognised the song, there was a knock at the door. I knew who it was. Valentine's humming came to an abrupt stop. Lol came quietly through to the bedroom to see if we'd heard. Valentine and I were both on our feet.

When Lol saw our faces, he said, 'Do you want me to answer it?'

I hesitated. 'No…I'll get it.'

I went to the door. Lol waited behind in the bedroom with Valentine.

The Caretaker was standing in the corridor. A younger man was with him; not the man we'd met on the day we moved in, a man I hadn't seen before. He stood behind the Caretaker looking at me over the other man's shoulder. The lights in the main corridors were bright and the two men seemed very distinct against the white walls. Two sets of eyes, strikingly similar, took me in.

'Have you a visitor in the flat?'

'Er…yes.'

'You haven't been to notify me. Why's that?'

'I was about to…We were just having dinner.'

'You should notify me of overnight guests *in advance*. Do you hear me? It's important, not least as a safety precaution.'

'Yes…I'm sorry.'

He was staring at me, purposely not speaking, willing me to be uncomfortable.

'We really didn't know he'd be staying. Or else we'd have told you.'

'You've had all day today. Why've you not been down?'

I could hear shuffling coming from behind the door of the flat opposite – someone listening to the conversation taking place in the corridor.

'Um. I'm sorry. We forgot to…'

'You've violated the rules of the property and it's been noted, Citizen. Misdemeanours such as this don't pass without record. A series of this type of incident and you'll start to feel the weight of the law.'

'It won't happen again, I promise.'

'You make sure it doesn't. As soon as you suspect a guest will be staying, you inform me. If it's after nine o'clock inform me via a written note and include the identification details of the visitor.'

The Caretaker handed me a form. 'Give this to your guest to complete and post it through my door immediately.'

'Yes, Sir.'

The younger man leant forward and spoke into the Caretaker's ear. 'Tell her about the ruling, father.'

The Caretaker turned his head a little to the side. 'I hadn't forgotten, Andrew.'

He turned back to address me. 'This will be the visitor's second night in the building, will it not?'

'We-ll, I'm not sure he's staying tonight.'

'Not sure?'

'Could you wait a minute?' I went quickly back into the flat. Lol was stood with Valentine, listening from the bedroom.

'The Caretaker wants to know if you'll be staying here tonight?'

Lol looked at us.

'You're welcome to,' I said, 'if that's what you'd like.'

'Thanks, that'd be great.'

I went back out to the corridor.

'He says he is.'

'Then I must remind you of the ruling that states that no guest is to stay here longer than three nights in any season.'

I lowered my voice 'He'll be leaving soon.'

'Make sure he does. Evictions can occur more easily than you'd imagine, Miss.'

The son nodded in agreement.

'I think you need to watch yourself, young lady...Two nights board at two and a quarter tokens per night. That'll be four and a half tokens you owe. The rate's just increased.' The Caretaker held out his hand.

I went to fetch my purse and paid him the money.

'Ensure the form is brought to me immediately. D'you hear?'

'Yes, Caretaker.'

The two men went away.

I went back inside and closed the door. Valentine and Lol came out to the kitchen. I sat down on one of the chairs and Valentine brought me a glass of water. All I could think was that I'd invited the Caretaker to my wedding. I was glad he hadn't come.

Lol went over to the notice on the door and read from the list of rules.

'It doesn't say here that you've to inform him about guests in advance. There's a camera above the entrances recording everyone going in and out anyway. He's coming down hard on you because you're from a Compound. Pass me the form. I'll fill the thing in and take it down there. Might give the old oaf a sleepless night if I don't.'

I sat reeling from the Caretaker's threats as the form got filled in beside me on the kitchen table.

Lol was downstairs handing in the form for some time. When he came back he looked pleased about something.

'Did you post it under his door?' I asked.

'No, I saw him instead.'

'Was it alright?'

'Yes. Now let's forget about it and do something else.'

'But Lol…'

'Mm?'

'What if he checks your name and finds you aren't a registered person?'

'I don't write my real name. I've got another one I use for forms. Marlon Jacamo Darlund…In a way I like it more than my proper one.'

'How come you've got it?'

'A boy died and I got given his name.'

'He *died*?'

'He committed suicide nine years ago and I've had his name since then. He'd be the same age as me. That's how come I can use it.'

'He committed what?'

'Oh, yes…It's another Streamlined word. It means he killed himself.'

Valentine gasped.

We'd never heard it called that. Occasionally, at the Compound people died in their booths and there'd be rumours passed around of them having done something to themselves but that was never what was officially said.

'They put on his Death Sheet that he died of an accident. But his mother said that it wasn't true...A woman from the Movement works in the Death Registry. She can delete deaths from the records and fix unregistered people up with part-time names. Or else with registered people from places like the Realm, she can give them new names if they end up in trouble. The names come off the Death Registry but they don't make it back onto the Census lists so there's no problem with that.'

'And she hasn't got caught?'

'We're not talking loads. Maybe two or three people a year who need her help out of all those that are dropping down dead.'

I thought it through. 'So how come you know his mother? That boy...whose name you've got.'

'I knew his address from the deleted Death Sheet and so I went round to the house. I told the woman that I'd heard about her son and wanted to offer condolences. I told her that I knew him a little. She was distraught and she invited me in. We talked about him, about how he died, and then we sort of became friends. I was like her replacement son for a while. She even let me stay in their home for a few nights. Her husband wasn't sure about it but he didn't say anything.'

'Does she know you use his name?'

'No. She doesn't know that.'

'But what about your own mother? Why didn't she register you when you were born? That's a serious offence.'

'She was in the Third Compound and she got pregnant. She was lucky though, she was massive and the pregnancy never showed, not even near the end. People just thought she'd got fatter. So the baby, me, never got taken from her. When she knew I was going to be born, she went outside the gates. She missed a curfew and the night's stamping, and got severely reprimanded when she got back in. She'd told them that she'd been attacked in the street by a stranger and that she'd been unable to make it back to the Compound in time. They didn't believe her, of course. She said they burnt her legs as punishment. But she was determined to have an unregistered child, a child born outside the City so to speak. To her it was worth it.'

'But what did she do with you? She couldn't bring you back to the Compound…'

'No, she had a friend on the outside who was affiliated with an earlier form of one of the Movements. She gave me to him and I was brought up by the group. She's still in the Third Compound, my mother. I met her a couple of times.'

I looked at Valentine. He seemed caught up inside his own thoughts, a weird expression on his face. When he became aware of me looking, he whispered, 'My mother and father died in a traffic accident. That's what they told me.'

'A traffic accident? Both of them?' Lol was shocked. 'Blimey, Val.'

I didn't understand what Valentine was talking about until I followed back through his train of thought.

'Oh no, Val! That's not it…Lol, he's thinking about the suicide. He's thinking it got his parents. Tell him. It wouldn't have, would it?' I wasn't even sure myself.

'Uh? No!...No, it's people on their own who do it. Mostly it's people who don't have anybody. Isolated people. They get low. It's rare that people with families, with children do it. Much rarer…'

Valentine's expression didn't change. He whispered, 'What about the shame? That could push them to it.'

'What shame?'

'…Of their son.'

For once Lol was too stunned to think of anything convincing to say.

The next morning was Monday and Valentine and I had to go to work. We assumed that Lol did too; back to selling Fountainade for his friend or whatever it was he did. He'd insisted, as on the previous evening, that he slept in the hallway again. We woke him as we were leaving for the Unit a little after eight o'clock so that we could say goodbye. I told him to let himself out and to post the key back under the door. He sleepily wished us good days at work and crawled off to sleep in the small bed.

We got back in that evening after work and found the flat empty. Lol had gone, but there was a note left on the kitchen table for us.

Thank you very much for the visit.
Hope to see you soon.
Love Lol.

Beside the note was a folded piece of paper. It was a copy of one of the Circle's from the Realm, the pattern they'd put on my foot.

Valentine seemed very taken with it. He wanted to stick it to the wall in the kitchen. 'So we can look at it while we eat,' he said.

I wasn't happy but I couldn't let on to Valentine that I knew what it was.

I thought that would be all we saw of Lol for a while. Maybe he'd contact us, I thought, and we'd meet up with him somewhere. I didn't expect to see him back at the flat.

But then, one evening a couple of weeks later, I kept feeling as though Lol was nearby. When I washed my hands at the sink, I felt as though he was stood beside me, waiting to use the taps. When I sat down on my bed, it was like he was already in the room. Then, not long before bedtime, I heard someone at the door. I opened it and it was him.

He came into the kitchen. His face was fresh from the cold night. He had a bag with him that he set down on the table. I was too surprised to say much. He apologised to me for turning up unannounced.

I felt a bit in awe of him and fumbled about setting some water to boil on the stove. Valentine emerged from the little room without his glasses, blinking his eyes when he saw Lol. There was a strange hush in the flat as we sat and drank the tea. It meant something, him coming back so soon.

I promptly took a note down to the Caretaker to tell him that Marlon Jacamo Darlund would be staying another night with us; officially his last visit of the season.

We discovered that the bag Lol had brought with him was full of items with which to bribe the Caretaker. He'd hardly bought anything of his own; just a couple of changes of clothes. He said that the first time he saw the Caretaker, he knew that he'd be open to 'sweeteners'. Lol said it was instinct, that he always knew. He asked Valentine if he'd mind sticking to Silver; Lol couldn't spare Fountainade. He needed what he had for the Caretaker.

'A bottle of Fountainade and a jar of olives and that bloke downstairs will be eating out of our hands. I guarantee it,' Lol said.

'Remember how he was the other evening though, when he came round checking up on us?' I reminded. 'He's so strict about the rules, Lol. I don't think you should try this…Please, at least just think about it.'

'That's the thing though; that sort's the best for bribing. They're so busy laying down the law to everyone else, they start thinking they're above it. They start thinking the rules don't apply to them, or at least not in the same way. Don't worry, I know what I'm doing.'

Don't worry, Neeve. Don't worry. It was something Lol would come to say a lot.

Lol spent his third night with us and ordinarily that would have been the last time he should have stayed. But the fourth evening passed without note. The Caretaker didn't come back to knock on our door. Lol said it was just a matter of keeping the man well stocked. From then on, when I saw the Caretaker in the corridor or on the stairs, he'd turn away and pretend to be seeing to a fixture of some kind or tending to the heating system. It was as if he wanted to trick himself into believing that we didn't really exist. At any rate, he didn't bother us again.

The fact of the matter was, Lol was moving in with us. Only, at the time, we didn't fully realise it. The gradual way in which it happened and Lol's lack of belongings meant that the significance of it passed us by.

We were finding security in a man who saw himself as being beyond the law – a precarious place to find safety, but for some odd reason it seemed better than the safety Valentine and I had been able to offer each other. When Lol came to stay with us we knew him only as Lol or Lollard. We found out later his real name was Linden Doiger.

'You don't share a bed, do you?'

It was late in the evening. Valentine wasn't in the room. He'd just got up and gone to the washroom. There was only Lol and me. He must have been waiting for a chance to question me.

'No…'

'You have separate rooms then?'

I just looked at him.

'I never see you even touch each other.'

I couldn't reply. I didn't know what to say.

'You're not really a couple are you?' His voice wasn't unkind. There was no judgement in it. He was gentle with the questions, but it was clear that he wanted to know.

'Did you strike a deal with each other to get out of the Compound? I've heard that happens.'

'Sort of.' I felt foolish. I felt stupid and so I started to speak without thinking. I didn't want Lol to think I was the one at fault. It all came out in a rush.

'He has a Bad Passion. He takes pills for it. I don't think he could form a proper union with someone even if he wanted to.' I stunned myself with my own words. I'd tried to blame Valentine.

Lol looked shocked at what I'd told him. Of course he did.

I bit my lip, chastising myself in my head, wanting to take back what I'd said.

Lol mumbled, 'What kind of Bad Passion?'

'I don't know. I didn't ask.'

'It could explain things. The way he is.'

Sounds of Valentine leaving the washroom came through the door.

I looked guiltily at Lol.

No more was said.

Over the days that followed, the three of us fell into step with one another. It wasn't difficult. Lol didn't make the flat feel cramped. It didn't feel like we were trying to accommodate another body. It was like there was suddenly colour and sound in the rooms whereas before there'd just been white walls and too much quiet.

When Lol made his special deal with the Caretaker, the Caretaker had stressed the problem of our neighbours. He'd told Lol that our neighbours would be suspicious of his presence. The Caretaker would need extra payment for informing them of the change in circumstances and for putting them at their ease. He'd have to tell them that Lol was a relative of Mr Frankland, that Lol was in need of assistance and so was being permitted to stay. In return, Lol would reward the Caretaker for the added inconvenience.

When Mrs Broxter from across the hall heard the news from the Caretaker, she came over to check things for herself.

I answered the door.

'There's a personage you have in there. A new lad. Where is he?'

'He's –'

'Let me speak to him.'

I went to fetch Lol from the bedroom.

'What're doing living here, laddie? What cause have you?'

'I'm here thanks to the kindness of my cousin, Valentine. You know, Mr Frankland?'

'You've not got the look of him. Not at all.'

'No.' He laughed. 'I'm always wishing that I'd been born with my cousin's good looks.'

Lol went on to spin out a story for our neighbour – an elaborate tale to explain how come he'd had to ask for help from his cousin, Valentine. He stood in the doorway to the flat with one hand in his pocket and the other one splayed against his cheek and earnestly told her a story – a funny, tender one to pull at her toughened, old heart-strings. I watched as the tightness in her face undid itself as she listened.

'Well, laddie, I can see you're thankful to your people for their help. By the time you've lived to my age you'll have seen too many who've had nowhere kindly to go,' she said.

She went back to her flat satisfied, lightly patting her chest with her twisted fingers.

There was no need to pretend now Lol understood our situation. I told Valentine that Lol knew we'd kept separate rooms. Valentine nodded blankly, keeping any reaction to himself. And from then on we took it in turns for the beds and the hallway floor. It became a sort of rotating game. Only, because I was always the one who went to sleep first, I tended to have the comfort and privacy of the small room.

We gave Lol a set of keys so that he could let himself in when he wanted. Valentine hardly ever used his. He didn't go out of the flat alone except for his trips to the clinic and so Valentine gave his set to Lol.

When we went to work at the Unit we missed Lol's company. When we came home in the evenings, we were glad if he was there.

Often we'd return to find him at the stove, preparing a meal, absorbed in what he was doing. The flat would be full of the smell of frying vegetables and the sound of his slurred singing. If we came home and found the flat empty, we'd conceal our disappointment; he couldn't always be there but things were better once he'd returned.

He'd bring back gifts for us from other regions of the City; treats from the market stalls, exotic-tasting things we'd never tried before. Lol knew the special places to go to find hard-to-come-by items. He knew the people to ask.

'I need to see your bellies grow bigger.' he said one day as he was unpacking strange canned foods from his bag onto the kitchen table; artichoke hearts and tins of pickled fish, 'Then there'll be more of you to love.'

We blinked at him, dumbfounded, as Lol casually put the cans into the cupboards.

It became obvious that Lol liked to recount stories. The stories he told were mostly about odd or comical things that had happened, things that had happened to people that he'd known. For all we knew, he might have made them up but, at any rate, they were compelling. It became our favourite pastime, sitting and listening to Lol. He never ran out of tales to tell us and he never told the same story twice. We grew more and more engaged by his company, more enamoured with each tale he told, with each of his deliberately self-abasing acts.

Hardly any of Lol's stories contained facts about his own life, however. When he recounted a tale that related to himself, it was more of a sketch, not rooted in time, not related to any other sketch. When we asked him questions about himself, just as before, he was evasive. The answers he gave were far-fetched, seemingly designed to make us laugh and forget he'd ever had a past.

For the most part Valentine would be quiet, just listening to Lol's anecdotes, or else to Lol and my conversations, but he wasn't ill at ease. Hearing the stories helped Valentine. I think they encouraged him to look back over his own past, to remember things he'd forgotten; pleasanter memories that had got buried under the not-so-happy ones.

Slowly, Valentine began to talk more, and not just when he'd drunk Silver. Once or twice, he even tried to come up with a tale of his own that he could share. He needed a lot of prompting, he related things stiltedly and didn't have Lol's gift for story-telling. In truth, he didn't have such big stories to tell. That didn't matter though. All that mattered was that the times when Valentine would sit wearing his darkened glasses, or when he'd take himself off to be alone in another part of the flat, were becoming less.

Sometimes, when Lol and I were alone, when Valentine was quiet in his room, Lol would ask me, *What was it like when so and so happened? How did it feel when such and such happened?* He was trying to get me to talk about my past too. I had no idea how to respond. No-one had really asked those sorts of questions – about the Vanishment and its aftermath. When I started talking, I found myself getting affected. It was strange; the upset seemed to come from nowhere. Lol said it was no bad thing. If I cried, it made him want to ask more. He'd rub my back and stroke my hand as I tried to explain it. Little by little, a heaviness I'd been carrying, grew lighter.

And Lol taught us how to use the Circle. I was wary at first. I didn't understand what it was or what it could do. All I knew was that Willa had badly wanted one and so I considered it wise to steer clear. But the Circle got to me. It worked on me through Valentine who took to it like a boat to water. The strange thing was, it felt good to use it. You could be more comfortable in your own skin when you did.

In so many ways things were better. It felt as though we'd stumbled headlong into a brighter time. Things seemed to get easier, they seemed to flow without as much effort. Even at the Unit, life wasn't as bad: out of the blue, Mr Spinks asked me back to his office and instead of penalising me for something I'd done wrong, he told me that my work had improved and that I could return to my usual work-station. I could fraternise with Valentine again. Without warning, life became more accommodating.

But it wasn't just that we were living different lives; it was that we were becoming different people. Because of the changes in Valentine, I stopped feeling the need to protect him in the way that I had. Lol adopted much of that role anyway. He did it instinctively with the strength of his enthusiasm and the strength of his fully inhabited body. Lol even took Valentine back for visits to the Realm so that he could dance. I stayed at home, glad that Valentine had somebody to take him at last. I didn't worry about them; it's as though I forgot to fret.

One night at bedtime, when I went to the washroom to brush my teeth, I got a shock when I saw myself in the mirror. It wasn't an obvious thing, but I noticed it. When I saw myself, my face reminded me of the one in the mirror when I was small, before anything had happened. My eyes looked wider and softer. It was like the muscles of my face had relaxed. The frown lines between my brows weren't as apparent. I thought, *the face I had at the Compound is disappearing.* It was like I was staring at my real face, the one that I was meant to have.

Chapter 10

We got back in from the fair at nearly one o'clock in the morning. We opened the front door and peered into the kitchen. The flat was dark and very quiet.

'Lol...?'

Nobody.

We stepped unsurely inside and made our way through the hall to the bedroom. We stood for a while in the dark. Neither of us could bring ourselves to turn the lights on. It felt better not seeing; Lol's absence was obvious enough without the lights. And it was better being hidden by the dark.

Valentine went to his room and poured two glasses of Silver. He came back into the big bedroom with the drinks. He didn't want to be alone.

The room felt like a piece of Lol's clothing that he'd worn and then thrown off. It seemed that traces of his shape were everywhere, even in the dark, even though his body was no longer there to fill it.

'We still have his wallet,' Valentine whispered.

'We should hide it.'

'Where?'

'In the communal room under a bench.'

'We should take the money out of it.'

We went together. We crept down the corridor to the communal room and hid the evidence.

When we came back we saw the flat with different eyes: there were other things we had to hide. I poured a full litre of Fountainade down the sink and put milk into the empty bottle. I took black market delicacies from the kitchen cupboards and emptied them down the toilet. Valentine tipped the remainder of his Silver into our glasses. There wasn't time to take in the significance of what we were doing; we did what was necessary.

When we'd finished, we crashed down on the bed, too tired to undress. We lay side by side, knocking back the drinks. Valentine had the Circle with him. He was clutching the paper against his chest.

'Maybe he'll come really late...'

'What do we do if he doesn't?'

'We go very early to the Realm. If there's no-one there, we put a note

under the metal door telling them we need their help and to come and find us...somewhere.'

Where? Where would we go to wait for them? We couldn't wait in the flat. The plans I had weren't workable. I felt we were trapped in our own home.

'Val...?'

'Yes?'

'Why did he turn like that?'

'I don't know.'

'I think it was our fault. We let him down. We should've -'

'Don't, Neeve. You'll go mad thinking what we could've done. Don't think like that.'

I still hadn't told Valentine about Lol's bad dream. If I told him now, it wouldn't do any good. He'd feel more to blame for what had happened. I thought about the other things I still hadn't told Valentine. He didn't know about the Circle that'd been burned into my foot. He didn't even know about my father's Vanishment. Even now he didn't know these things. I'd never been able to bring myself to tell him.

We lay side by side in the dark, my mind trawling through different possible scenarios; what if after what if after what if. My whole body was alert to the least little click or scratch; the slightest sound that could be Lol, that could be the Guarda.

'I'm not too comfortable on the floor. D'you mind if I lie on the bed?' Lol said.

We were sat on the rug in big bedroom, listening to stories.

'No. Not at all.'

Lol pulled off his shoes and went and lay down on the mattress. He lay on his belly with his head at the foot-end of the bed so that he could continue with his tale.

After a little while, he interrupted himself again to say, 'It's much better on here. Why don't you come up?'

Valentine and I obediently raised ourselves to our feet. Standing by the bed, we hesitated, uncertain of how to arrange ourselves. I sat down at Lol's feet and Valentine did the same on the other side of him, our legs dangling awkwardly over the edges of the bed.

Lol turned over onto his back to look at us.

'D'you know what? I've never met two people as reserved as the pair of you,' he joked, nudging us with his feet. 'Starchy and Prim; that's what your names ought to be. Don't be alarmed but I'm going to dare you to do something, alright? Neeve, I'm going to challenge you to smell Valentine's knees.'

I looked at him. 'Uh…why?'

'Because it's a dare. You don't ask why with dares. Val, roll up your trouser legs…'

'But you haven't finished with what you were telling us…What happened to Mr Clauden after he got his shoes back?' I asked.

'Well, that's basically the end of the story. He just made sure that he never returned to the Foyler District and then that's it.'

'Oh.'

'Are you going to smell Valentine's knees then?'

'Don't people's knees just smell of skin?'

'You'll need to smell hard, that's all. Come on, Val.'

Valentine reluctantly rolled up his trousers.

I bent over his legs as he lay them out across the bed. 'This is silly…'

'Smell anything?'

'They're…um…nice.' They smelled lovely but I didn't like to say.

'Well done, you.'

Then Lol challenged Valentine to touch my vertebrae while I lay on my stomach on the bed.

'Start at the top, at the base of Neeve's skull, and then work your way down.'

But it was too ambitious a task. Valentine got as far as my shoulder blades, touching very lightly, and then gave in.

Lol didn't insist. 'Oh, well.'

There seemed to be a sort of conviction in the way Lol wanted us to be familiar with each other. Still, he knew better than to push too hard. Chinks in our reserve were starting to fall away and we were scarcely aware of it.

Later that evening, Lol put his arm over Valentine's shoulder and said softly, 'What are those pills I hear you taking late on, in the kitchen, Val?' And then he gave Valentine a shake, a gentle shake, as though Val was a pill bottle himself.

Valentine gaped at him, astonished.

Lol had asked the question as though he didn't understand the significance of what he was saying, although I knew for certain that he did. He wanted to hear about the Passion from Valentine's own mouth.

Valentine turned to me; a panicked look that said, *what do I do?*

As carefully as I could, I said, 'You can tell him, Val.'

Valentine shook his head.

After a few moments he said, 'You tell him, Neeve.'

'Wouldn't it be better if you did?'

He sat shaking.

Lol said, 'Don't say if it's difficult.'

'I can only say it to one –' Valentine's voice broke off.

'I'll go out,' I said.

I went and sat in the kitchen.

Everything in the flat was quiet. I couldn't hear voices from the bedroom. I couldn't hear anything. I sat and waited and after a while there was the sound of footsteps across the floorboards and the conspicuous click of the light being switched off. Maybe it was easier for Valentine to say it in the dark.

I heard nothing until the door swung open a little while later and Valentine rushed to the washroom. I heard the sound of him locking himself in and then water being splashed repeatedly. The taps were running continuously. It was just the same as that day at the Compound when Valentine had told me.

Lol crept into the kitchen. His face looked tense now.

We kept our voices low.

'Did he say?' I whispered.

'Yes, but not much. He doesn't seem to know much about it himself, does he?'

Even that was more than I'd discovered.

'He said the Passion's one of the severest you can have. That's why they had to purge it so early.'

'The severest. Blimey.'

'When I asked him what kind of Passion it was, he just said that it had a "Listing of ten".'

'What does that mean?'

'He said ten was the type of Passion. He wouldn't speak after that.'

'They asked about the Listing when we went to the Engagement interview at the Commission. I didn't know what they meant.'

'Mm. But *ten*. It doesn't tell us much. I wonder if we could find out from somewhere.'

'He'd have told us if he wanted us to know.'

'Maybe that's why he told me. Maybe he wants us to find out. Maybe he doesn't even know himself.'

'P'rhaps...' I wasn't sure.

The Census form for our district arrived through our door. I'd tried to forget that it was coming. When it arrived, we had to fill it in as though all was normal at number 92, no mention of Lol's presence in our flat.

The three of us sat, bent over the form.

'Give me the pen, Neeve. I'll fill it in. You don't have to make such a meal of it.'

'We need to be really careful, Lol. They're on the look out for discrepancies. We need to get it right.'

Valentine said, 'Neeve, your hand's shaking. Your writing will look odd. Maybe we should wait.'

'We can't leave it, Val. We'll just keep putting it off.'

Lol said, 'Give the pen to me, Neeve. I'll make a start on it. I'll just tick the boxes. You can fill in the writing sections when you're calmer. I know what I'm doing.'

I put the pen down. 'But you've never even filled one in.'

'I've studied the forms at the Realm. I know all about them.'

Lol started going through the pages. He read the questions out in order and then waited for us to agree an answer before ticking each box.

As I watched him working through the form, I thought how easily one criminal act can lead to another and then another. I wondered if we'd set off a chain.

I was getting up to go to the small room to sleep one night. Lol took hold of my hand.

'Why don't you sleep here?' Lol said pointing to the big bed. 'You could sleep here while Valentine and I chat. We'll talk quietly. We won't keep you awake. It seems a shame for you to always go off at night into the other room.'

Valentine looked shocked. Neither of us understood where Lol was heading with his suggestion.

'But whose turn is it in the big bed?' I asked. 'Where are they going to sleep?'

'It's my turn. I could sleep in there too. What I've been thinking is that it seems impractical to have a big bed and only one person in it each night. One person always on the floor.'

I was looking at him, uncertain, the way that Valentine had looked at me so often in the past. I'd never shared a bed with someone in my life. Not properly, not a whole night.

'It'll be alright, I promise, Neeve. This way Valentine can sleep in the small bed. He can't insist on having the hallway carpet again. He says he's alright down there because he doesn't sleep much, but it's not right.'

'...I need to go and change into my night-clothes.'

I went to the washroom and undressed. I washed without noticing what I was doing, I was too busy fretting.

When I went back into the big room, Lol was telling Valentine a story about somebody, a woman called June.

I slid myself into the big bed.

'Goodnight, Neeve,' Lol said.

'Goodnight.'

Lol continued with his story. He spoke with his voice lowered so that I could sleep. I lay and listened to his anecdote. He told how the woman's house had caught fire and how she'd only just escaped from the blaze, how she'd been diagnosed with a sickness of heart, how she'd fallen from a towpath into a canal, how her husband had been arrested in a case of mistaken identity. The thing was, all these events had occurred within the month of June in various years so one day she applied to have her name changed. Her request was granted; she got a letter back saying that her new name was Margaret and after that no more bad things happened.

I fell asleep and only woke up when Lol came to bed. I felt the mattress move as he lay down beside me. I pretended I hadn't woken. I seemed to fill so much of the bed. I made my breaths small, trying to compensate. Behind me, Lol shuffled himself into a comfortable position. I lay, waiting to hear his breathing slow. I tried to rest. I was married to Valentine, not Lol. I shouldn't have been sharing a bed with another man.

Lol was moving us slowly in a certain direction. I wasn't sure exactly where he was leading us, but it seemed the destination was already clear in his mind.

I don't quite know how, but the bed rotation stopped. Lol continued to sleep beside me in the larger room, and Valentine, making no mention of the new arrangements, moved back into his own.

Then, a couple of weeks later, Lol tried to question Valentine about his pills again.

'Have you ever stopped taking them just to see what happens?'

Valentine shook his head.

'Not even for a day?'

'No.'

Valentine took his pills with clockwork regularity. Every day, every night at the same times, no matter what, he'd go to his supply. It was like his body knew to do it even without his mind getting involved. It seemed automatic to him, like breathing.

'Don't you even wonder about stopping?'

'Yes. I've wondered.' His voice was guarded.

But Lol wouldn't accept it.

'Are you sure you need them?'

'I have to take them. It's the law.'

Later, at eleven o'clock at night, when Valentine went to take his medicine, I knew something was going to happen. Lol followed Valentine out to the kitchen. The look on his face alarmed me and I went after him.

Valentine was in the kitchen undoing the lid of the bottle. Lol walked up to him and pulled the pill bottle from Valentine's hands. Before Valentine could do anything, Lol had hurled the bottle out of the room. The brittle plastic hit the hallway wall and broke open. Tablets showered all over the floor; dozens and dozens of bright red pills on the dull green carpet.

Valentine let out a yelp of distress. He bolted past Lol, into the hall and fell on his knees. He scooped a handful of pills and poured them into his mouth. He clenched his jaws and tried to swallow. His mouth was too dry though. They wouldn't go down.

He choked the pills back up again and had to spit them into his palm.

He remained there in the hall, unmoving except for the rapid motion of his breath. He kept hold of the pills he'd tried to take and sat guarding the rest, not daring to move away from them.

Lol stepped into the hall.

Valentine wouldn't look at him.

'Val,' Lol murmured.

Valentine stayed silent. His face was flushed.

'I didn't mean to break the bottle. Sorry.'

Lol went back into the kitchen. I heard him take his jacket from the hook on the front door. He called out, 'It's the situation I'm angry at, not you. You know that.' Then he opened the front door and went out.

I stood in the hallway and gazed at the pills on the carpet. There was an empty space in the random pattern they'd made as they'd scattered across the floor; an empty space where Valentine had frantically scrambled with his hands.

I crept by him and went to the kitchen. I filled a glass with some water and found a cup in which to collect the pills. Then I went back and knelt beside Valentine.

I passed him the glass. 'Do you want to swallow one down?'

Valentine took a pill and I began to gather up the rest. They were hard and shiny, rolling away when I tried to get them.

Valentine raised his head. He said, 'What does he want?'

'I'm not sure…He doesn't mean you any harm, Val, I'm sure of that…He must think what he's doing's for the best.'

Lol came back in around midnight. Valentine was still awake in his room and I was awake in the big bed. Lol had brought confections with him; a bag of currants in coloured icing. I don't know where he could have got them from at that time of night. He went in to give the confections to Valentine. I tried to act cheerful, as though nothing had happened.

A few days later, when Valentine and I were at work, Lol went through the flat searching for Valentine's medicine supply. When the time came late that evening for Valentine to take his dose, he couldn't find his pills.

Lol admitted to it immediately, 'I took them.'

Valentine looked destroyed. 'Wh-ere…?'

'Away. Out of the flat.'

Valentine's expression was uncomprehending. He could hardly take in Lol's words.

'You can have them back, I promise. Just go a few days without them. It won't show in your tests when you go back to the clinic. Give it a few days and see what happens. You can have them back. I promise I'll give them back to you.'

I uttered a vague, 'Oh, no…'

Valentine just stared helplessly into space.

'You might find things out about yourself that you never knew. You can see what you're like without the medicine inside you.'

Valentine let out a short, desperate wail; a helpless cry of complaint.

Lol brought both hands up to his face. He looked perplexed. 'Look, just give it six days. Six days from today. That means the last two days will be Saturday and Sunday so you won't even have to go outside if you don't want to.'

Valentine stared ahead at nothing and shook.

Lol said, 'Come and look at the Circle, Val. It'll ease you.'

Valentine allowed himself to be led towards the bed and Lol tried to make him comfortable with pillows under his head and shoulders.

Valentine stared at the symbol, or maybe just at the wall.

'This isn't right, Lol,' I whispered.

'It'll be alright, Neeve. Don't worry.'

'But poor Valentine, he's petrified.'

'I know it seems harsh but it's only six days, Neeve. Trust me. Something incredible might happen. This is his big chance to find out.'

There was no point arguing. I knew nothing I said would get Lol to return the pills.

It was summertime and the flat was hot. The stifling atmosphere of our rooms only served to make the pressure on Valentine more intense. I felt bad about it, like Valentine was part of a bad experiment, but I couldn't help watching his behaviour over the following days, watching to see if the effects of the pills would wear off, waiting to find out what the effects of the pills actually were.

Each day, Valentine pleaded repeatedly with Lol for his pills. Each time he stammered out his request Lol would speak comfortingly to him, hold him, tell him how brave he was, how there was only a few more days to go, how important these six days could be for him and then tell him he couldn't have the pills. Valentine had no choice but to use the Circle over and over as he tried to reconcile himself to what Lol was doing.

There were changes almost from the first. The initial difference was startling; Valentine grew tired. Very tired. On the second night, after an evening of Circle-staring, Valentine turned over on the big bed and fell asleep. It was 8-45 in the evening. He slept for ten hours solid. Normally he got by on only four or five.

Then, when Valentine woke the next morning, he knew that he'd dreamt. With amazement in his voice, he told me what he'd seen. The dream was only short but it was vivid. He'd dreamed of a herd of beautiful creatures who lived on the Moon. The animals were pure white and they had white horns growing from the tops of their heads. The animals had gone to stay on the Moon when living conditions had become hostile. The Moon was a good place for them – their white coats made them invisible on the pale surface.

I'd never known Valentine dream before. At least he never remembered any when I asked.

On the third night, Valentine tried, in the most vehement manner he could muster, to demand his pills back.

'But it's only been three days,' Lol said. 'Think of what's already happened in this short time. You've slept well. You've even dreamt.'

'That's why it shouldn't go on…It – it's too dangerous.'

'But, Val –'

'I don't know what will *happen*.' He blurted it out. You could hear the panic in his voice.

'But it's so important to find out. You'll discover who –'

'I already feel that I'm not myself. *Already*.'

'Give it just three more days. Just three more. Until Sunday remember? I swear after that I'll give them back. You can take as many as you want then.'

That evening, before Valentine lay in front of the Circle, Lol took him out to the bars for Silver. After only a couple of drinks, Valentine got so tired, he fell asleep where he sat and Lol had to bring him home again.

It seems strange but at no point did I think about asking Lol to leave. Similarly, Valentine never came to me with doubts about Lol's presence in our flat, or about his influence over us. Lol was our armour. Even if the armour felt uncomfortable, too heavy to bear sometimes, we weren't about to take it off.

The next step seemed inevitable. I was almost waiting for it to happen.

Five days into the experiment, late on the Saturday afternoon, after Valentine had survived all week at work, Lol suggested that we celebrate the achievement. He gave us both Fountainade to drink.

'It's a special time,' Lol explained. 'I can spare a glass or two each for this.'

Valentine gulped his drink down hurriedly.

Lol said, 'I think we should take it in turns.'

'In turns for what?'

'Playing a trusting game. If we play a game it'll be a way of seeing if there's been a change in Valentine since he stopped the pills. Neeve, you should go first.'

'How come I have to?'

'Because Valentine's too nervous and I'm too hasty.'

'But I'm nervous about it as well.'

'Yes, but we're doing this for Val, Neeve. It's for him that we're doing it. This could be his only chance.'

Both Valentine and I knew what playing a trusting game meant. We'd played them with Lol before. That's how we'd discovered that Valentine and I were no good. Valentine was especially bad. Lol could just about get Valentine to fall slightly backwards. Valentine would allow himself to be caught and held, but only briefly. His participation was never anything to speak of. That's as far as it went. Any further and he'd cut out. He'd just go dead.

The three of us sat together on the floor of the big bedroom. Valentine and I were gazing at our laps. Already my body was feeling the effects of the alcohol.

'Stand up, Neeve.'

I slowly stood up and Lol did the same.

But instead of the usual trusting game, Lol reached over and nudged my shoulder, pushing me so that I fell towards the bed. I teetered momentarily and then he pushed me again, harder this time. I fell onto the mattress and Lol followed, sitting himself beside me.

'What's going on?'

'You have to trust me. It's a trust game, remember?'

'And first we must remove the sock-es.' He put on a funny voice. He seemed to be pretending to Valentine that he was giving a demonstration.

With his bitten, inelegant fingernails, Lol started to take off my sock. As I stared at his concentrating face, I remembered the night at the Realm when Nolan Jonker had done the same.

Lol turned to Valentine, 'Could you close the curtains? The sun's too bright.'

I laughed nervously, feeling the bed judder beneath me as both socks were removed. This was going to be strange. I closed my eyes. I couldn't look.

Lol began. I felt one hand at first. I could feel it through my short-sleeved summer blouse. It reached for my stomach and I flinched with the touch. His hand slid across my waist and down my left leg all the way to my feet. I felt him tugging at my toes. He rubbed my sole where the Circle had been.

I opened my eyes. 'Lol…I'm not sure about this.'

'Don't worry.'

Then there were two hands on me. Both were Lol's. He moved them slowly to begin with but then gradually he speeded up and then his hands were swooping over me, over my hair and face and arms. It was hard to keep up with where they went.

'Sweet Neeve.' Lol stated it like a fact.

He leaned over and kissed my cheek.

I tried to smile at him.

Then Lol reached over to Valentine. He took hold of Valentine's wrist and brought his arm towards me, making Valentine press his hand against me. I felt the difference in temperature between their two palms. Lol kept Valentine's hand held there; insistent that he keep the contact. Then four hands were on me; Lol's two warm, confident hands and Valentine's cold ones touching me uncertainly. Sometimes Lol tickled, but mostly he stroked and glided. I could feel him behind my ears, at the back of my neck, under my knees.

He began to unfasten the buttons on the front of my blouse.

'This isn't right.'

He worked around my hands, where my hands gripped my clothes. He undid the buttons he could get to. He went slowly and carefully. I suppose I let him because of the Fountainade I'd drunk. He carried on until the last button was undone.

Then he tried to ease my blouse off, wanting to guide my arms out of it, but I was squirming with embarrassment at my nakedness, ashamed at the size of myself.

'I feel ugly.' The words came out of my mouth; three plain words, as though my body was speaking, not my brain.

'How can you say that? With that face? Look, Val, look at this lovely woman before us!' Lol exclaimed.

I pulled the blouse closed over my front. 'I want to keep it on. I feel cold.' I knew the room was red hot from the day's sun but still I was shivering with nervousness.

'Really? Fair do's. Try to relax and we'll warm you up.'

Lol's hands continued to glide over me. It happened without my meaning it to; I could sense the different parts of me waking up as they responded to the touch. Lol managed to push aside the material at the bottom of my blouse. He put his mouth on the exposed skin and kissed. After the kiss, he gently bit the place where he'd put his lips. My body shot awake even though I was ordering it to be quiet. None of this would've happened without Fountainade.

Lol pointed to my arm. 'Val, kiss Neeve here.' It was a command.

Valentine moved his face a little closer to me.

'A bit nearer…'

Valentine came closer still. Then hurriedly, in a fraction of a second, he pressed his mouth against the skin near my elbow and withdrew again. He pulled himself away and lay further down the bed. My throat tightened and my eyes began to itch, moved by Valentine's attempt. I stretched my hand out to him, trying to give reassurance.

Lol had moved further down the bed too. He was facing Valentine across my body.

'Shift over, Val,' he whispered.

Valentine moved back and Lol made a grab for my legs, pushing them apart.

Kneeling over me, Lol slid my skirt further up towards my waist. I began to shake. He held on to my thighs. I could feel his breath moving up the inside of my leg. My cheeks burned. I squeezed my eyes shut. I could hear myself laughing, but it was a weird, embarrassed laugh and I didn't know how to stop. Then suddenly I *had* stopped. Air rushed into my lungs and my head veered. The intimacy of what Lol did made me gasp. It was like my body was tightening around a single rigid nerve – elastic being twisted around a stick. It was too much. It was an effort just to say, 'No…Stop.'

That time, Lol didn't insist. Instead, he turned to Valentine.

He pulled Valentine from the mattress and took him to the three-way mirror on the dresser. I lay, a blurred heap under the bedclothes, watching aghast. I could see our reflections; Lol and Valentine, big in the foreground, and me further off in the background of the glass. Lol was making Valentine look at himself, making him watch himself being undressed. In the same focused manner as he'd tried to unclothe me, Lol was stripping Valentine. My mind was shot but I knew what was happening. I knew that it shouldn't be. What did he think he was doing? His aim was to bring me and Valentine together – I'd thought that it was. *We're doing this for Valentine,* he'd said. I'd thought he'd meant to demonstrate the ways of a married couple.

I watched the spectacle as it was doubled and tripled in the little side-mirrors. Lol exposed Valentine's skin bit by bit: chest, shoulder, arms. I couldn't take my gaze away. So much of Valentine's skin. His chest was flat and his nipples were dark. Veins stood out in pathways down his arms – an effortlessly graceful body. Lol put his nose against Valentine's shoulder and smelled his skin.

Lol had stripped Valentine to the waist and now he was taking off his own clothes. The room was getting hotter and more stifling. I wiped the sweat from my palms on to the sheets. I saw how much paler Lol's body was than Valentine's. The muscles in his arms were larger and rounder, the skin thicker. Fine hairs lay flat across his chest.

Lol took hold of Valentine by the waist of his trousers and pulled him back towards the bed. He led him to the mattress and laid him beside me. Then Lol lay down too. Valentine couldn't bring himself to look. He blinked a couple of times at the ceiling, then, to shield his eyes from whatever was about to happen, he bent his arm across his face; a child-like action, as though he thought he could make the room disappear by hiding it from view.

Lol took up Valentine's free arm and kissed it. I stared at him. He glanced back at me and grinned. Then he made his way, recklessly, up towards Valentine's neck. Valentine just let him. I had an impulse to speak; warning words that would stop him. But I didn't. Couldn't. The whole room seemed to tip under the weight of the danger.

Lol bit Valentine's neck and then angled his face towards his own, forcing Valentine to remove his shielding arm. He kissed him and then drew back to see Valentine's expression. He smiled at Valentine's amazed face and then laughed. It was a daring sort of laugh. It frightened me.

Lol had hold of Valentine's hair, trying to keep him still. Valentine was half-trying to stop Lol from doing whatever he was doing. His hand was over his own mouth, suppressing the noises he was making beneath his palm. I should've turned away but I kept looking.

I couldn't see Lol's face, he'd moved so that his back was towards me, but I could see Valentine and he looked half-mad. I watched his hand as it reached out to touch, only to recoil once contact was made. Still, his hand kept reaching, seeming not to know where it meant to go.

Nowhere else in the City, I thought. *Only here. Terrible. Terrible. Terrible.*

Lol paused and turned to me briefly. 'Don't be shy…Help me.' His face was flushed.

He was giving me access to Valentine's body; something I'd tried hard to stop longing for. Here he was, giving me what I'd always wanted, but my hands were frozen, stalled by what was taking place. All I could do was try to lean in and feel Valentine from inside. I emptied my thoughts towards him in the hope it'd come.

I didn't have to lean far. His feelings were immediate and obvious. It's like his body was shouting them out. There they were, Valentine's responses inside me. They had his unmistakable texture. The feelings weren't unpleasant, still I had to grip myself around the waist because the sensations were so strong. I could feel Valentine's anxiety giving way, caving in on itself.

Suddenly, it felt as though everything was rushing inwards. It was like living a lifetime in a second. The force of what Valentine felt seemed to hurt him. I felt an ache shoot through my body, into my head. It was like I'd been slammed on the back of my skull.

Something strange was happening. For a moment, the Valentine I knew wasn't there. For a moment it was like clouds had moved away and in the gap that was left was a part of him I didn't recognise; a remote part suddenly become more distinct. It was strikingly intact, untouched by the troubles he'd had. *Like the feeling from the Circle,* I thought. I opened my eyes and looked at him. He was lying very still on the bed.

The feelings started to drift off. I leaned in closer to catch the tail-end before they disappeared. I felt like I'd been fused very tightly together only to be unravelled, forced to come apart again.

Valentine didn't move. Even after several minutes he was still motionless. Lol got up and pulled him over so that he could see his face. Valentine looked like a happy dead man.

'Valentine?' Lol drummed the mattress anxiously with his fingers.

Again, it was like the first time Valentine had used the Circle; very hard to get through to him.

'Valentine...?' Lol shook him by the arm.

Valentine stirred beside me. He made a cat-like sound at the back of his throat. His eyes opened slowly. He blinked, then looked at Lol. He didn't do or say anything, he just closed his eyes again. I stared at the perfection of his profile in the semi-dark room.

We lay on the bed. My head was swimming from the alcohol. I didn't sleep. Lol and Valentine slept but I lay there as though on guard; a vague sense of something looming over us, keeping me awake.

It was so hot. The sheet that was over us got thrown to the floor. Despite the heat, even in their sleep, Valentine and Lol seemed to be fighting for the best spot – the place flanked by the other two; a slow, sleepers' game to reach the middle. I wondered how they could rest. Somebody needed to be alert for the trouble when it hit.

Eventually I must have slept because when I opened my eyes the sky outside had started to get dark. The room was still warm though. I had perspiration on my chest and legs and I was still dizzy from the Fountainade. The silhouetted curve of Lol's back was beside me. I couldn't see anything of Valentine, he was obscured behind Lol. I wondered if either of them were awake. I lay listening to the sound of our breaths mingled together into one chant-like hush.

Lol rolled over. He was facing me then and I could just about make out his features in the dark. His eyes were closed.

'Lol...?'

'...Mm?'

'Are you awake?'

'Mmm.'

'Have you slept?'

There was a pause when I thought Lol must definitely be asleep. But then, without opening his eyes, he whispered, '...Haven't been asleep...I've been saving myself...Waiting for you to wake up.'

'Lol?...Did you ever think...think you ought to be on the pills? Maybe we both should?'

His eyes were open now, his voice low. 'I don't know how come they never put *you* on them.' He was grinning, not serious at all.

'Yes, but– ?'

'I think you should be drugged to the eyeballs.'

'But don't you ever wonder if they'd have given you pills if they'd known? If you'd been registered?'

'Who knows? Probably. They give out pills for all sorts. Don't worry, Neeve...It's important to do these things. You can't live a half-life. It's too heart-breaking. I won't let you.'

I breathed in and then slowly out again, trying to let go of the fear I was holding.

He said, 'You think I'm bad but I'm not...You're too ashamed of things that ought to make you glad. Both of you...I can't bear it.'

Valentine shifted in the bed.

'Is he still asleep?'

'I don't know.' Lol said. 'Want me to find out?'

'No.'

It was too late; Lol had reached over and nudged Valentine. Valentine jerked awake. Drowsily he came round and raised himself up on one elbow.

Lol moved to lie on his back so that he could see us both.

'It must be my turn...' he said, only half-joking.

We stared at him, stock still, not knowing what to do.

'I'm that appealing?' he whispered.

Lol stroked his hand along my leg and then slid himself closer toward me. Valentine was watching us. The situation was bizarre. Somehow Lol managed to position himself half under me. I felt huge and wanted to move out of the way, but Lol didn't hesitate. It shocked me how at ease he seemed. He acted as though what was happening was the most natural thing in the world. I, however, may as well have been a beginner like Valentine. I felt strange about the femaleness of my body. In comparison to the sleek bodies of the men, I felt conscious of my rounded shape.

I thought I knew what to expect. I'd had experiences in the Sixth Compound. Patrollers on the night shifts came into the booths of the inhabitants. They could make you wish you were locked up safe in the containment cavities for weeks on end. A few times I'd had relations with Compound residents; hurried, emotionless encounters that dispelled one type of loneliness only to bring on another. It made you wonder why you did it. But anyway, those experiences were nothing compared to what happened with Lol.

Lol was affectionate and definite. Maybe the confidence he had gradually began to infect me too; I was able to let go of some of my embarrassment. Scarcely-formed sentences appeared in my head: '*So this is how it...feels to be kissed...held...fondled.*'

And then it wasn't just Lol, it was Valentine too.

Valentine was moving shyly nearer. He reached over to us. One tentative touch each. I watched, silent, as a more definite embrace was given to Lol. A hand moved to my face then, and there it was:

not a kiss like at our wedding, not a kiss for show, a different sort of kiss. I felt a fraction of Valentine's grace conferred into my awkward body and the looming danger I'd sensed seemed to slink back, away into the dark.

Chapter 11

My forehead, my back, my palms were sweaty – just from the effort of making it home with the pills. I came through the ground floor entrance of Canal Bank Court and a man in uniform was standing there waiting.

'I need to check your shoulder bag, Miss. New regulations.'

The man took my bag and I stood as he rummaged inside it, searching amongst my things. I was squeezing my fingers into fists and pushing them into my thighs. The man's eyebrows rose when he caught sight of the pills. He lifted the jar to more clearly see the label and then coughed, embarrassed, and put it back. He searched awkwardly for a few seconds more before handing back the bag.

I made my way away from him, towards the stairs. I was weak and needed to sit but by then I was desperate to be in my own space. I went slowly up and didn't stop until I reached the flat.

Inside it was strange. I was alone in the kitchen but I was alone in a place where too much had happened. I leaned over the sink and ran cold water from the tap. I splashed myself with it, letting my shirt and jumper get soaked. I felt a little better for it. Dr Merlevede's orders were going through my head…the first thing you do upon reaching home…I scrambled for the jar of pills in my bag. I looked at the name printed on the label, N. Glynnan.

I managed to open the lid but it was too dark inside to see. I tipped the jar and four pills fell into my hand. They were tiny, triangular, greyish-purple in colour. Not like Valentine's. I picked one. It looked little and lethal between my fingertips. I put it on my tongue and closed my mouth around it. It felt hard and foreign and it tasted bitter. I walked to the washroom.

I stood in front of the washroom mirror and pushed my tongue out at myself. The pill was stuck in the middle of it by my saliva. The pill had turned white, the purple colouring worn off, smeared over my tongue. I closed my mouth. My body was cold now from the wetness of my clothes. I could see my reflection shivering in front of me. I was about to tip my head back and swallow the pill when I heard a voice in my head:

Not yet.

I leaned forward and felt the pill drop to the front of my mouth, just

behind my teeth. I opened my jaw and the pill fell into the sink. I turned
on the tap and water carried it away, out of sight.

I woke up in an empty bed. Valentine was no longer in the room.
He must have left much earlier, in the small hours of the morning,
escaping to the privacy of his room. It seemed as though the
bottom, the top, the sides of my life, had been blown apart and
away. I lay under the covers, too stunned at myself, too shocked by
what had gone on, to be able to move.

Lol, however, was triumphant. I could hear him in the kitchen,
singing in a loud and joyful voice. I suppose it was hard for him,
being with us in the flat; he couldn't bear to see us so alarmed. In
the end, when he realised he couldn't lift our mood, he went out so
that he could be jubilant without us there to dampen his spirits.

I stayed in my room for almost the entire Sunday, unable to face
Valentine. I tried hard to make myself feel normal again but I was
petrified of going outside. By the time evening came, I realised I'd
have to leave the flat. Otherwise it would be impossible to leave for
the Unit the following morning.

I went up the street to the late shop as a way of trying to
overcome my anxiety but I was sick with nerves. It was as though
everything was watching me – not just the people I passed, but
inanimate things as well – traffic, buildings, lamp-posts. I felt that
the whole City was alert to my movements, acutely aware of what
had gone on.

Lol came home very late that evening.

Valentine had waited for hours that day to sneak from his room
for food. But Lol came back in while he was at it. I heard the front
door and then his voice briefly. I went through to them. There they
were, like two vehicles crashed together in the kitchen.

Valentine was adamant that he wanted his medicine back. You
could see it in the clenched set of his jaw.

'Give me the pills.' Beneath his darkened glasses, his face looked
distorted, almost twisted in on itself.

Lol unzipped his holdall. Dozens of medicine bottles were
inside. I think all along Lol had been hoping that somehow
Valentine would choose not to go back to his pills.

But Valentine wasted no time. He took the whole holdall, along with a glass of water, into his room. I wondered how he did it; I wondered if he had to spend ages trying to psyche himself up to taking a pill. I imagined him sitting on the bed with a tablet in his hand, thinking everything through before he could bring it to his mouth. Maybe not. Maybe he downed several right away.

Monday morning came and we had to face the world again. Valentine and I had to return to work.

Lol helped me to get Valentine moderately prepared for the Unit.

As I was easing Valentine into his coat, Lol asked, 'You *are* glad you stopped taking the pills, aren't you? It was only a short time, Val, not even a week.'

It took Valentine a long time to respond. 'I don't know…,' I thought that was his answer but then, '…who I am.'

'You're the same person as before.' I said. 'You're taking your medicine again and now everything will be just like it was.'

Valentine had his hand over his face. His body was rocking without him seeming to realise. From under his fingers, he let out a sob, '*How can it?*'

Valentine wore his darkened glasses for the walk over to the Unit. The fresh air seemed to compose him a little. From a short distance away you couldn't really tell that he wasn't fit to be out. It was only up close when you could hear and see his jaw jittering constantly, that you knew something was wrong.

That day we sat in front of our screens and performed our tasks as best we could, but our minds were scrambled. Mistakes must have been made. Maybe to the people at the Unit, we were just as we always were – just as peculiar perhaps. But we weren't right. I didn't know how to feel. I didn't know *what* I felt. Part of me was furious with Lol for what he'd done. Another part of me, a quieter, lesser part maybe, was grateful beyond measure.

And going back to the pills wasn't a simple matter. Valentine had been desperate to go back to them but he couldn't do so without a sense of loss. He'd caught a glimpse of another self; a man who slept and dreamt, who'd experienced things. Now he had to be rid of that person. He had to stuff him away. Afterwards, always, he'd know there was something extraordinary locked up. He had an idea now of what he was giving up.

A letter arrived from Dean, Mauran's husband.

Some time ago, Valentine had written to his sister to thank her for her wedding gift and Mauran had replied saying that the decorating was taking longer than she'd thought and it didn't look as though they'd be able to come to visit for a while. In the meantime, she promised to keep in touch by post.

Then this new letter came. Valentine opened it immediately. I stood beside him in the kitchen, reading it over his arm.

Valentine,

As you know, for some time, it's been an intention of mine and my wife's to begin a family. Gladly now I am writing to inform you that Mauran is with child, this being the fifth week of her pregnancy. I hope that you will respect our wishes therefore, and cease contact with us while Mauran is pregnant. I'm sure you'd agree that it is unwise to subject her to situations of a potentially stressful nature. I urge you to respect our wishes and make no attempts at contact over the forthcoming months.

Furthermore, once the baby is born, as I'm sure you'll appreciate, it will be necessary to restrict your contact with the child. Although, regrettably, we can never be entirely sure that your condition will not be passed on to our offspring, we must not allow inappropriate environmental influences to over-shadow the child's upbringing.

I'd be grateful for your co-operation in these matters.

Regards,

Dean Pettenger.

Valentine let the letter fall from his fingers. It landed on the table, all stiffness and creases, refusing to lie flat.

I put my hand on Valentine's back. His whole body was quietly quaking. I stroked his shirt and he turned towards me. He gave way, letting himself collapse onto my shoulder.

So many of the placards around the City were about family life. They affirmed its many benefits. Slogans warned also of the pitfalls of other ways of living. Even if, like Valentine, there was only a slim chance of you ever starting a family, it didn't stop you longing. It was hard-wired into us; *Family Life.*

What's more, Valentine was the type of person for whom a family would have meant everything, had things been different. Coming on the back of the pill experiment, Valentine's loss of contact with his sister, and her future child, hit him hard.

Despite my and Lol's efforts to cheer and distract him, Valentine lost interest in things. He started to go off his food, even the meals that had been cooked by Lol. He mostly only managed soup; food he didn't have to chew or make an effort to swallow. As he grieved his latest hurt, the previous losses and troubles he'd endured seemed to flood back into him.

After the pill experiment, Valentine felt like a criminal. I don't think he even thought about contesting Dean's demand. He believed himself to be utterly wrong, and therefore beyond claim over anybody.

Even Lol made no mention of confronting Dean. I suppose he figured that with Valentine's brother-in-law being a member of the Guarda, things could get so much worse if we tried to protest.

'Have either of you been to see the City Museum? The one in the Imperial Sector?'

'I haven't…and Valentine's never spoken about it.'

'Maybe we should try that on Saturday. A day out. A bit of a diversion. Valentine could lose himself in the crowds. Feel more anonymous.'

I didn't know what to do for the best. I was running out of ways of helping Valentine, ways to preoccupy him.

'We can read the Museum's version of things and then I could tell you what really happened. It's quite funny, the history they've invented. It'd make you laugh.'

I was uneasy about the idea but I let Lol persuade me. He seemed convinced the day out would lift our spirits.

We woke up early to take the trains to the Imperial Sector. It was said that the Imperial Sector was the oldest part of the City – the very centre of it. The buildings in that region were large and very grand; governing offices of one sort or another. Lol claimed that if a person walked far enough in a straight line from the Imperial Sector, they'd eventually walk right out of the City.

The last time I'd been to the Imperial Sector was with my mother when I was a child. She'd taken me to see my father's name written on the Record of Vanishments in the main square. I didn't understand what had happened to him, or maybe I wouldn't believe her. Either way, she'd taken me there to show me his name and I'd screamed all the way home on the trains. She'd had to put a handkerchief in my mouth to quieten the noise. My father's name wouldn't be there now. It'd be long gone. Now there'd be a whole list of new ones.

It was busy on the trains. There wasn't room for us to sit together. I was glad of it. It was weird being the three of us out in public. When it was just me and Valentine going back and forth to work, I could try to convince myself that we were still innocent. But with Lol beside us, there was no way that I could.

I looked over at Valentine, to where he was sitting in the carriage. He seemed washed out, like it was taking all his strength just to be there. He'd only agreed to come with us because now he was terrified of being alone in the flat.

We alighted from the train and came up from the tunnels into a far corner of the main square. As we came up into the sunlight, I felt as though the day had something bad in it; like the day was a trap and it was waiting for us to step inside. I wanted to turn around and go back down.

'Lol, maybe we shouldn't do this.'

'It's just a Museum, Neeve. It's not like we're going to visit the Guarda Confines.'

He was right. I told myself the feeling was due to upsetting memories. *The past's clouding things. It hasn't anything to do with today.*

It was mid-morning. Sunlight fell into the square, unobstructed. In the centre was a monument. Statues of five famous men stood on top of towering pillars; I didn't know their names or what they'd done, but they must've been people who'd achieved great things for the City. At the base of the pillars, there was the Record of Vanishments, and also the names of other lesser offenders. The tablets of listed criminals had been placed on the ground so that they'd be looked down upon by the statued leaders, and also so members of the public could walk around the monument and tread on the names of the guilty. If people wanted, they could spit. The lists had been carved into blocks of powdery rock so that they could be more easily crushed. That's how it was when I was there with my mother. I'd been told they still did it that way but I wasn't going to go near the monument to find out.

'The Museum's that way.' Lol was pointing over to the other side of the square.

'Can we walk around the edges in the shade? The sunlight's making me dizzy,' I said.

'Okay then.' Even Lol seemed quieter than usual.

We moved, three small figures in a big world, awed by the proportions of the place. As a child, the main square had seemed too huge to comprehend; the largest expanse of open ground I'd ever seen. I expected my eyes to see it differently now, but even as grown adult, it seemed vast.

'There's something going on over there. Looks like a rally.'

I followed Lol's eyes. Far over on one side of the square a covered stage had been set up with rows of chairs in front. People were beginning to assemble and take up places in the audience. They looked small from where we stood.

We walked in the shade of the buildings. I took Valentine's arm. His body was already noticeably thinner from not eating properly. Also, now that he was back on the pills, he wasn't sleeping again. Before the experiment, Valentine's lack of sleep had never tired him. Now he seemed exhausted.

Lol was staring over at the crowds gathering in front of the stage.

'Have you seen rallies here before?' I asked.

'Yes, frightening. Look, they're bringing in Compound inhabitants to make up the numbers.'

Willa-Rix had told me about that. She said that at the Sixth Compound they made the C-wingers go because they were the political dissenters. She said it was done to humiliate the inhabitants.

We stopped and watched as people from one of the Compounds, linked together by wires binding their hands, were herded by Patrollers out of two large vehicles and made to stand in rows behind the seated audience.

'They put the Compound people at the back so that if somebody shouts obscenities towards the stage, they won't be heard.' Lol explained. 'And the trouble-maker's dealt with without disturbing the seated audience in front. Can we go nearer and see?'

'…Alright.'

I trailed behind him with Valentine.

We came to a stop a little way off from where the Compound inhabitants had been made to stand. The rows of seats were filling up. Lol's eyes were fixed on the stage where important-seeming people were assuming their positions. Up there the seating had been arranged in such a way as to suggest rank and status; the chairs were tiered, each row slightly above the one in front. Above the stage was a big banner that ran from one side of the construction to the other – 'Stand In The Face Of Enmity. Righteousness Is Ours.'

'What's *enmity?*' I asked Lol.

'Hatred, opposition, that sort of thing.'

Valentine and I were reluctant bystanders. We were waiting for Lol to finish with the rally so that we could move on. The heavy presence of the Patrollers and Guarda was making me anxious. I couldn't help staring at the Compound inhabitants. I kept thinking, *Not so long ago that was Valentine and me.*

I saw someone I recognised. For a moment the unfamiliar surroundings confused me and I wasn't sure. Then I realised; I was looking at the back of Willa-Rix's head. I could see her tightly curling auburn hair, the familiar angle of her neck and her bony shoulders. She was standing in the audience at the end of a row, about ten or so rows in front of us.

'There's Willa.'

Lol looked at me quizzically.

'My friend from the Compound. The one who got us passes to the Realm.'

'Really? I'd like to meet her. Introduce me, will you?'

I hesitated. I looked around to see if there were any Guarda or Compound Patrollers nearby. There were, but none of them were paying attention to us. They were busy monitoring the crowd.

'Okay…but we'll have to be really careful.'

He nodded.

We inched down the rows of the audience towards Willa. We stopped a couple of metres to the side of her.

Lol coughed and Willa-Rix turned her head. She saw us, smiled and turned back to face the stage where sound-equipment was being set up.

We moved nearer.

'So you've come for a fun day out too?' Willa said.

'We've come to see the Museum. We didn't know about this rally,' I replied.

'The Museum?'

I wanted to be quick, to get the introductions over and done with.

'Yes. Willa, this is Lol. He's from the…club. Lol, this is Willa-Rix.'

'How do?' She nodded her head towards him and again turned to face the front.

Lol said, 'Nice to meet you.'

'So you're getting in on things at last?' This was aimed at me.

I was about to deny it but she was right.

'You've got a Circle?' Lol whispered.

'Yes, indeed. And we're coming along with it. Some of the things that have happened…' Willa indicated the woman standing next to her. 'This is Verna. She's been doing incredible things. She's our champion.'

The woman turned to us and smiled. She had a striking face. Her features were very even. They looked as though they'd been smoothed off; as though something had been to work on them, eroding anything that didn't fit there. And her hair and skin were the same sandy colour as her eyes. Nothing jarring stood out against the even ground of her face.

'Verna's seen the edge of the City. Imagine that.'

'The *edge*?'

'I know, girlie, but Verna saw it.'

'You're sure?' I said.

'Yeah. The Circle pulled Verna clean out of her skin. Out and out until she'd reached the edge of the City.'

Verna nodded.

'I once heard another group of Circle-users say something similar,' said Lol. 'They claimed that they'd flown over the City with their minds.'

'What was there, though? I mean at the edge?' I asked.

'A wall. A wall higher than anything in the world, swarming with Guarda at the foot of it. And then the true sea. That's what's limitless, Neeve; not the City but the sea.'

'Yes,' said Verna. '…Beautiful.'

Several Guarda were coming around the edge of the audience. They were moving up our side of the crowd. I looked at Willa and Verna. There were suddenly dozens of things in my head that I wanted to ask. Willa looked at me warningly. We had to stop.

Quickly, before we separated, Willa, staring ahead, whispered, 'When I can get out of the Compound, I'll come to the flat and tell you more. I'm on Barricade Time. They aren't letting me out right now, but I'll try and come soon.'

'Okay…'

We moved off, Lol and Valentine and I, further back down the rows before the Guarda got near. We walked away and merged with other people who'd gathered to stand and observe the rally. I watched as two of the Guarda walked to the spot where we'd talked with Willa-Rix and Verna. They seemed to be addressing Willa with questions – I saw the fervent nods and shakes of her head. Then the Guarda applied a shock to her shoulder and moved away, in the direction of the rest of the group. Willa couldn't even nurse her arm; her hands were held together by wire.

'I told you the Circle was amazing,' Lol said into my ear.

'Yes…'

A man was on stage tapping a microphone with his hand. The little movement was amplified around the square. The sound boomed and echoed against the buildings.

I wanted to believe what Willa had said: Verna had seen a wall at the City's edge and then the true sea.

'Can we stay for a few minutes? I just need to get the gist of what the rally's about,' Lol said. 'We can go to the Museum straight after.'

But Valentine looked like he badly needed to sit and rest. We left Lol watching the stage and made our way further back to some wide steps that surrounded a smaller stone memorial. Some people were already gathered there to view the proceedings.

We sat down amongst the crowd. I wasn't really paying attention; I was busy thinking about what Verna and Willa had said about the edge of the City. What if the City really did have an end? What if it really did stop somewhere? I tried to imagine the true sea; the flat line of the horizon and the plane of water that ran from there. Nothing else. No buildings or people. Kilometres of nothing but air and water. The wind carrying every bad sound away. The true sea; I wanted to believe in it.

I couldn't see Valentine from where I was positioned, a few steps below him. I only knew there was trouble when I saw Lol coming towards us. At first he was walking but then he broke into a run. He flew past me, up the steps and plunged himself into the mass of bodies swarming around Valentine.

Someone shouted, *'Eye Offence'* and what before had been just a commotion, seemed to turn, in an instant, to chaos.

I stood uselessly watching. Lol seemed unstoppable. He dragged Valentine out of the frenzy and away.

Within seconds, Guarda were at the memorial. People surged towards them, shouting out their accounts of the disturbance.

When I looked about again for Lol and Valentine, I couldn't see them. I thought, *He must have got so tired that he forgot the ruling.* Valentine must have shut his eyes as he sat there, too exhausted to keep them open. I hurried away, before anyone could accuse me too.

I rode around the tunnel-trains for a long time. I used all the money I had with me, money that I'd intended to spend at the Museum, on travel tickets. I didn't want to go home to the flat. I was dreading finding Lol and Valentine weren't there. It seemed, from the accounts of people in the crowd, that the two of them had run down into the tunnels but I hadn't been able to find them below ground. I hoped it meant that they'd managed to escape the Guarda. I'd seen Guarda in the station, wandering the platforms, seeming to conduct a search amongst the waiting travellers, but that wasn't unusual; the Guarda were regularly down in the tunnels.

I sat in various seats on various trains, vacantly, restlessly travelling, staring numbly out at the black tunnels, avoiding my own eyes reflected in the windows. Whenever thoughts of Lol and Valentine became too fretful and intense, I'd get off at the next station and find another train, distracting myself that way. I lost track, several times, of whereabouts I was and then I had to scramble to make sense of the coloured lines on the tunnel plan above my head. To some extent, I was eased by the continual movement of the carriages. The speed of the trains kept agitation from completely overcoming me.

Evening came and I had to return home. I walked slowly, stalling for time, as I made my way along the street and then up the flights of stairs of Canal Bank Court. My hand shook as I put the key in the door. I paused before turning it, listening for traces of Lol or Valentine. Or for the presence of other voices; voices I didn't recognise.

I turned the key and pushed open the door. I stepped into the kitchen and nearly jumped out of my skin. Lol was stood in front of me.

He put his finger to his mouth, advising me not to speak. He whispered, 'Valentine's in bed...He's taken the Circle to help him rest.'

Before Lol had finished his sentence I'd already begun to cry. It was a noiseless sort of weeping, the sort that comes when you haven't the strength left for anything else. Lol took me into the big bedroom. He put his arms around me and I cried into his clothes.

'I thought they'd got you...' I sounded feeble and childish.

'No...We managed to lose them in the tunnels. The platforms were busy. We were lucky.'

I nodded my head against Lol's body, letting the weight of it be supported by his chest.

'I put Valentine to bed as soon as we got back. He'll be okay.'

Valentine didn't emerge from the small room that evening and Lol and I were quiet. We didn't have the energy for a proper conversation. For supper we had the uneaten soup that was meant for Valentine, and then went to bed a couple of hours earlier than usual because it was too exhausting trying to stay awake.

I didn't sleep deeply that night. I had fitful dreams in which everything was jumbled and nothing made sense. Then, at some point during that long drawn out night, I sensed Lol awake beside me and that woke me too.

I didn't get up, not straight away. For some reason, I lay motionless, pretending to sleep, watching Lol as he lay quietly next to me in the bed. Eventually, Lol rose and went to sit on a chair over by the window. I watched him as he smoked a cigarette, dragging hard on it as he inhaled. His face looked troubled. He seemed upset. When he started on his second cigarette, I pretended to wake up. I lifted myself from the bed.

'What's the matter? Why are you up?'

'I had a dream. It woke me, that's all. It's alright. I'm coming back to bed now,' he said. 'I'm just going to finish this cigarette.'

But he didn't come back. He left the room.

I waited for a few minutes, then I followed him out. Lol was standing in the kitchen. He still looked distressed. I got him to come back with me, into the warmth of the bedroom.

'What was your dream? It must've been horrible to upset you this much.'

'I don't want to tell you.'

'No, not if talking about it'll make you upset again.'

'It's not that. It's because it's so bad. It'd upset you as well.'

'I'll be alright. It's just a dream. You can tell me if you want.'

'It was awful, Neeve. You'd hate me if I told you.'

'Don't be silly. I *couldn't* hate you. Maybe you'll feel better for getting the dream off your chest.'

He was quiet for a long time.

Then he said, 'I hit Valentine.'

I might even have flinched when he said it.

He looked at me. 'I bloodied his face up.' The fingers of his left hand involuntarily flicked as though it was re-living the moment in the dream.

'…His face was so bad and bloody, that perfect face of his…He was crying, begging me to stop but I kept hitting him.'

I stared at Lol, stunned by what he was telling me.

'We were in the street…People were watching.'

He stopped then, seeming to wait for me to comment. I tried to think of something to say.

'Maybe you're angry about yesterday and so it came out in your dream…because you might feel angry after what happened even though it's not Valentine's fault and…' I was talking rubbish, speaking off the top of my head.

He nodded, appearing to acknowledge what I'd said but I could tell by his face that he wasn't really listening. He bit his lip. His agitation was almost making his mouth into a leer.

'And then I – I started on you…I ripped your shirt. Your lip got cut…I wanted you to fight back. I was yelling at you to fight back but you wouldn't. I woke up dreaming I was hitting you. I woke up and there you were, in bed, asleep. You looked so…It was like my dream hadn't finished. I couldn't bear it.'

I interrupted, 'Looked so what?'

'Exposed...You looked so exposed. I hated it. It was like my dream hadn't finished. I wanted to shake you and get you to wake up. And then lying in the dark, I started feeling it myself. Like I was the same as you and Valentine. It scared the life out of me.'

'But everybody feels like that. They especially would after what happened at the rally. The dream doesn't mean anything... Everyone feels like that sometimes.'

He turned to look at me. 'No, they don't, Neeve. I don't know anybody else like that. Only you and Valentine.'

It felt as though he really had hit me in the stomach.

In the firmest voice I could manage, I said, 'I think we should go back to sleep now. We need to *rest*.'

I couldn't hear any more from him that night.

Lol went out early the next morning to fetch provisions for Sunday lunch. He said that we weren't eating properly, just having soup. He said we'd all feel better if we ate a decent meal. He made no mention of what had gone on in the night-time, no mention of his bad dream.

Valentine stayed in his room for most of the morning and so I went out to see if I could find some darkened glasses to replace the pair he'd lost. I trawled through the different stores in our area but couldn't find anywhere that stocked them. Only corrective-vision glasses were available. The following morning, Valentine would be forced to go to the Unit without the glasses. He'd hate it, it wouldn't do him any good but I had to stop searching and go back to the flat. Being left alone in there would only make him more anxious.

I went home and waited for Valentine to emerge. Sometime around mid-afternoon, I heard him go into the kitchen for some water. I went through to see if he was alright. I got a shock when I saw him. The colour in his face had all drained away. He was a sort of pale grey. And his eyes had their terrible haunted look. They seemed to flicker, unable to keep steady even as he looked at me. I felt frightened. I was reminded of what Lol had told us about people purposefully taking their own lives.

I spoke useless words to fill a gaping space, 'Lol's gone to buy lunch...He wanted to know what your favourite food was.'

Valentine didn't respond in any way.

In my head an image replayed itself: the empty frames of the darkened glasses being kicked away from him, lost amongst the feet of the crowd.

'...I told him mango.'

Valentine had only eaten mango a few times in his life. It was expensive. You could buy it in the markets in dried, orange strips.

'That's your favourite, isn't it?'

Valentine nodded but I got the sense that he'd have nodded whatever I'd said; my words weren't registering. He took his water and went back to his room.

I was ill at ease and restless. I went and lay down on the bed in the big room but it was no good. I couldn't stay put. I left the room and went out the front door. I walked down to the communal room. The corridor smelled of Sunday meals being cooked in the flats.

The communal room was empty apart from an elderly man who was asleep in a chair. Everyone was indoors having dinner. A broadcast was being transmitted on the screen. I sat a few rows back from the man and tried to watch.

The programme showed a family in their home. The movements of their lips and the words being said weren't in time with one another; a *spoken-over* showing, where parts of the dialogue had been Streamlined. It wasn't even a good one; the words the characters were saying contradicted the expressions on their faces.

I tried to watch but I was too agitated to settle. I got up and went to the window.

Down on the street, a man was walking along the pavement. In the flats opposite I could see a woman putting water on her window-box of dried-up plants. A dog was running across the road.

Tick, tick, tick.

Time was passing, bringing the future closer with each second. How did a person ready themselves?

I looked down at my arms resting on the windowsill. By my elbow was a short plastic pen that somebody had left behind. I picked it up and ran the nib against the tip of my finger. There was no ink in it. I looked back at the man dozing in front of the screen. He was fast asleep.

I slid myself along to the end of the windowsill and, behind the curtain, I started to write on to the wooden surface. I wrote with the pen's non-existent ink. I practised my name: Neeve. The pen left no trace of the letters.

I wrote my name again. NEEVE. This time I pressed harder and the pen nib carved slight indentations in the wood. I wrote my name a third time, going over the letters I'd just done, pushing down with force. NEEVE. Much clearer now. I looked at it. It was good to see the word. Proof of me having been there. I wasn't even worried that the Caretaker might find it.

Lol came back in with bags of shopping. He'd bought Valentine some mango along with several other items to cook for us. The mango that he'd bought was *fresh* – the type of food only he knew how to find.

Lol spent the afternoon preparing a meal and when it was ready, he called us in to eat. Part of the reason for his extravagant cooking had been to coax Valentine from his room. Lol wanted us to share a meal together and he refused to let Valentine eat alone. It wasn't easy getting Valentine to come out though. He only joined us after much cajoling and bothering on Lol's part. Valentine sat on the bed and mechanically ate his meal. I don't think he was even able to relish the experience of eating fresh mango.

Lol was in the kitchen between courses, putting the finishing touches to the next dish.

Valentine said, 'I need to get to the club. Neeve, ask Lol to take me to the club. I can hide there. Tell Lol to take me tonight.'

He was convinced that the Guarda would be arriving imminently to convey him to the Confines.

When I asked Lol about taking Valentine to the Realm, he shook his head.

'I'll gladly take him to see somebody but it'll cause him to suffer. The Movement can offer a person protection; it can take people in and give them a new identity in a different part of the City. But to do that Valentine would have to leave his whole life behind – you, this flat, his family, his job. He couldn't come back again. As soon as he didn't turn up for work, as soon as he was absent from the flat, they'd come looking for him.'

'Couldn't I go with him?'

'Neeve, it's not like accompanying someone to the dentist when they're frightened. You'd both have to be *seriously* in trouble before you thought of giving your lives up like that. It's a very big deal. Only people who've committed serious offences, people who're being hunted down, take that route. It's forced upon them. They don't *choose* it. Valentine's got nothing to worry about. The Guarda aren't after him for Eye Offences. They didn't get near us yesterday. People are so petrified of them. They think the Guarda can work miracles. Honestly, tell Valentine not to fret.'

I didn't want Valentine to go and I wasn't ready for us to give up the lives we'd built. I wasn't ready for things to change. I went and relayed to him what Lol had said, that Lol believed his leaving would be a mistake.

That night Lol stayed up late on his own in the kitchen. By the sounds of it he got out one of the bottles of Fountainade that he'd brought to give the Caretaker. I lay in bed, listening to him steadily drinking, mumbling old songs, singing the parts he could remember the words to.

At the Unit the next day, Valentine allowed me to care for him. He had no choice. He couldn't properly function without my help. I brought him his meal tray in the noontime break and held his hand under the table in the refectory as he sat, not eating, shielding his face with his free hand, trying to get by without the glasses. Nowhere felt safe to him now: not the Unit; not the flat. Only in the privacy of his bedroom using the Circle and drinking the Fountainade that Lol had given him, could he feel slightly freer of things.

While we were at work, Lol went out looking for a place that sold darkened glasses. Like me, he came back empty-handed.

'It's as though he owned the only pair in the City,' Lol said.

Lol began to talk quite fanatically about a fairground he'd seen one day while he was out. The way he spoke to me about it was odd. He seemed fixated. He was almost ranting.

'It's not far. It's pitched near to where the old botanicals used to be on Michael Row, that patch of land. I could take us there tonight.'

'I can't think where you mean.' Lol knew our region of the City better than we did now.

'You know, the old gardens?'

'No.'

'Never mind. I saw it. It's big. Loads of rides. We need to get out of this flat, Neeve. We need to do something *enjoyable* for a change. That's what Valentine needs. He needs to get things in perspective. We'll go there, get on some fast rides. They'll spin Valentine round till he's too dizzy to remember his own name, let alone what half his troubles are.'

'Lol, we tried that two weeks ago with the Museum and just look what happened.'

'We never even got to the Museum. That's why it didn't work. I mean it about the fair, Neeve. It's something *physical* for us. Air and noise and speed. It gets you out of yourself. And the food they sell is great. Smells wafting round the place. Valentine'll be so hungry he'll want to eat the stall where they make it.'

But Lol's excitement didn't seem fuelled by his usual delight in things. Something else was driving him.

'I don't think Valentine'll agree to it.'

'No?' Beneath his enthusiasm Lol seemed angry. Agitation was straining his face. 'Well, we can't have him fucking festering in his room forever.'

He didn't even apologise for cursing.

'Please, Lol, don't be cross…I'll go and speak to him. See what he says.'

I went and knocked on Valentine's bedroom door.

Valentine didn't want to go to the fair. Of course he didn't. He didn't need to tell me why. I knew he didn't want any part in another trip arranged by Lol. He was too afraid to go out and he was too afraid to be left indoors on his own.

'Lol will understand that you don't want to go.'

'Don't tell him I don't want to go.'

'No…I'll say that we're staying in because we've had long days at work.'

Valentine remained in his room while I let Lol know that we weren't going to the fair.

Lol rolled his eyes. 'This is Valentine's doing, isn't it?'

'Lol, please…' I lowered my voice to a whisper, 'He just needs more time. He needs time to feel alright again. He doesn't have his glasses any more, remember?'

'Okay, we'll go without him.'

'But he's frightened of being alone. One of us should stay with him. Why don't you go on your own?'

Lol didn't reply. He strode into the kitchen, got our coats from the back of the door and went into Valentine's room. 'Put this on, Valentine. We're going out.' He said it like an order, like he wouldn't take no for an answer.

Valentine was too weakened to even think of disobeying. After a few seconds of shocked silence, he did what he was told. Once Lol saw that Valentine was complying, he said more gently, 'You can't stay in here indefinitely, Val. There's just no good reason for you to hide like this. You need a *life*.'

I wondered what would have happened if Valentine had refused, if Lol would have dragged him from the flat.

Chapter 12

The room was in a state. Our belongings were strewn across the floor. There was the hole where the floorboards had been pulled up. I didn't notice it at first. It was only as time passed, as daylight crept back in, that I saw it all. I looked over at the place where Valentine and I had stood, the Guarda beside us. It was stupid but I almost wanted to go and be there again, the last place we were.

On the floor, where we'd stood, I saw something. It looked like paper. A screwed-up ball of paper. I hauled myself out of bed and went over to it. It was lying there like it was waiting for me. The ball was very tightly crushed, as if it couldn't be made any smaller. Before I'd even unravelled it, I knew what it was.

I took it to the bed and unpicked it, smoothed its creases out with my hand. Valentine's Circle; the one he'd clung to the previous night. It seemed like a gift he'd left purposefully for me; a kindness to help me escape.

I just have to look at the Circle and then nothing will matter.

I pinned it to the wall above the bed.

It was difficult at first. I couldn't even keep my eyes on it. My mind was skittering about and I wasn't able to follow the lines across the paper. I had to keep bringing my eyes back to it. But gradually the pattern steadied me, my mind slowed enough to try. The lines started to move.

There was a noise. One, two, three, it went. One, two, three. The noise was pulling me out of the sway of the Circle. In an un-guessable amount of time I was back in the room.

The front door. Someone was knocking. They're back.

Panic flooded my body but in a habitual way as if that was how my body would always react now; its one stock answer to everything.

The knocking came again. One, two, three...

It was a hesitant knock. Not the knock of the Guarda.

I heard a voice. Someone was calling through the door. I didn't want to see anyone. I didn't want to see anyone ever again.

'Mrs Frankland?'

I didn't recognise it.

'Mrs Frankland, it's the Caretaker.'

It wasn't the Caretaker's voice. This voice was lower, softer.

'Could you open the door?'

There was something gentle about the voice to which, in my state, I couldn't help but respond.

My face was wet, maybe I'd been crying. I wiped my face on the blanket and got out of bed. I walked to the kitchen and stood behind the door.

'Mrs Frankland?'

I called through the wood, 'Yes?'

'You're expected at work. A representative has just contacted me from your Unit. He said that you hadn't come in this morning and that you're expected.'

Work…I'd forgotten all about it. It was an effort to think back. A few days ago I'd been living a relatively ordinary life.

I opened the door.

A man in the Caretaker's uniform stood in the corridor.

He said, 'You're wanted at work, Miss.'

I was confused. 'Where's the Caretaker?'

'He was dismissed yesterday. I'm the new Caretaker. Temporarily.'

'Why was he dismissed?'

'I believe for possession. And falling prey…' Then his voice went quieter, 'to inducements. I believe he's been taken for questioning.'

The man looked embarrassed as he said it. I wondered what he knew of my situation, of Lol and Valentine. I could feel the effects of the Circle leaving me rapidly. It was difficult to look him in the face.

'Mrs Frankland? Remember your work. You're to be there within the hour. The man said to inform you that you won't be penalised for the time you've missed, but you must go to work.' Whatever he knew about me, he was affording me some dignity.

I stammered a 'thank you'. The man nodded and went away.

I returned to the bedroom and sat on my bed. A voice in my head said, Get yourself ready. Find your clothes…

The man who'd followed us into the dark became visible again in the glow of the fair-lights behind the Tower. He reappeared, shaking his head. Another man, the one with Lol's coat, began gesturing with it, waving it vehemently as he spoke. The group stood, consulting with each other for a while, gazing at the wasteland until, eventually, they left to go back to the main drag of the fair.

We sat in silence, scarcely able to breathe, staring at the mass of lights, letting the sounds of the rides crash over us. I couldn't see Lol well, but I could smell him, smell the mud. Over the top of the noise, I realised he was shivering.

'Are you alright? Lol?'

'...Um?'

'Are you hurt?'

He coughed, trying to find his voice. 'My hip and shoulder a bit. I'm cold.'

Valentine took off his coat and gave it to Lol. He took it and wrapped it around himself. He said, 'I need to move. To keep warm.'

'Let's get back to the flat. Can you walk?'

'Not there. I need tea. I'm freezing.'

'Okay, I'll go and get you something.' I looked around. I was worried about returning to the fair and being recognised by the young man from the Tower.

'No. I need to move. I'll get it.'

'But you're covered in dirt. You'll get stopped.'

He took off Valentine's coat and his own muck-covered jumper. With the side of the jumper that wasn't soiled, he began wiping his hair and face. As far as I could tell in the dark, he was mostly just making it worse, spreading the mud around.

'It's busy in there. No one'll notice.' He sounded irritated. I didn't want to argue with him.

He got up, steadier now. He took a step towards the fair but his hip hurt. He took another and this time kept hold of himself, rubbing the sore spot to ease it.

Before Lol could move off, Valentine said, 'Why did you do it?'

He was braver than I was. I was going to let the event pass.

'Do what?' Lol knew what he meant. He just wanted Valentine to say.

'...Jump off.'

Lol was bent over with his hands on his knees now, trying to take deep breaths. He faced the ground as he spoke. 'I didn't jump off...I fell.'

A pause and then, 'It looked like you...you let yourself fall.'

'Did it? I don't remember it that way. Maybe I'm concussed.' His voice had a mocking edge to it.

Almost inaudibly, Valentine said, 'It wasn't like you.'

Lol pulled himself upright. 'Wasn't it? I thought that's what you liked about me, the both of you.' He said it like a provocation. 'I *do* things while you stand around gawping like a pair of feeble-minded loons.'

'So, then…you *did* jump?' I asked, unsure.

'Oh, *get lost*, Neeve! Both of you can get fucking lost. You're just a pair of institutionalised Compound freaks who can't think for themselves.' He started wandering away. He went limping jerkily on his bad leg, heading for the fair.

He only went a few metres and then he turned. He hadn't finished yet.

'When I met you, I couldn't believe it, I thought you must be Contemplatives only you didn't know it because no-one'd told you. Not just one Contemplative, but two. Two of you. Imagine that? I thought, with a bit of help from the Realm you'd be away. You'd be free. Flying.' His voice was more desperate now. 'What an idiot…' He hit himself hard on the head. 'Look at the pair of you. *Just look at yourselves.*'

He spun away and set off again for the fair. We watched him go, standing there just as Lol had described us – a pair of loons. His words didn't make much sense to us, not then. He walked a few more steps away from us before he stopped and threw Valentine's coat to the ground, leaving it lying in the dirt. We stared after him, watching the wind billowing about inside his thin shirt as he went shivering towards the lights.

We were stupid; we couldn't bear to let him out of our sight. When Lol got uncomfortably distant, we started to follow him, even though he'd been cruel and insulting. Perhaps if we'd let him alone, Lol would eventually have cooled off and come home, but instead we trudged after him.

Maybe not though. That night, it was almost like something in him *wanted* to get caught. It was as though his return to the fairground was a second attempt – the fair-workers hadn't got him for his jump from the Tower and so he'd gone back to give them another chance.

We trailed after Lol, back into the noise and hustle. We could see him ahead of us, bobbing exaggeratedly about in the crowd because of his limping walk. We kept our heads low but our eyes up, watching for trouble. We saw people's faces as Lol passed them; wide-eyed glances as he went by. He seemed not to notice or care. He was heading for the confectionery stall.

We stood some distance from him, hiding behind the Squeeze-Dolls, as he queued to be served. He was lit up by the lines of coloured bulbs decorating the stand. His unkempt state was more marked than I'd realised. His trousers were streaked with mud where he'd wiped them with his jumper. Dark patches remained on his neck and his hair was caked. Mud was visible around his nostrils and at the corners of his mouth and eyes. Wherever a layer of dirt had been wiped away, the mud that remained had dried and cracked giving him the appearance of a much older man. People in the queue kept their distance.

Lol reached the front of the line. The confection-seller seemed to take a slight step backwards when she saw him. She pointed at his face and spoke. It must have been something like, 'What happened to you?'

Lol's reply was very brief. Something like, 'I fell.'

The confection-seller spoke again and Lol touched his face, nodding absently. He gave his order and the woman turned to prepare the food. I watched Lol as he watched the woman. She fetched him a hot drink and something from the grill, wrapped in paper. Lol reached into his pockets, searching about for his money.

Valentine said, 'His wallet, Neeve.'

I still had it after Lol had thrown it from the Tower. I blundered over with the money and hurriedly handed some citizen tokens to the lady. I scarcely acknowledged Lol. I didn't want people to know I was with him. I walked away, back to my spot behind the Squeeze-Dolls where I wouldn't be noticed.

After a few minutes, Lol limped over to where we were hiding. 'What're you doing behind here?'

It was obvious, it would be to any normal person. It was so obvious I couldn't think how to answer him.

He was trying to unwrap the paper from around his food but his hands were shaking and he was holding the hot drink.

I felt nervous addressing him, even just offering him help, 'D'you want me to hold your cup while you eat?'

'Okay.'

He'd bought some pieces of sweet-dipped, grilled pear. Without speaking he turned and offered us a share of it from the opened packet.

'No, thanks,' I said.

Valentine shook his head.

We stood silently as Lol chewed his food.

'Are you warming up?' I asked.

He nodded. His eyes were losing their fierceness. Now they were just turning glassy and dark.

Lol finished eating and I passed him his cup.

As he stood drinking, I said, 'We should probably head off soon.'

All I could think of was getting out of the fair, returning to the flat. Once we were there things could get back to normal.

Lol nodded and downed the rest of his hot tea in a couple of mouthfuls.

'C'mon then,' he said.

Before Valentine or I had the chance to take a step, Lol was off. The way I'd figured it, we'd take a short-cut out of the fairground to avoid being seen but Lol had a different idea. He was walking straight back into the main drag.

We followed him, only now the distance between us was deliberate. We couldn't risk getting close. I wished Lol would hurry but his hip was hurting, slowing him down. I found it hard not to rush, to hang back. In the end though, it made no difference how fast we went because before we'd even got in sight of the exit, Lol had got himself into more trouble.

We saw him up in front, hobbling over to a family as they stood considering a ride. We watched as he approached and then briefly addressed the mother. The woman turned to him. She looked shaken by whatever he'd said. Then Lol dropped to his knees in front of her and grabbed hold of her skirt, clutching the material tightly in his hands. The woman's face dropped in disbelief. She tried to retrieve her skirt from Lol's grasp, not pulling so hard at first until she realised that he wasn't going to let go and then she began yanking at her own clothes.

The woman's husband began gesturing vehemently at the alarming man at his wife's feet. It looked absurd. Two small children were staring, baffled, at their parents and at Lol. They seemed not to be able to tell whether it was just another part of the fairground's standard showy entertainment, or a real and true danger.

Lol and the husband were both vying for the woman's skirt, yelling at each other. The woman was now just trying to keep the garment from being pulled completely off her body but Lol kept a firm grip. He pressed his face into the material. He was half-shouting, half-mumbling something into it, his voice too muffled to hear. The children started to cry.

Lol shouted again, louder this time, 'My wife!...'

Other people, passers-by, had noticed the fuss and were staring too.

'We've never seen this man!' the woman implored, 'Never in our lives!'

'My wife. My wife!' Lol wailed the words at the bewildered woman. He was rubbing the skirt material hard into his face, pushing it into the sockets of his eyes with his fists.

The Guarda were coming. Somehow I knew that they were. I couldn't locate them; but it felt as though they were everywhere at once. There was a roughness in my head, the feeling of running your hand over gritty rock. There was something impersonal to it too. I knew it was them.

'My wife!'

Suddenly, there they were. Two uniformed shapes launched themselves out of nowhere. They made a grab for Lol's arms, one on either side of him. They tried to force him from the woman, but he wouldn't let go. He was ripping her skirt. The Guarda had to prize Lol's fingers from the fabric one by one until his hold had been released.

I took steps backwards without thinking, taking Valentine with me.

Lol was a like a dead load then. He made no attempt to resist or stand. He collapsed and the Guarda had to bear his weight. But they were big; I'd always thought of Lol as tough, yet against the two Guarda he looked suddenly smaller, weaker. They pushed him to the floor, his face pressed hard into the ground, his hands pinned behind his back. One of the Guarda held a gun-like thing to his neck. A sharp click and Lol went very still.

It must have taken them just seconds to remove Lol from the area. In my memory though, it'd play back in slow-motion – tears travelling gradually down his face forming paths through the pale, dried mud on his skin, each grain of dirt moved aside by the water as it fell.

He wasn't dead. They'd paralysed him from the neck, you could tell from the look on his face when they took him; he was still conscious. The Guarda pulled Lol's head back by his hair and he saw us watching. Who can say what the expression on his face was: a glare; a grimace; a frown? His face was compacted by too many feelings; a mixture of feelings that could only belong to Lol. No-one else could look like that.

I lowered my gaze to avoid his eyes. We'd done nothing to help him.

The Guarda heaved Lol away. I kept my eyes on the ground but I could sense when he was no longer there.

When I raised my head a Guarda was approaching the woman and her family for questioning. I stared at the dark patches on her skirt. Dark patches in the material where Lol had cried into it.

'We have to go. Quickly before…' I didn't finish the sentence. I didn't need to. We were already leaving.

But we didn't go far. We went back and hid behind the Squeeze-Doll machines. We couldn't bring ourselves to leave, not immediately. We couldn't leave without Lol, without being certain he wouldn't return. We hoped he'd remember the Squeeze-Dolls and come to find us. It was stupid but we waited, rigid and frightened in the cold, watching the comings and goings of the people, believing that if we just stayed there long enough, Lol would appear. We waited until they started turning the lights out on the rides. Until it was closing time at the fair.

I gazed over at a ticket booth. Inside a ticket-seller was finishing up for the night, pulling the drawer out of his till. A yellow bulb illuminated the booth and the man inside it. I watched as the ticket-seller took his coat off the back of a chair with his free hand and put it over his shoulder.

Valentine said, 'The lights are nearly all out…' His pupils were huge.

The fair had emptied around us. A little way off, a man was

going about with a torch, shutting-down rides, looking for stragglers to cast out.

'…They'll have taken him to the Confines by now. They'll know about him jumping off the Tower.' Valentine's jaw was shaking as he spoke.

We headed out of the fairground, in the vague direction of Canal Bank Court. We were afraid of going home, though. We didn't know how long it'd take for the Guarda to find out where Lol had been staying. We didn't know where to go.

'Could we stay with your sister?'

'No.'

I remembered Dean's letter. 'No…'

'Dean'd call the Guarda if we turned up there,' Valentine said flatly.

We'd led such an insular life, there was no-one to go to.

'We'll have to try the Realm.'

Valentine was right. It was our only choice. I thought of the people there that I knew by name. Bonny. Nolan Jonker. Some of Lol's other friends. If we went to the Realm we'd be handing ourselves in for their protection. We'd be joining the Movement.

I looked at my watch. There was time to get over there on the tunnel-trains but we'd have to find a nearby station and we didn't know the area. There was a late-night shop further ahead, up the street. We made our way towards it but we were both shattered, we couldn't walk fast.

We asked for directions from the shopkeeper. The man's voice was slow and dawdling as he explained the way to the station. I tried to listen while my head raced on ahead to the trains. As we left, the man called out from behind us, 'Thank you so much for your custom.'

We walked as quickly as we could manage. After Pollat Road, we were on to Marsden Street. Then we turned into Pretto Street.

'Neeve…'

Valentine had called out to me. I turned. He'd stopped ten or so metres behind. I went back to him.

'What if the Realm's shut?' he whispered. 'What if it isn't a club night?…Chances are it's not.'

I could feel all the energy running out of my body. There

probably wouldn't be anyone about when we got there. We could arrive and if the Realm was closed, we'd be too late to get the tunnel-trains home. We'd be stranded. We couldn't wander the City all night. We'd have to sleep outside and then the Street Sweepers would find us.

Exhausted, I said, 'We should still risk it. We can't go back to the flat.' But my voice was sapped of its strength. There was no motivation behind what I said.

'Yes.'

We stood, neither of us moving. It might have been a minute before either of us spoke.

I said a preposterous thing, 'What if Lol's there?'

'At the Realm?'

'No, the flat. They might give him a Cautionary and release him. I mean, he didn't *harm* anyone. Maybe we're getting too worked up. He might just come home.'

The thing was, we were very, very tired. We weren't thinking straight. I didn't feel good about travelling across the City to give ourselves over to people at the Realm. Now, added to that was my blind, wild hope of Lol coming home.

Somehow, we managed to talk ourselves out of getting on the trains that night. We were cowards, I suppose. All we could think to do was go back to what we knew and hope the life we'd been living would still be there.

'Lol...?'

The flat felt stark and empty; not like home at all.

We wandered about the dark rooms keeping close together, not quite able to give up, trying to half-convince ourselves that Lol might actually be there, that he might step out at us at any moment.

The minutes passed quietly by though. We were forced to allow the reality of his absence to sink in.

We did what was necessary without thinking all that much about it. We must have known, deep down, that we were in danger but neither of us properly acknowledged it. We set about hiding Lol's things and getting rid of all the black market items he'd brought into the flat. I hoped the neighbours weren't woken by the sound of the toilet flushing over and over as things were washed away down the pipes.

Valentine saw to the final item, pouring the last of his Silver into two glasses. We crashed down then, exhausted, onto the bed. Valentine lay holding the image of the Circle against his chest as though it was armour that could protect him from danger. We knocked the Silvers back and made a vague plan for ourselves, that we'd go to the Realm the next morning if Lol hadn't come home. We lay side by side, huddling together, trying to find consolation in each other as though Lol was still there to bridge us. Maybe Valentine craved the closeness as much as I did. I could feel him trying to draw me inside, like he wanted to suck comfort in through his skin. I put my arm over him and held on.

I went over and over Lol's behaviour that night, trying to find a reason. In some well-meaning, ill-thought-out way, we'd become Lol's project, his grand plan. In the light of his dream, Lol's actions at the fair seemed like a test; his final provocation to force daring out of us, a last effort to make us stronger.

But I could see his actions also as though they were a type of punishment; the price he might make us pay for not living up to his plans. Or maybe even as his own punishment, done out of anger at himself, as though he knew his efforts to help us weren't working – worse than that, that he was actually doing us harm – and so he'd had to pull himself away. Only he couldn't leave. He'd become too involved. He'd got the Guarda to take him instead.

What I couldn't believe was that Lol had acted that way knowingly. Nobody would choose that. The cost of that sort of behaviour could be so high. Not only for Lol.

I thought about all that had happened since our time at the Compound. I wondered if Valentine wished I hadn't forced him out, if he regretted it. I wondered if he secretly blamed me. I lay quiet, too afraid of the answer to ask.

I never found out if Valentine slept, if his insomnia kept him awake through those long hours. Sometime in the small hours of the morning, before we'd woken, before we'd had the chance to even think of going to the Realm, our flat was raided.

A sound seeped through into my sleep. As I woke up, my brain grappled to make sense of the noise. At the same time, images of the previous night came rushing back into my thoughts: the fairground; Lol; the Guarda.

The sound continued, getting louder and more definite. Someone was knocking on the door. We froze.

There was a voice, so booming it was as though the person was standing at the end of our bed.

'Open this door. Open it or the door will be opened by force.'

Then, 'Mister Frankland, Mrs Frankland, we know you are inside.'

We rose from the mattress; two mindless figures following a command. We didn't acknowledge each other. We moved through the darkness in a daze.

I remember the black uniforms as the door was opened; the door frame filled with the Guarda and the lights from their torches. Impossible to say how many men.

'Is this the dwelling-place of Linden Doiger?'

You couldn't see their eyes. They wore visors over their faces. We stared blankly. I'd never been up so close to the Guarda.

'Is this the dwelling place of Linden Doiger?'

Maybe Valentine shook his head. I don't remember.

'A man was arrested at a fairground on Michael Row last night. Linden Doiger. We believe he was residing in this apartment. We need to search the property. Step aside.'

Lights were switched on at the walls. Guarda pushed past us into the flat. A blur of black uniforms. When the dark shapes had passed inside, we were marshalled into the main bedroom. Air was only getting into my lungs in small snatches – rapid, jolting breaths.

The Guarda were swarming over everything, handling our belongings. One of them stood very close to me. I was disorientated. It didn't register it at first; a gun was pressing into my back.

Guarda were passing in and out of the bedroom. Black-gloved hands sifted through our things, interested in everything; a half-drunk cup of decoction left by the bed; the photograph of Valentine's sister; Lol's cigarettes that we'd forgotten to get rid of, hidden behind the books. As the room was pulled apart, every item seemed to betray us, to pronounce our guilt.

I could see Valentine out of the corner of my eye. It was the first time I'd properly noticed him. An armed Guarda was with him.

Another approached with a machine in his hand. He held it up to Valentine's mouth.

'Speak your name.'

At first he couldn't. Valentine made a noise with his mouth but it wasn't a word. He needed to swallow but he couldn't. He tried again, 'Val-entine...'

'Your full name.'

He spoke slowly, one word at a time, pausing for breath between each, 'Valentine... Duvante...Deyan...Kristic...Frankland.' His beautiful voice in that room full of Guarda.

The machine made a sound and the Guarda studied the results displayed on the tiny screen. He wandered away, taking the machine to show another man. They were discussing Valentine, 'A Listing of *ten*.'

Then both Guarda came over, invisible eyes staring at Valentine from behind the visors. 'You're on medication?'

'Yes.' Hardly a voice at all.

The Guarda had another instrument in his hand. 'Hold out your arm.'

Valentine obeyed, raising a shaking limb from his side. The Guarda forced his arm higher, straight out in front. Then he pushed back the sleeve of Valentine's shirt. He did it like he was handling an inanimate thing, not a person at all. Valentine's skin was exposed. It must have been my fear heightening everything, but I was struck by the sight of it. It seemed to have an effect on the room, the space where we stood.

Valentine couldn't keep his arm out. A Guarda had to hold it while another pressed the needled-instrument into a vein and took a blood sample. I felt the needle as though it were being pushed into my own skin and my body gave a spasm. The Guarda beside me jabbed the gun warningly against my side. I'd been feeling Valentine's intense distress only I hadn't realised – it was identical to my own. The feeling was amplified beyond what I could take.

The Guarda who'd taken the sample stepped back to study the machine, waiting for the results to show. It seemed to be taking a long time. Maybe there was something wrong with Valentine's blood.

A different Guarda addressed Valentine, 'You recognise the corrupting nature of your disorder?'

'Yes.' A whisper.

'It is a serious offence to in any way curtail the taking of your medicine. You know that. If you refrain from controlling your condition, you endanger other citizens. You put others at risk with your Listing.'

I didn't understand. Valentine couldn't be a danger to anybody.

The reading finally came up on the machine. Two Guarda lowered their heads to view it. One of them turned and looked briefly at Valentine but said nothing.

Then they came to me. The machine was lifted to my face.

'Your name.'

'Neeve Frankl-and.' My voice cracked on the last part.

Suddenly, there was a flurry of activity on the other side of the room. The Guarda reading my voice was momentarily distracted.

They were pulling up boards from the floor. The shelves and the dresser and all the other surfaces had been cleared. Our things were scattered across the floor. The Guarda had found something. A book was being passed between them. The cover looked old and faded. The Guarda were flicking through the pages. I could just make out its title; 'Tranquil States for Beginners'.

'A Thought-Refusal book.'

'Do an eye-test. See what they know.'

Several more Guarda came over. They held us so that we couldn't move. A man took hold of my face, his hand clasped around my jaw. I couldn't see his eyes but he seemed to be staring right into mine.

The book was held up before us.

'Do you know of this book?'

I couldn't move my jaw to speak. I couldn't even move my head to shake it.

There was a pause and then the question was put another way. 'Have you seen this book before?'

Again, the questioner paused, giving the Guarda time.

'Does this book belong to you?'

Neither of us could respond but it wasn't our answers that interested them.

The Guarda holding my face spoke, 'The eyes corroborate, Sir.'
Then the Guarda with Valentine, 'And the male, Sir.'

Another voice; it was the Guarda with the name-reading machine. 'Sir, the girl has familial histories: two Vanishments.'
Discussion went on around us. I couldn't tell who was addressing who. They spoke of my family. Valentine must have heard it all.

Then, despite the terror I was feeling, there was something besides just that; something else vying for my attention. I turned my attention towards it. I peered at Valentine. It was coming from him. He was staring straight ahead, but something was happening as he stood there.

There was a subtle sound in my ears. Something sounding like air was blowing quietly through them. The noise wasn't distinct but it was growing stronger. Somehow I knew Valentine was experiencing it, that what was happening was inside his body – I was getting it through him.

My vision blurred. I tried to blink it away and my sight cleared again, but only for a few seconds before the mist took over. I didn't know what was happening. I checked the Guarda; none of their dark, hazy shapes were paying attention. It seemed to be happening only to Valentine and me. A pressure was building up – like someone pressing against my forehead. The airy sound-movement in my ears was gathering speed, becoming more of a ringing. It became faster and more intense and soon it was resonating through all of me. The pressure increased. I closed my eyes. I was giddy. It was like a plug had been removed and now water was gaining momentum, swirling down a hole, spinning inside me.

Then suddenly it stopped. There was a popping sound and everything went silent.

I opened my eyes. My vision had come back, but it had come back better than before. Things looked crisp. I was struck by the clarity of my own sight.

I heard sounds from the room. I was aware of the man standing at my side, his gun pressing against me. I could hear him breathing – sounds amplified and more defined. There was movement; the Guarda finishing their search. I watched as they moved around the room. I was shocked because I was *alright*. I viewed the scene not wanting to change it. The Guarda's presence seemed neutral. I stood watching, my body effortless, not tensed. I felt light, marvelling that I wasn't terrified.

To the left of me was Valentine. I could feel him clearly. He seemed shocked by what was happening, but underneath the surprise he was calm too – the sort of calmness you'd get after using the Circle, only multiplied. Whatever had occurred, he wasn't afraid. And my dread was lessened because of him. I thought, *Maybe he's giving it to me on purpose, trying to share the calmness?*

A Guarda came over.

'Unlawful material has been discovered in this apartment. The evidence suggests it is solely the property of the Interned.' The words didn't mean very much. They were mostly just noise. 'Neither of you will be charged with possession. You should have picked your house-mate more carefully, Citizens,' he said laughing.

Then the Guarda addressed the others in the room. 'Move out. Bring the Listing. Leave the other.'

By *Listing* they meant Valentine. Guarda came towards him.

He's going. The thought blasted through me.

The Guarda caught Valentine as his body gave way, before it hit the floor. He collapsed but not from fright; his body just went by itself.

I watched as they took him, handling him like another piece of evidence even though he was the most alive thing in the room. I glared at him, willing him to see me. He turned his head, twisting it back but I was out of his range of vision. I caught a glance of the side of his face. I saw one eye; almond shaped and clear, no fear fringing it. Then he was gone.

The room emptied of black-uniforms. Heavy boots left. I heard the front door shut. The clarity and effortlessness had vanished. I'd been sucked brutally back into the world.

I curled in on myself. I lay in darkness so total and unchanging that I began to doubt the sun would rise, that it would ever be morning. Everything around me seemed hostile and strange. The room felt bad, like something had been left behind by the presence of the Guarda. But there was something else; a trace of what had happened to Valentine in the last moments – a slight breeze through all the dense, panic-ridden air.

It's stupid what you think at such times. In my head I saw the neighbours at their doors, watching as Valentine was taken. I wasn't ashamed of them having seen. I was envious; I wanted to see him as they had – a few seconds more.

I had to find a way to occupy my mind. I had to find a way of keeping it from running over what would be done to Lol and Valentine. I started to count. I lay in the dark counting anything I could think of. I counted the teeth in my mouth, feeling each one with my tongue. ...*Thirty, thirty-one, thirty-two*... I'd count thirty-two teeth and then I'd do it all over again. ...*Two, three, four*...

Time began to twist in on itself. Slowly the room lost its hostility and it became a nothingness instead. It did it so easily, as if that's all it'd ever been.

I wondered how it'd happened; all the things I'd never meant to do that I'd ended up doing. There wasn't anything *to* do now. No more plans or schemes could be made. All that was finished with.

...*Linden Doiger*. Somehow, the name managed to creep into my mind. It caught me off guard. *Linden Doiger*, I didn't know that person. I thought about what had been hidden under the floorboards, hidden from Valentine and me in our home. Lol, Lollard, Linden, Marlon Darlund – which one of them had put it there?

I looked around the room, at all our scattered belongings. The bookshelf was empty apart from one big book. Not Lol's book. It was *Essential Guidance for the Modern Marriage* – the gift from Dean and Mauran. My mind drifted back to our wedding. I remembered the conversation I'd had with Mauran – the way she'd come over to me in the reception room as soon as I was alone. Her face was flushed. She'd been upset. The words had come out of her in a rush.

'He's flawed. You know that. We didn't know they'd let him marry. When he was a child, they said they weren't sure if he could. I'm his sister. If I have a baby, they say there's a chance it could be like him. He's good to you, isn't he?'

The question took me by surprise. Was she doubting his

goodness? Her uncertainty infected me too: how would I even know what a good person was? 'Yes.'

It was such an intimate conversation to be having with a person I'd only just met. Suddenly, I was gripped by the urge to know.

'What was he like as a child?'

'Even with the pills he was strange,' she said. 'He'd climb naked onto the roof of the house. Neighbours in the flats opposite saw him and alerted our parents. He didn't realise that there was anything wrong in what he did. He said he wanted to feel grit and breezes on his skin.'

We were like criminals conspiring against Valentine.

'After the scolding he got for that, he went the other way. He hid himself in the smallest, darkest places possible. He'd get himself trapped. It would take us ages to find him.' She looked at the floor then and said quietly, 'He liked the feel of my mother's coat. He'd lie inside it.' Her voice trailed off.

'Valentine said that you lived with your grandfather?'

'After the accident, that's where we went. The nurses from the clinic did home visits. They told grandfather that he wasn't strict enough. I don't think grandfather knew what to do with him.'

'Sorry...I don't know about the accident? Valentine never told me.'

'Our parents came off the road. Straight into a wall.'

The shock of talking about it had jolted us out of something. We remembered that we didn't even know each other and the conversation evaporated. Later, when Mauran had left the Commission, Valentine asked me what we had discussed. I'd had to lie to him.

I lay in bed in the flat wondering how long it would be before Mauran received the news of Valentine's arrest. Would Dean find out sooner because he was with the Guarda? I wondered if Mauran would come to the flat, distraught, blaming me for what had happened. I remembered what she'd said that day at the wedding: *I know you'll look after each other.*

The paper had been squeezed into a tight ball. I saw it lying on the floor, small enough not to be noticeable amongst all the mess and wreck of our room. I didn't know what it was at first. I got up and went over to it. *The Circle.* When I unravelled it, I saw the strange pattern inside. Somehow, during all that had gone on in the raid, Valentine had thought to leave it behind. He didn't need it any more. The Circle had helped him and now he'd left it behind to help me. I went back to the bed and stuck the paper on the wall above it. I lowered myself down on the mattress and tried to focus. I wanted the shapes to take me over. I just wanted to escape.

A repeated sound summoned me back. I came back from the Circle like I was having to drag my way back through centuries in a single moment. I didn't want to return.

Someone was calling to me. I could hear the voice but didn't recognise it. The kindness of its tone drew me towards it.

A man was at the door. The new Caretaker.

'A representative has just contacted me from your Unit. He said that you hadn't come in this morning and that you're expected.'

Somehow I managed it; I got myself to work. My anxiety was constant now. It was becoming oddly normal.

I walked through the Unit's entrance hall and felt the presence of the security cameras above my head, clinging to the wall. I looked up. The cameras were like small dark birds, their lenses pointing like sharp, accusing beaks. Beneath one of them was a monitor, its screen alternately displaying views from other cameras in the building. I'd seen Valentine and me on that screen many times, moving across the entrance hall. Now I was struck by his absence from my side. It was like seeing a picture of yourself with half your features missing. The upraised angle of my face as I gazed at the screen made me look foolish and lost, childishly hopeful. Then I disappeared. The view switched to another camera's; another corridor white and indistinguishable, interchangeable with all the others. It struck me how easily I was wiped from the screen. I didn't mind; it didn't hurt to disappear.

I went to the lifts. One was waiting, its doors open. I stepped in and felt the lurch of movement as it began to ascend. I watched the floor numbers change. *Four…five…six.* As they went higher my anxiety increased. Their regular sequence alarmed me; something cruel in their unalterable order. *If only nine could flash before six, there might be a chance…*At eleven, the lift beeped and stopped.

I walked to the office. I could see people through the glass in the door. They were in their uniforms at their work-stations, staring at screens. The sight terrified me.

I went in and sat at my desk. I turned on, waited for my screen to show and punched in my code. Mr Spinks would be waiting for me to report to him but I couldn't.

I gazed at my screen. I felt the eyes of my colleagues at my back. I couldn't remember what I was supposed to do. I stared at the cursor, watching it as it flashed. Over and over, it left an empty space, then returned to fill it. There, then not there, then there again. As I stared, the flashing seemed to slow, the cursor staying away for longer and longer. When it went, I wanted to go with it. I wondered, *when things vanish, do they all go to the same place?*

I heard a voice behind me.

'Glynnan?'

I had to drag my eyes from the screen.

It was Mr Spinks. He'd called me by my old name.

'Somebody to see you, Glynnan.'

I must have looked blank because then he made his words slow and deliberate. 'Leave your work-station. Come with me.'

I followed him to his room.

A man was waiting for me there. Mr Spinks said, 'this is Dr Merlevede.'

'Take a seat, Miss Glynnan.' Again, my old name.

I sat down.

'You've suffered quite a shock recently.' The skin on Dr Merlevede's face was shiny. His mouth slanted downwards at one side.

'Y-es.'

Dr Merlevede turned briefly to give Mr Spinks an assuring look, then he turned back to me.

'We've learnt a good deal about your domestic affairs recently, Citizen. It seems you got yourself into a bad situation…Tell me, what's your assessment of what happened?'

He was watching me, checking to see if I was listening, if I understood what was being said.

'Uh…'

'How do you think the predicament in which you found yourself came about?'

I looked at him. I didn't know.

'Do you realise, Miss Glynnan, that it was actually due to the fact that there is something very wrong with you?'

'No.'

'That's actually why it happened, isn't it?'

He nodded at me then, as though he was being kind, giving me a clue, giving me the answer.

'Y-es.'

Mr Spinks said, 'Yes, Dr Merlevede.'

I turned to Mr Spinks, bewildered as to why he was answering the doctor's question. I realised he was correcting me.

'Yes, Dr Merlevede,' I repeated.

'And what exactly do I mean when I refer to your *domestic affairs*?'

'You mean…my…home.'

'I mean your *private* life, don't I, Citizen? Which in your case was abhorrent.'

I withered inside.

'Tell me, Citizen, what have you learned from your error?'

I was looking at his face, trying to guess what I should say.

'That…That it wasn't…'

I was interrupted. 'That you are not right, Citizen. You learnt that you are not right. It was hoped that in your marriage you would have a mollifying influence over your spouse. But, unfortunately, the opposite was the case; you were weak and weakened further by certain objectionable influences. You know to what I refer?'

'We –'

'Miss Glynnan, you allowed an *unregistered* citizen into your home and lived with him as though you were his spouse. You did this whilst being legitimately married to another.' He coughed. 'There are other, more heinous transgressions still which you allowed to take place. It is our belief that the atrocities stem from your one main, core defect. Miss Glynnan, it is unusual for conditions such as yours to go undetected. There must have been some grave error of classification at the time of your birth. We're looking into the cause of this regrettable mistake.'

There was a pause.

'We can assist you, Citizen. Would you like us to do that?'

I nodded vaguely.

'To begin, we need to address your marriage status. Your marriage to the Listing will obviously be annulled. As of today you will be returned to your maiden name and any wedding rights that you might call upon in the future will be voided to prevent you from further error. Also, as your marriage status has been annulled, your claim on your current property is now invalid. You will be returned to take up residence in the Sixth Compound, C-wing. The Compound Executives will be in contact with you regarding this matter. Do you understand everything that has been said to you up to this point?'

I nodded.

'Do you understand me, Citizen?'

I managed a breath, 'Yes.'

Mr Spinks made a noise at the back of his throat.

It didn't register.

He said, 'Yes, Dr Merlevede.'

'Yes, Dr Merlevede,' I repeated.

'As for the imbalances in your disposition, you may be wondering how we can help you with that. We must assign you a Listing; a category establishing the acuteness of your condition, a category by which you can henceforth identify yourself. Your Listing is highly significant as it will prescribe your movements and actions. To step outside the precepts placed upon you by your Listing is a very serious offence. I am going to help you by prescribing some interim medication that will enable you to resist the behaviours associated with your Listing. Do you see?'

'Yes, Dr Merlevede.'

'Good girl. You'll be given an appointment time for a full assessment shortly. And you'll be assigned a clinic which you will be called to attend regularly.'

He held a jar of pills in his hand. It was as though he'd conjured it from nowhere. He held the jar in front of me so I could read the label. 'The end to your problems, Citizen.'

My old name was printed on it: *C.f.: N. Glynnan.*

Dr Merlevede passed me the jar and an accompanying leaflet of instructions.

'Take this medicine. One tablet on your tongue and swallow it down with a glass of water. Do this three times a day, every *eight* hours. The clinic will, perhaps, prescribe a more accurate type of medication. Then they will monitor your progress. You'll be our experiment, Miss Glynnan. We'll be monitoring the progress of this unique case. Now, there's no need for you to be at work today. Mr Spinks and his colleagues need time to decide what to do about your position; whether you are to continue to work here or whether he needs a replacement. Return home and take your medicine, that is today's vital requirement. The question is, will you need to be escorted?'

'...Er.'

'I'm wondering if you can you be trusted, Miss Glynnan? I'm wondering if you're capable of conducting yourself in the correct manner?' His voice was getting louder as he spoke. 'Do we need to monitor your every word, your most minute gesture, Miss Glynnan? In short, I'm wondering if there is hope for you as a citizen of this City?'

I gazed at him, stunned.

'Is there?'

I nodded weakly.

'There is?'

'Yes.'

'Any further transgressions will not be tolerated.' He leaned towards me and whispered, 'You are infinitesimally close to a similar fate as your former spouse, Miss Glynnan. Only the error of diagnosis has prevented you from it thus far.'

He sat back again. 'Commonly there is sickness and headaches with the first doses of the medicine. Return directly to your home therefore. Take the medicine upon arriving. This will be the first thing you do. After that, every eight hours, every day. A health inspector will call to see you in the morning to ensure you've complied with the medication procedure. The taking of these tablets is *compulsory*. What does compulsory mean, Citizen?'

'It –'

But Dr Merlevede was already answering the question. 'It means it is an *offence* not to take them. If your medicine is stolen or misplaced you must go directly to your clinic. Now then, notification of your forthcoming Listing assessment at the clinic will be sent to you shortly. Also the date of removal from your current property and the decision regarding your post here. Do you have any questions before I adjourn, Citizen?'

Dr Merlevede began writing something on the paper he had in front of him. I didn't think I had questions, my mind was too shot. But then something came. The words emerged, hushed and urgent, my last chance to know. 'Sir, what's meant by ten?'

'*Ten?*'

'A Listing of ten?'

The doctor looked shocked and then angry. He tilted his head back and looked down at me.

'A Listing of ten denotes a complete inversion of the appropriate response, its corollary being the most extreme digression from custom. It is the utter inability to manifest within the usual patterns. Other than that, I cannot say. I am forbidden in my role as a doctor to discuss it any further with a citizen of the City.'

'Can I see him?' The words had come before I could help myself.

'*See who?*'

I said his name. The word seemed too good to be spoken out loud. 'Valentine.'

Mr Spinks said, 'She means the spouse. Frankland.'

Dr Merlevede's voice rose sharply. 'Goodness! Of course no!' He raised his arms up as if to block further requests. 'Enough now.' He flicked his hands down the legs of his trousers. 'Enough of this…enquiry.'

Dr Merlevede rose from his chair. I was exasperating him. He began collecting up his notes to put in his case.

The meeting had come to an end.

Mr Spinks stood up. 'Thank the doctor for his time, Glynnan,' he said.

'Thank you, Dr Merlevede.'

Mr Spinks came over to me and escorted me from the room.

Once outside, he stopped. Closing the door behind him, he looked at me and said, 'Take your fetid clutter from your workstation and get out.'

As I walked away I heard him muttering 'Listing' derisively under his breath.

I walked from the Unit, far away enough to breathe. Nothing seemed real.

I looked at the sky. The sun was overhead, reaching the streets from directly above; the way it never normally was when I left the Unit. Even the angle of the sun was saying that life would be different now.

I kept floundering on my way home. I'd stop dead in my tracks, too overwhelmed to carry on. When I tried to walk, the pills rattled in my bag, banging against my side with each step I took. I had to slow right down to lessen the noise. Every time I passed a pedestrian I thought the pills would give me away; everyone alerted to the sound.

A man in uniform was waiting inside the entrance of Canal Bank Court.

'I need to check your shoulder bag, Miss. New regulations,' he said.

I kept my eyes low as he searched inside my bag. He picked out the pill bottle and read the label. I squirmed in my shoes; my body trying to turn itself inside-out.

He handed the bag back to me and I stumbled away, over to the stairway. Holding onto the banister, I hauled myself up. I dreaded that I'd meet a neighbour; someone looking at me with their too-knowing eyes. I couldn't handle an encounter like that.

I let myself into the flat. As soon as I was inside, the events that had occurred there crowded around me like angry, complaining citizens. I turned away, over the kitchen sink and let cold water splash onto my skin and clothes.

The pills were waiting for me in my bag on the table. *Take the medicine…This will be the first thing you do upon arriving home.* I reached inside and found the bottle. I twisted open the lid and tipped some pills into my hand. I placed one on my tongue. Bitter. A strange chemical taste.

I went to the washroom and looked at my face in the mirror. It had changed. The defensive look had come back. My eyes looked mean and frightened like they had in the Compound. I opened my mouth and gazed at the pill stuck to my tongue. I was about to swallow it but suddenly there was a voice in my head.

Not yet. The voice was telling me to wait.

I let the pill fall into the basin and turned on the tap. The pill was lifted, taken away by a rapid swirl of water.

I didn't know what the pills would do. I didn't know which parts of me they'd knock out. I imagined them moving through me, destroying whole clusters of feelings. I didn't want to feel how Valentine had felt; my life so watered-down and sparse, but I had no choice. I had to take the medicine, only there was something I wanted to do before I did. *One more thing. One more thing before the pills.*

I hesitated at the door to Valentine's room. I wanted to go in, to feel nearer to him but I couldn't. I hadn't been in there since he'd been taken. I didn't want to see what the Guarda had done to it. I went into the big room and lay down on the bed.

I removed my wet clothes and put on my nightdress even though it was the afternoon. I lay under the bed clothes, keeping warm. I was going to pretend that part of me was Lol so that I could be assured in what I did, so that I could feel something definite, something I'd remember even when the medicine was trying to make me forget. A little victory before the onset of the pills.

I began slowly. It was difficult not to rush because every moment that passed was another one where I still hadn't taken a pill – another moment of misconduct. I had to try and block that out. I wouldn't let myself give up.

I reached down, under the covers. Gradually, I felt it. It felt as though my body was a heavy chain that ran from a mooring, deep into the water. What I was doing was making the chain shift. It was like I was heaving that bulky, old chain out link by link, and where the metal had been submerged, the links were thick with rust. The metal groaned and creaked as the chain was moved. I was hoisting it up bit by bit, pulling myself loose, clear of the water. Then, when all of the chain was finally out, I let go. I just let it drop. It went crashing back down with a weighty, thunderous noise. Everything went quiet.

I drifted for a while. I thought I'd cry but I didn't. I should have got out of bed and gone to the kitchen where the jar was waiting for me on the side of the sink. In my mind's eye I saw myself unscrewing the top, tipping out a pill, throwing it to the back of my throat. But I couldn't bring myself to go and do it.

As my mind drifted, Willa's voice came into my head, '...The true sea. That's what's limitless, Neeve. Not the City.' And in the background, Verna, '...Beautiful...Beautiful.'

Beautiful. The word linked me inevitably to Valentine. An image of him appeared. It was a clear enough mental picture but it was what it was; a memory of a lovely face I'd known. He was beyond me now in the same way that he was beyond the Guarda and the City, beyond even himself. I thought, *Nothing can touch him. He's worked himself loose.*

On the tail of Valentine, thoughts of Lol followed. Lol, who'd seen something in us that we couldn't see. Lol, who'd tried to hold back the City and give us the space to...*to what?* I couldn't even think. He'd tried to coax us off the bank, to get us to stand in the current with him, to keep us steady inside it. Only how could he have the strength for three people? The City wasn't a place where you could be strong for others for long. It was hard enough being strong for yourself.

Lol hadn't shielded us from danger, he'd taken us to it. Perhaps I should've been more angry but the mistake seemed partly ours. We'd expected something from him that he couldn't give. We believed he could shield us from the City. Maybe nobody could do that.

I thought about the future; the next days, waiting for notification to come. I was to be housed in the Sixth Compound, this time in C-wing with the other dissidents. I was to be given a clinic to attend. My marriage was being annulled. I wasn't allowed to marry again. There were so many plans and propositions for my life. I knew I was this person and that she was persisting but it seemed a nonsense without Valentine and Lol. Everything had stopped and by some oversight I'd carried on when I wasn't meant to. *Neeve Glynnan*: it seemed like a flimsy idea now, like a transfer sticker that could be scratched off my surface, another sticker, another name put on in its place.

My eyes caught a flicker of yellow at the window. It was early evening and just starting to get dark. In the dimming light, from the corner of my eye, I saw something yellow. I turned my head: a tiny bird hopping along the ledge on its stick legs, flitting carelessly about. I looked hard at it, unsure whether or not I was seeing right.

I could no longer trust my mind to make proper sense of things.

A canary…They don't live wild. They don't fly in the cold September weather.

Maybe it's escaped from one of the richer houses, a cage door accidentally left open…

The bird hopped, looking at me sideways with its head cocked. It moved into a patch of evening light and its colour flared up. Its feathers were so bright, radiant against the grey City.

Aren't you cold out there?

The bird was my ally. I thought it understood what had happened. I didn't want it to go but it did a few more hops along the ledge and then, with a flutter of its wings, it flew off.

Come back little bird…

I closed my eyes, trying to hold the colour of its feathers in my head. But behind my eyelids, things were more confused. Thoughts were mixed together in the upheaval of everything. I heard my mother's voice, *'Don't expect so much, my girl. Don't expect so much from this world.'* The same words as before but this time the meaning had changed. I'd always thought she was telling me that I wouldn't amount to much but now the essence of the words seemed different. She was trying to tell me that the City couldn't give me what I wanted; the City was limited and wasn't able to offer much. The City was simply the wrong place to look.

Her words made the City seem smaller. In my head, the City grew oddly, unexpectedly small, so small that it seemed its laws couldn't impress upon me. I saw my old life: my booth and the curfews. I saw it with the addition of the pills. And now, with the opportunity of a future marriage denied me, I'd be at the Compound till I was an old woman. It seemed clear, like a decision was being made inside me. I wouldn't take the medicine and I wouldn't go back to the booths. It would be like being made to be dead when you'd only just come alive. There was no point. I'd be better off being properly dead.

I could follow Valentine, maybe. Find that elusive thing; what it was he'd discovered in the Circle – what had discovered him. I could follow Valentine's tracks in the hope I'd understand. Until I knew how he'd worked himself loose.

I wasn't even all that afraid.

The rhythm of my wings was calming. There was something hypnotic about the steady repetition of the movement. I was above the City, looking down at everything, all the streets and buildings. Canal Bank Court was down there, so was the Unit and the Sixth Compound, the house where I'd grown up. It was all down there in the City.

I could go wherever I wanted, any direction. What was striking was how weightless I was, how unfettered. I could go anywhere but I was flying to the centre. I was approaching the Imperial Sector.

I could see the monument up ahead. I could see the five figures stood high on their pillars. I could see the pigeons that flapped and landed about the famous stone men and the ones that flapped about in the square below. I could see people circling the pillars, hitting their feet on the slabs to wear away the writing. I flew lower and saw the stones where the Vanishment names were carved.

As I got near, other birds saw me and flew away. They sensed something different perhaps, and were afraid. I circled the pillars, flying low, round and around, just over the heads of the crowds. I saw words completely trampled in places, others where letters were still readable. I flew to the recently laid stones, the place where the stones were newest and freshest.

I hovered above, looking for a V or an L. I read 'Lewis', 'Vanda', 'Vincent', 'Lisalotte'...Then for a moment I thought I'd found them. My eyes caught on two names. There was a second's confusion in my head. Verna Rus – Thought Refusal Crimes. Willa-Rix – Thought Refusal... My wings failed me. I faltered mid-air, battled to recover myself. Somehow I managed to swing my weight away and up. Up and up, away from the names of the Vanishments.

I flew to the top, the very top. The higher I went the windier it became. I flew right up and perched myself on a statue's head, curling my claws around the stone furls of its hair, holding on tight, panicked inside my tiny frame.

The monument was the highest point. Higher than any building. The view was huge. I felt giddy with the wind. Giddy from the swell of fear in my chest. I gazed at the City's horizon. My eyes strained to its furthest reaches. The air was hazy. I squinted for a glimpse of a giant wall, the glint of waves on a sea. The City disappeared into the blur of the distance.

Far out, an orange sun was going down. I stared right at it with my black, beady eyes, not flinching, letting it burn away everything that my eyes had ever seen. Then, with my burnt-out vision, beneath the orb of the sun, I saw that the air glistened; specks of moving light. It could have been water.

Everything has to end somewhere...

The evening sun shone over the City as though it was liquid, as though the City itself was a wide, metallic sea. The sun made a line of reflected light reaching toward me across the sea-City; a line of dazzling yellow-gold over all that grey.

Fly out, Neeve. Keep flying till you come to the edge. Get to the true sea.

I uncurled my wings and took off. I launched myself into the air and flew at the sun, letting the skill of my feathers carry me. I swerved to the left and the line of sunlight followed. I swerved to the right and it did the same. It was like a game; the line of light chasing me, teasing me, coming to get me. I went towards the sun and the yellow of my wings merged with the deeper yellow of the evening. I flew and felt Lol and Valentine. I could feel them with me almost, very near. It was like they were in the dusk somewhere, larking about, moving as though they were one being with four arms and four legs, dancing around, laughing in the wobbling line of light.

Epilogue

A fan is whirring in a Guarda Department sub-office at the Headquarters of Law. The heating system is blowing hot air into the huge room but it's still cold. Rain is blustering against the windows. The afternoon sky is dark.

At a desk, a young man works diligently in front of a screen. There is a clock on the far wall. The young man looks up to check the time as he types.

He is updating information concerning the status of current criminals: Arrest, Trial, Imprisonment, Vanishment. He is working through a list of names and details. He turns a page in the file from which he takes the statistics.

The young man is surprised.

The file reports a Disappearance. Disappearances are rare. He runs his finger along the words. An offending citizen has gone missing, cannot be traced. There have been no sightings for fourteen days. The person is considered dangerous; a Listing. A search is underway.

The young man shudders, partly from the cold, partly from unease. It troubles him that an offender might be lost to the City in this way. There is a photograph of the criminal's face. He glances at it for a moment. He isn't sure but he thinks, almost hopes, it is there; he thinks he can detect a reprehensible quality in the woman's rounded, unprepared face.